CONTEMPORARY AMERICAN RELIGION

CONTEMPORARY AMERICAN RELIGION

An Ethnographic Reader

EDITED BY

PENNY EDGELL BECKER

AND

NANCY L. EIESLAND

ALTAMIRA
PRESS

A Division of Sage Publications, Inc.
Walnut Creek • London • New Delhi

For information address:

AltaMira Press
1630 North Main Street
Suite 367
Walnut Creek, California 94596
E-mail: explore@altamira.sagepub.com

SAGE Publications Ltd.
6 Bonhill Street
London EC2A 4PU
United Kingdom

SAGE Publications India Pvt. Ltd.
M-32 Market
Greater Kailash I
New Delhi 110 048 India

Printed in the United States of America

Library of Congress Cataloging-in-Publication Data

Contemporary American Religion: An Ethnographic Reader / Edited by Penny Edgell Becker
        and Nancy L. Eiesland
        p. cm.
    Includes bibliographical references and idex
    1. United States—Religion—1960—Case studies. 2. United States—Religious Life
    and Custom—Case studies. 3. United States—Church History—20th century—
    Case studies
    1. Becker, Penny Edgell. 2. Eiesland, Nancy L., 1964–
    BL252.C66 1998
    306.6097309045—dc21   97-33744
                                                         CIP

    97 98 99 10 9 8 7 6 5 4 3 2

Production Services: Zenda, Inc.
Cover Design: Joanna Ebenstein

CONTENTS

ACKNOWLEDGMENTS

We owe a debt of gratitude to a number of individuals who have assisted us throughout the process of compiling this volume. On behalf of all the authors, we would first like to thank all those who shared their stories with us and allowed access to their lives and settings of worship for the puposes of our research. Our colleagues at Cornell University and Emory University provided good advice and valuable suggestions. Thanks are due to all the chapter contributors for their cooperation and timeliness. Mitch Allen and Erik Hanson, our editors at AltaMira, guided us helpfully throughout. Thanks to David Becker and Terry Eiesland for their steadfast support and practical help through this and many other projects. As editors, we appreciate one another and the friendship that has made this opportunity to work together not only possible but also very gratifying.

ABOUT THE AUTHORS

Penny Edgell Becker is an assistant professor in the sociology department at Cornell University who received her doctorate from the University of Chicago in 1995. She is interested in religion, culture, and social change. Her most recent work is a study of how congregational cultures fall into institutionally specific patterns that shape identity, mission, and internal organizational process (*Culture and Conflict: The Moral Order of Local Religious Life*, working title, Cambridge University Press, forthcoming). She has also analyzed 19th-century Catholic gender ideology. Her next project will examine how religious institutions adapt to new family forms.

Nancy L. Eiesland is assistant professor of sociology of religion at the Candler School of Theology at Emory University. She received her doctorate from Emory University in 1995. Her revised dissertation, *A Particular Place: Exurbanization and Religious Response*, is forthcoming from Rutgers University Press. This work highlights how the religious ecology of a once small town was altered by incorporation into a metropolitan region. In addition to her work in social change and religion, Eiesland has published in the area of physical disability and social status.

Shoshanah Feher received her doctorate in 1995 from the University of California, Santa Barbara. She has published articles on new religious movements and Judaism in North America, as well as on the intersection of religion with gender and ethnicity. Her contribution in this volume is based on her doctoral dissertation, which in revised form, *Passing over Easter: Constructing the Boundaries of Messianic Judaism*, is forthcoming from AltaMira Press. Feher is currently doing postdoctoral work at the University of California, Los Angeles, School of Medicine, for which she is studying the role of religion in women's illness experiences.

Edward R. Gray is a doctoral candidate at Emory University. He received his M.A. from the Pacific School of Religion. His dissertation, "Shifting Sacred Ground: California Catastrophe and Its Moral Meaning," examines the moral logics of civic and religious institutions after the 1906 San Francisco and the 1989 Loma Prieta earthquakes. He is also working on a study of performative iconographic representations of the assassinated Harvey Milk, the first openly gay public official in the nation.

Matthew P. Lawson received his doctorate from Princeton University in 1996 and is visiting assistant professor of sociology at Brandeis University. He is an associate editor for *Sociology of Religion* and has published in *Research in the Social Scientific Study of Religion* and in *"I Come Away Stronger" : How Small Groups are Shaping American Religion*, edited by Robert Wuthnow.

Michael McMullen is assistant professor of sociology at the University of Houston, Clear Lake. He received his doctorate from Emory University in 1995.His revised dissertation, *The Atlanta Bahá'í Community: On the Religious Construction of a Global Identity* (working title) is forthcoming from Rutgers University Press. His areas of interest include the sociology of religion, complex organizations, and conflict resolution and mediation. He continues to research the American Bahá'í community, as well as various conflict resolution programs in the corporate and nonprofit sectors.

Timothy J. Nelson received his doctorate from University of Chicago in 1997. He is currently interviewing nonresident, low-income fathers in Camden, New Jersey, and studying an African American congregation in Philadelphia. His published work includes several articles in *Sociology of Religion*.

Janet Stocks received her doctorate from University of Pittsburgh in 1995. She currently works as center administrator for the Center for Integrated Study of the Human Dimensions of Global Change at Carnegie Mellon University. The chapter she contributed to this volume comes from her dissertation. Her current research includes the analysis of the democratization of science and of public participation in complex policy decisions.

Scott L. Thumma received his doctorate from Emory University in 1996. He is currently a research associate with the Hartford Seminary Center for Social and Religious Research. He has published chapters and articles on evangelicalism and homosexuality, religious conversion, megachurches, and congregational research methods.

Elfriede Wedam is a research associate with the Polis Center at Indiana University–Purdue University, Indianapolis where she codirects the Faith and Community Project. She received her Ph.D. in 1993 in sociology from the University of Illinois at Chicago where she was also a member of the Religion in Urban America Program. Her work on the small groups movement in religion was published in *"I Come Away Stronger."* Her dissertation on the pro-life movement is part of a larger interest in the diversity of moral cultures in a pluralistic society. Much of her current writing examines how members of new and old immigrant congregations construct racial and ethnic identities and mobilize for change in post-industrial urban contexts.

Robert Wuthnow is the Gerhard R. Andlinger Professor of Sociology at Princeton University where he is also director of the Center for the Study of American Religion. He is the author of many books on contemporary American religion, including *The Restructuring of American Religion, Sharing the Journey: Support Groups and America's New Quest for Community, God and Mammon,* and *The Crisis in the Churches: Spiritual Malaise, Fiscal Woe.*

EDITORS' NOTE

Throughout the volume, the authors use the following conventions for quoted material. Emphasis is noted in italics, with a statement in brackets following that indicates whether the emphasis is the speaker's or the author's. Pauses are indicated by the word pause in brackets, i.e. [pause]. Self-interruptions are indicated with a dash, and an ellipsis indicates the author's editing of a speaker's quote. All other editorial clarifications appear in brackets at the end of the quote.

DEVELOPING INTERPRETATIONS

Ethnography and the Restructuring of Knowledge in a Changing Field

PENNY EDGELL BECKER AND NANCY L. EIESLAND

Interpreting Contemporary American Religion

Each scholar in the sociology of religion must eventually give her account of the American religious situation. What are the sociologically relevant features of religion in its diverse cultural and organizational manifestations? Trained during the last decade, the editors and contributors to this volume have faced this interpretive challenge during a period of significant intellectual change and reorganization.

Three noteworthy changes in the sociology of religion have shaped our account of religious life in America: the reassessment of secularization theories that have long been a dominant paradigm within the field; the increased numbers of women studying religion and the emergence of feminist analyses within the sociology of religion; and the heightened attention to local religious practices and organizations. The appraisals of secularization theories have been conducted both among those who see their enduring utility (e.g., Lechner 1991) and by those who argue the existence of a paradigm shift (e.g., Warner 1993). Whatever else has been accomplished by the debate among secularization theorists and skeptics, it has challenged scholars to "flesh out" such disembodied trends as differentiation, privatization, and religious decline. Too often, our analysis of changes in American religion are organized as a straightforward narrative of decline, a lament for lost community and public influence that captures more about the experiences of white, middle-class members of "mainline" religions than it does about American religion as a whole (see Holifield 1994).

For sociologists who maintain that social location matters, the fact that growing numbers of women sociologists of religion have altered the theoretical terrain should come as no surprise (Maduro 1996). Not only have women scholars offered varied perspectives on religious power and women as research subjects, they have also reexamined the narratives about religious life through the lens of gender. For instance, what does privatization of religion mean when women's experience is taken as the norm? Attending to the changes wrought in American religion as women's paid workforce participation has increased, as more women have joined the ranks of religious professionals, and as family forms have been altered necessitates that old lines of interpretation within the sociology of religion are broadened and that new lines are advanced.

Finally, interpreters of religion have increasingly shown interest in analyses situated in particular places, mapping territory close at hand rather than offering maps of American religion divided broadly into left and right, liberal and conservative. The trope of a liberal-conservative divide is invoked as characterizing the entire religious field, despite evidence that this divide applies primarily to religious professionals and other elites and may not characterize the field as a whole or organize the daily practices, individual beliefs, or congregational culture of most believing persons (see Ammerman 1997, 1994; DiMaggio, Evans, and Bryson, 1996; and chapters by Becker and Wedam in this volume). On the ground, among religious groups and individuals, these maps too often fail to account for the diversity and complexity of everyday religious life.

As observers of this complexity, we are persuaded that adequate interpretive frameworks for religious life in North America must acknowledge complicated relations among religious groups, subcultures, and the larger culture. They must note the depth of complexity within any single religious tradition, organization, or ritual expression. And they must take into account the intricate interplay among what sociologists call "levels of analysis." How do individual beliefs relate to organizational forms and institutional culture? How do changes in one level, say the emergence of the megachurch as a form of organization, stem from and affect changes in the others? How do we understand the effects of modernization on American religion? What are the appropriate theoretical models for describing changes in affiliation, commitment, and authority? And where are the exceptions or countertrends?

Some scholars have led the way in providing better accounts of contemporary American religion by providing a more varied and subtle analysis of religious change. For example, Robert Wuthnow's (1988) use of the term "restructuring" has provided a way to talk about change in religious organizations and institutions without assuming a uni-directional force, whether that be a teleology of progress or a lament for inevitable decline. In asking questions about organization, power, and resources, this framework also suggested an analytical approach that avoided the universalization of a white, middle-class (and often male) religious experience. Recently, Phillip E. Hammond's (1992) work has continued this very promising focus; his categories of "individual-expressive" and "communal-expressive" allow one to analyze how religious belief and involvement provide differing bases for identity in contemporary society, ones that crosscut liberal and conservative camps. Wade Clark Roof's (1993) work on baby-boom spirituality and Nancy Ammerman's (1997) study of congregations in changing communities are two examples of work that socially locates and particularizes religious experience while also addressing the relationship between religion and social change and displaying an awareness that a simple right-left dichotomy is inadequate to map the American religious landscape.

The work showcased in this volume continues this trend of constructing more adequate interpretive frameworks for understanding American religious experience, practice, and organization. Rather than achieve such understanding through large-scale surveys of individuals or comparative studies of congregations all over the country, this volume features ethnographic accounts, for a particular purpose. Ethnography, we argue, provides an excellent set of tools for developing more adequate narratives of religious change, a more nuanced understanding of the differences between individual belief and practice and organizational culture and process, and a map that refines our knowledge of religious cultural cleavages and religious experience.

Studying Contemporary American Religion

Restructuring, we believe, is a useful metaphor for two kinds of changes. One is a set of intertwined changes in American religious organization and expression in the post–World War II era. (This is the meaning that Wuthnow, who coined the term, had in mind.) But restructuring is also a useful way to think about the process of reinterpreting our scholarly practice and about our attempts to come up with better maps and better stories—a better interpretive framework—with which to understand the changing religious landscape.

Ethnography, we believe, can be a generative location for the restructuring of scholarship on a changing social reality, not just a place from which to debunk work that has gone before. Ethnography is a scholarly practice in which these two restructurings can inform one another. Do old templates make sense of newly restructured forms of religious organization and identity? And does the ethnography of these emerging religious spaces change our way of conceptualizing American religious life? The contributors to this volume are engaged in trying to answer these two questions.

First, each contributor examines a "region" of the restructured religious landscape. The traditional congregation, for example, now exists in a context of special-purpose groups from singles' fellowships to prayer groups to political action organizations. One chapter analyzes how second-wave feminism has altered norms of leadership within most religious groups—even those who have rejected women as clergy. As the gay and lesbian movements prompted more people to come out, these individuals have created new venues for the expression of their spirituality, whether they be new denominations or established bars catering to a specific clientele. Whereas earlier waves of suburbanization created bedroom communities, today's deconcentration often occurs in exurban rings around edge cities where megachurches stake their claims. These large congregations not only have a different internal structure than that of traditional congregations, but they relate to their communities in new ways, stretching the concept "local church" that is so much a part of our assumptions about community life. Drawing on their own historical tradition as well as a new awareness of globalization, Bahá'ís challenge this local-church understanding philosophically as well as organizationally. There are new settings, new movements, and new interpretations.

Our contributors also look at the old-made-new, or the restructuring of traditional discourses and identities in ways that our traditional scholarly maps and stories would not predict. From the Metropolitan Community Churches (MCC) to new ethnic and immigrant groups, from feminist evangelicals to those who combine faith and therapy, from gays who sing gospel to those who forge a style of moral reasoning that rejects liberal relativism and conservative certainty, we see an ongoing negotiation with and interpretation of religious meaning and practice in our society. There is continual creation and reconfiguration of religious discourses and identities.

Ethnography is a particularly appropriate tool in analyzing periods of rapid social and institutional change. Ethnography is a method uniquely suited to challenging the conventional wisdom, for subjecting large-scale theories to empirical examination, for generating data on new phenomena, and for generating new theories or insights on the subjects we thought we already knew. Ethnography is a form of rendering an account that does not emphasize formalism or move to theoretical closure in a premature way. It allows for the expression of emergent understandings, partial accounts, and contradiction. But this is not to say that ethnography has no place at the table as we refine our more abstract and theoretical understandings of American religious life.

Ethnography has an important role to play in this period of theory testing and theory building, as we debate the significance of the empirical changes we see around us and try to understand the causes and consequences of current trends. Ethnographic analysis can deflate our tendency to overgeneralize from our own data (or experiences) to all of American religion. In this volume, the work of Timothy J. Nelson does more than suggest limits to the validity of a rational-choice approach to understanding religious commitment. It also underscores that the nominally universal assumptions of that approach are, in fact, often rooted in a white, middle-class, Protestant experience.

Ethnography can also make us aware of the inadequacy of our most frequently used theoretical categories. Liberal and conservative are not adequate to explain the moral reasoning and political mobilization in the groups that Elfriede Wedam studied, and there are factors that cross-cut a liberal-conservative divide in the conflicts that Penny Edgell Becker writes about. Michael McMullen's essay on the Bahá'ís shows that the boundaries between public and private need reconceptualizing in order to understand a globalizing religion. Nancy L. Eiesland highlights the importance of attending to local changes in religious environments.

Ethnography can also make us think more critically about the linear narratives of disembodied trends that still pervade our work. When Edward R. Gray and Scott L. Thumma describe the Gospel Hour at a gay bar in Atlanta, they demonstrate that secularization and sacralization may exist side-by-side and that religion can provide a social and cultural space to renegotiate identities thought to be mutually exclusive. Modernity and its ongoing divisive effects on identity is one story; reintegration or reconfiguration of identity is another story. Janet Stocks's work on evangelical feminists and Shoshanah Feher's account of Messianic Jews tell this story; the very phrases "evangelical feminist" and "Messianic Jew" attest to creative integration. Matthew P. Lawson's study of how religion can be a resource for bolstering personal identity and coping with intimate relationships tells this story of creative integration on an individual level.

Narrating Religious Life

This volume showcases work by people who are just beginning the task of restructuring our understanding of a changing religious landscape and so itself is offered in the spirit of critical and open-ended inquiry that ethnography fosters. This work suggests that to understand the ongoing restructuring of religion and the ongoing development of an adequate set of concepts with which to understand it, we need to pay particular attention to the local construction and negotiation of religious identities as creative spaces for religious innovation.

In the first part of this volume, authors consider the pursuit of religious identity in contemporary American religion. Feher explores the quest for identity in the interstice between Judaism and evangelical Protestantism. Highlighting the shift from ascribed to achieved identity as one of the hallmarks of modern society, her study underscores the communal labor necessary in fashioning anew individual and collective identities from seemingly incompatible sources. Using life-history narratives, Lawson investigates the intersections between religious symbols and individual biographies. His careful examination of the four O'Doul women's religious trajectories reveals the religious creativity that is provoked by cultural and personal crises. He contends that religious converts may take the interactive routines practiced in ritual and apply them to transform face-to-face social relations.

The emergence of the Gospel Girls as an institution on the Atlanta gay scene exposes the dislocations that religious identities sometimes encompass. Among the regulars interviewed by Gray and Thumma are numerous southern gay males whose religious identities were formed, in part, by southern gospel songs. Drawing on gay and evangelical cultures, the Gospel Girls create a precarious haven against the strangeness and vulnerability of their social world. In her study of evangelical feminists, Stocks also highlights the dilemma of "outsiders within" or individuals whose views challenge the legitimacy of religious world views and organizational norms of which they are part. She examines the strategies that some women employ to maintain a commitment to the organizations that challenge their feminist views, and she explores the processes of disengagement followed by other evangelical feminists who disaffiliate with these same organizations.

In the volume's second part, the authors take a new look at religious organization. Becker's study of conflict in local congregations offers new ways of understanding the dynamics of communal identity and boundary clarification as well as the moral rhetorics through which public debate and decision making are conducted when issues of social inclusion arise. Elfriede Wedam's study of moral reasoning in two anti-abortion groups reveals a moral ethic of care and a moral ethic of justice. Both studies suggest that the absolutism necessary for a culture war is not easily sustained in local face-to-face religious groups, that religious moral logics are more complex than they are sometimes thought to be, and that our maps of religious culture need to include cleavages that crosscut a liberal-conservative divide.

Nelson, Eiesland, and McMullen examine the religious landscape. Nelson's study of the factors that limit commitment and foster distrust in a poor African American congregation reveals the inconsistent assumptions in rational-choice approaches to religious commitment and the illogic of applying these assumptions, based in the white, middle-class religious experience, to other settings. For Nelson, the landscape itself, the environment, is its own variable with its own effect on commitment and styles of belonging. Eiesland studies how a megachurch in an exurban setting forces a reconfiguration of the local religious ecology. Again, the environment becomes an important part of the analysis of internal religious organizational dynamics in her analysis of the effect a megachurch has on three neighboring congregations. As a result, Nelson and Eiesland demonstrate that our work on religious environments needs elaboration and development beyond our previous understandings. McMullen's work questions the whole issue of what is the relevant environment. In his study of the Atlanta Bahá'ís, McMullen finds that the dynamics of localizing a global religious identity mean interacting with the local environment in a different way than other religious groups do. Likewise, he challenges the assumption that the local environment is necessarily the anchoring frame of reference for a local religious group.

Robert Wuthnow's conclusion highlights the compatibility between the theoretical focus on religious culture in the sociological study of religion and the use of ethnographic methods to explore these diverse cultures' logics, narratives, and practices. He clearly reflects the views of authors when he writes, "culture is what makes religion interesting."

Through the ethnographic approach, the authors in this volume explore and illustrate the utility of applying cultural and institutional forms of analysis to the study of religious life. Ethnography does not yield statistical generalization, but it can lead to theoretical generalization (Snow and Anderson 1991). In this volume, ethnographic accounts add to our understanding of the construction of religious identity for nontraditional groups, the drawing of moral boundaries, and the religious and cultural categories that organize experience and shape decision making for individuals and groups. We learn about new religious spaces and changes in the landscape that reconfigure the relationships between religious organizations. We learn a bit more about feminist, gay, African American, and Bahá'í religiosity. We learn how individuals, through rituals and narratives and moral discourses, reintegrate cultural elements from widely divergent parts of their backgrounds to find healing, provide a rationale for political action, or construct a new model for intimate relationships.

As editors, we would suggest that these studies, taken together, cause us to reconsider a linear narrative of religious decline and secularization in favor of a more complicated understanding of religious restructuring, just as they force us to develop a more complicated map of the moral and cultural cleavages that structure religious life. They force us to acknowledge the social locatedness of some of our previous, ostensibly objective, theories. They suggest that the effects of modernization are complex and may not be linear, and that the study of religion on its own terms through cultural and institutional analysis can provide a more adequate way of examining the complexities of religion in a modern society. And, they show that ethnographic analysis is a tool that is flexible enough and rich enough to contribute something unique and worthwhile to our ongoing reinterpretation of this large and complex phenomenon we call American religion.

References

Ammerman, Nancy. 1994. "Telling Congregational Stories." *Review of Religious Research* 35:289–301.

———. 1997. *Congregation and Community*. New Brunswick, NJ: Rutgers University Press.

DiMaggio, Paul, John Evans, and Bethany Bryson. 1996. "Have Americans' Social Attitudes Become More Polarized?" *American Journal of Sociology* 102:690–755.

Hammond, Phillip E. 1992. *Religion and Personal Autonomy: The Third Disestablishment in America*. Columbia: University of South Carolina Press.

Holifield, E. Brooks. 1994. "Toward a History of American Congregations." Pp. 23–53 in *American Congregations*, Vol. 2., edited by James P. Wind and James W. Lewis. Chicago: University of Chicago Press.

Lechner, Frank J. 1991. "The Case Against Secularization: A Rebuttal." *Social Forces* 69:1103–19.

Maduro, Otto. 1996. "Introduction." *Social Compass* 43(4): 459–65.

Roof, Wade Clark. 1993. *A Generation of Seekers: The Spiritual Journeys of the Baby Boom Generation*. San Francisco: HarperSanFrancisco.

Snow, David A. and Leon Anderson. 1991. "Researching the Homeless: The Characteristic Features and Virtues of the Case Study." Pp. 148–73 in *A Case for the Case Study*, edited by Joe R. Feagin, Anthony Orum, and Gideon Sjoberg. Chapel Hill: University of North Carolina Press.

Warner, R. Stephen. 1993. "Work in Progress toward a New Paradigm for the Sociological Study of Religion in the United States." *American Journal of Sociology* 98(5):1044–93.

Wuthnow, Robert. 1988. *The Restructuring of American Religion: Society and Faith Since World War II*. Princeton: Princeton University Press.

Chapter 1

MANAGING STRAIN, CONTRADICTIONS, AND FLUIDITY

*Messianic Judaism and the Negotiation of a
Religio-Ethnic Identity[1]*

SHOSHANAH FEHER

"We are *mishpoche*,[2] the family of the Lord. We are here together to relax and to fellowship. Good *Yomtov*[3] and happy Passover. Tonight we celebrate our freedom, just as *Yshua*[4] taught his disciples." These opening remarks greeted almost 700 people, seated at round tables, in the converted gymnasium of a nondenominational Christian fellowship. It was spring 1993, and Adat haRuach's Passover seder had begun.[5]

This group of Messianic Jews faces a particular problem of negotiating an intersection of identities that are usually considered mutually exclusive. Examining how they do this became the focus of this ethnography. The opening remarks of Adat haRuach's seder were made by the Messianic rabbi who stood on the stage as he welcomed the evening's participants. A trim man of 40 with piercing blue eyes, he wore a pale brown suit, a tie, and a white *kippah* (skullcap). The wall behind him was decorated with a large Israeli flag, flanked by flags displaying Judean lions also in white and blue. The participants wore their best clothes and joined in the festive mood. All the men wore *kippot* (skullcaps); for those who did not bring their own, white ones were provided at the entrance.

Rabbi Jason[6] began by explaining the traditional seder foods in the center of each table and the new meaning of each item (as of the Passover itself) for Messianic Believers:[7] The *zeroah* (lamb shankbone) represents the means of redemption, the blood of the sacrifice, and the way in which *Yshua* haMashiach[8] became the *Pesach* (Passover) sacrifice. The *baytzah* (roasted egg) stands for the burnt offerings of the Temple period. The *maror* (bitter herbs) represents the bitterness of slavery and the terrible bondage of the oppressed.[9] The *charoset* (sweet apple and nut mixture) is a reminder of the sweetness of the redemption. The *karpas* (green spring herbs) speaks of life.

Rabbi Jason went on to describe the *matzoh tasch*, a pillowcase divided into three compartments. During the seder, three pieces of *matzoh* (unleavened bread)[10] are placed in the case, one in each compartment. The rabbi explained that the three compartments represent the unity of God

> For those of us who are Messianics, it makes perfect sense to us. It is such a beautiful picture of God, isn't it? . . . God is a oneness, a unity, with plural names. God is revealed as three persons: God, the Mashiach, and the Holy Spirit. Each has a distinct role, but all are one.

Wrapping the three matzoh in the case and pointing to the middle matzoh, Rabbi Jason said that, during its preparation, the matzoh is "perforated, and it is pierced and striped." As he pointed out, Isaiah says "the Messiah will be pierced through for our iniquities and will be striped." In other words, the matzoh has holes because it has been pierced, and the stripes are reminders of the stripes on the Messiah's back from the whipping he suffered at the hands of the Romans.[11]

As Rabbi Jason broke the middle matzoh, called the *afikomen*, he said

> This makes sense to us Messianic Believers, doesn't it? At this time, we wrap up the middle matzoh. After He was broken for our inequities, He was enshrouded. So do we now. He was hidden for awhile and buried. He will come again.

The symbolism, the rabbi explained, is clear: breaking the middle matzoh symbolizes the breaking of the body of *Yshua*. By wrapping the *afikomen* in linen, we remember the wrapping of *Yshua*'s body in linen after the crucifixion. When the broken half of the matzoh is placed under the pillow, *Yshua*'s burial is reenacted. After the meal is over, the pillow is removed, just as the stone covering the door of *Yshua*'s tomb was removed by the angel. Then the wrapped *afikomen* is taken out and unwrapped, signifying the resurrection. For Believers, breaking the matzoh into small pieces and eating them after the meal signifies the Believer feeding upon *Yshua*, the Bread of Life.

Rabbi Jason told the gathering that they celebrate Passover not only to commemorate the affliction and redemption in Egypt, but also to remind them of Yshua's redemption and affliction:

> Visitors, we're glad you had the nerve to come join us.[12] We don't want to put you on the spot, so this can mean just the *afikomen* [in the traditional sense] to you. But, we'll all partake together. It's what is in your hearts that matters. If you are a Believer and are redeemed, you can partake in the full meaning. If not, partake and thank God for the redemption of Egypt. But ask yourself: Why not receive the full redemption of God? You may not be a Believer, but the spirit of God may have tugged at your heart [tonight]. If you're a Jew and feel you can't turn on your people, we're here to tell you, it's the fulfillment of your Judaism. . . . Let us bow our heads and pray.

We closed our eyes and prayed. During the altar call, three "new sheep" (converts) went to the altar, having accepted *Yshua* into their hearts. Near the end of the seder, Rabbi Jason reminded us that

> There will come a time—some day, some year—when we will all call out *Baruch Hashem!*[13] *Adonai H'abba!*[14] *Yshua* is the Messiah. . . . It is a taste of what will happen in all seders of all nations.

At the end of the service, Rabbi Jason and two other men picked up their instruments. At their sides, two women dressed in blue and white sang and clapped as they swayed to the tunes. At the foot of the stage, many participants enthusiastically joined in dances reminiscent of Israeli folk steps, weaving their way between the stage and the dinner tables.

This seder serves as a metaphor for Messianic Judaism in general and Adat haRuach in particular. It attempts to bridge Christian and traditional Jewish ideologies by showing the Jewishness of Jesus' roots and how Jews, as believers in Jesus, can maintain the traditional rituals of their childhood. Congregants have done this by recoding Jewish ritual and infusing it with Christian meaning. This community has acknowledged Passover to be the Last Supper, the Eucharist, and simultaneously has given the holiday a new, *Yshua*-centered meaning.

Passover is only one example of Messianic Judaism's constant decoding and recoding of Jewish ritual and Christian meaning. The Messianic Judaism identifies with its parent communities, the Jewish and the Christian, and borrows elements from both. At the same time, however, it is breaking away from them to form a new community of its own. Many Messianic Jews grew up in the Jewish community; yet the Jewish community does not regard them as members. Nor does Messianic Judaism fall neatly into the Christian community because of its strong ethnic identity, values, and norms associated with being Jewish. Rather, it is a community of overlaps: Jews appropriate Christian imagery, and Christians appropriate Jewish culture. The way in which congregants in the Messianic community negotiate identity parallels the way the group negotiates its standing with respect to its parent communities.

The Messianic community works constantly to define its identity. In this chapter, I examine the degree to which Messianic Believers identify with their parent communities, which have traditionally called for exclusive identification (also see Nippert-Eng 1996; Zerubavel 1991).[15] I show how Believers remove preexisting fences and how, in turn, they produce new fences. I discuss Messianic Jews' identification and distancing mechanisms regarding the traditional Jewish community; then, their relationship with the Christian community; and finally, the ways in which Messianic Believers produce new sets of norms and form their own community.

Adat haRuach (Community of the Spirit), located in California, is one of 125 Messianic congregations in the United States; it is among the largest, drawing about 150 worshipers on any given Saturday. The congregation is diverse in members' ethnicity, age, and marital status.[16] At Adat haRuach, the proportions of Jewish and Gentile Believers is about even. Respondents told me that the proportion of Jews in East Coast congregations is significantly larger because of the religious demography of the region.

To become as deeply involved in the congregation as possible, I became a participant in the congregation's activities, including weekly services, the Women's Ministry, Bible study and bimonthly *Havorah* (fellowship), and social events ranging from birthdays and luncheons to consecrations and shabbat dinners. Although always aware of my status as an outsider, I came to feel like a welcomed member. In my time at the congregation, I had the chance to get to know and converse with all the members and regular attendants. I formally interviewed 20 sets of people, ten single congregants and ten couples.

Half of the interviewees were Jewish, and half of the group were members of the congregation.[17]

This study is a prime example of the cultural construction of identity, one which could not have been developed by postulating a theory in advance. Only through the ethnographic study of the community could I learn that Messianic Believers invest energy in this kind of "culture work" and "boundary work" (Becker 1994; Nippert-Eng 1996). When I set out to study Adat haRuach, my theoretical framework reflected my interest in Jews' involvement in new religious movements. I had posed the question "How do Jews reconcile their Judaism with their new Christian identity?" I found, however, that most adherents were trying to Judaize Christianity or to Judaize their own somewhat secular Jewish identity. In other words, my ethnographic work shed light on a whole set of cultural issues the existence of which I had not suspected previously (also see Nippert-Eng 1996).

Messianic Believers' Identification with the Jewish Community

The Messianic movement, and certainly the congregants of Adat haRuach, strongly identify with Judaism, and both Jews and Gentiles strive to be more Jewish in their involvement in the world. Because ethnic Jews have a stronger claim in this regard, there exists a cultural stratification within the group. Messianic Believers hold that Judaism is transmitted by descent. Within the Messianic Jewish movement, an individual is Jewish if he or she has one Jewish grandparent. Even though cultural upbringing is irrelevant to their definition of Jewishness, Messianics acknowledge that being Jewish has strong cultural manifestations. Messianic Believers identify with the parent Jewish community in four major ways: language, Holocaust memory, Zionism, and the construction of biography.

The use of Yiddish is one of the most obvious examples of Messianic identification with mainstream Jewish culture. According to Markowitz (1993), Royce (1982), and Waters (1990), language is the most effective cultural attribute in maintaining solidarity and integration in an ethnic group. At this level, language does not serve the primary function of communicating meaning, as it did for ancestral generations, but rather of communicating culture in a more general sense. Reviving a language is frequently one of the first strategies of groups that are strengthening or re-creating their identity (Royce 1982). For the American-born, the foreign language of their immigrant ancestors is not primarily a linguistic tool but a source of nostalgia and cherished memories. Often it is the "silly phrases" that remain among the native-born generation, and, from this level of knowledge, they learn the language of their ancestry (Waters 1990).

Messianics try to attach themselves to cultural aspects of Judaism by recapturing Yiddish phrases. Even Jews who grew up with no Jewish culture sprinkle Yiddishisms in their everyday language. Rabbi Jason himself was not brought up in a culturally Jewish home and had to learn everything "Jewish-wise." Rabbi Jason says that while he was growing up, the extent of his Jewish knowledge was "Passover is matzo ball soup." Today he freely uses *oy gevalt, sechel,* and *mazel tov* in his sermons and in daily conversation. These Yiddish expressions are particularly striking when combined with Christian elements, as when Rabbi Jason speaks of "the *chutzpah* of the New Testament."

Gentile congregants have made an effort to pick up Yiddish expressions as well. When I visited Diana at her home, she offered me tea and cookies to "*nosh* on." During prayer time at services, a woman made a plea for "this world that's a little *meshugeh. . . .* " One of my roles in the community was as a "Jewish expert" because of my standing as a member in the traditional Jewish community. I was often asked to translate Yiddish expressions: "What do *schlemiel* and *schlemazel* mean? Or *sechel*? How do you spell that?"[18]

Holocaust memory also unites Messianic Jews with the rest of the Jewish community. Messianic Jews identify with the Jewish victims of the Nazi genocide. Tammy says she wants to make *aliyah* (immigrate to Israel) someday because, "my bottom-line belief is anybody that's a Jew is not going to be welcome here [in the United States] sometime." Kay says that her future children will be Jewish, and adds, "No one is going to tell me I'm not Jewish. I'm going off to the gas chamber with everybody else if that day ever comes." To Nicholas's dismay, his brother does not consider himself Jewish and tries to "be really Aryan in his lifestyle." Nicholas shakes his head and adds, "But then, if we get another Hitler, he's gonna die just [because of] his [last] name alone."

Messianic Gentiles do not identify with Gentile persecutors and therefore do not carry the weight of Christian responsibility for Jewish persecution (also see Harris-Shapiro 1992:212). Mike, a Messianic Gentile, invokes the Holocaust while recalling a media image. "When I saw those bundles of *tallit* ready to be burned . . . it was like destroying the very soul of the people, even more so than just killing them. . . . That's how strongly I feel."

Messianic Jews seem unable to comprehend how their people, Jews who have been persecuted for most of their history because of their Jewishness, can shun Messianics in turn. Both explicitly and implicitly they express the attitude that if they, as Messianic Believers, had lived in Germany in the 1930s and 1940s, their Jewishness would have been enough to cause Hitler to consider them Jewish and have them killed. The idea is chilling. If their Jewishness was good enough for Hitler, it should certainly be good enough for the Jewish community.

In general, Messianic Jews are not politically aligned with the Jewish community, with the notable exception of support for the State of Israel. Messianic Jews have strong Zionist leanings (also see Harris-Shapiro 1992). Adat haRuach members talk about making *aliyah*, and the congregation sponsors yearly trips to the Holy Land. Some respondents have been interested in visiting Israel since they were young. Jessica, a Gentile Believer, read the Old Testament at age 13 and was struck with a desire to visit the places mentioned in the Scriptures. Fifteen years later, she went. Others are Zionists from afar. Nicholas, for example, says

> I want to see Israel come into its own and want to see God fulfill things in Israel. I'd love to see the Temple rebuilt, and all that aspect. I'd love to go and see these things that other people have seen, the Temple restoration committee. . . . I'd like to see Israel just say, "No more of this. Get out." To take the land back.

For other congregants, membership in Adat haRuach has changed their relationship to Israel considerably. The Flynns took their first trip to the Holy Land with a church group, but in retrospect, they are aware that it was not a Jewish experience. The emphasis, they explain, was on seeing where Jesus walked: "It was very detached from anything Jewish. . . . It could have been here in southern California, the way we interacted with people." Before they go to Israel again, the Flynns would like to learn some Hebrew in order to experience the trip at a more Jewish level.

The local Messianic gift shop stocks many items from Israel, both traditional Jewish and secular articles such as: *tallit, kippot, menorahs* (traditional candelabra), Jewish jewelry (Star of David necklaces and the like), *mezuzot* (prayer scrolls affixed to doorposts), paintings of Israel, photographs of Jerusalem, and the Israeli flag (as well as other items with the same blue-and-white color combination).

For Messianic Gentiles, the close identification with Jewish culture means incorporating bits of the culture into their lives, learning about and sometimes creating a culture, and digging into the past to unearth a personal connection with Judaism. Shelly, for example, asked her father about their ancestry. Her Danish grandparents' name was Davidsen, and she thought it might reflect a Jewish background. (Actually, it did not.) Her father still teases her about her interest in their (possibly) Jewish ancestors and asks her laughingly, "You want to know about the Davidsteins?"

Even if Judaism is not part of their own past, respondents want their children to be Jewish. Illana's husband grew up in a family of Gentile Believers; none of his ancestors was Jewish. Illana feels strongly that her son (who was one-and-a-half years old at the time of my fieldwork) must marry a traditionally (matrilineally) Jewish woman so that their children, in turn, will be recognized as Jewish by the State of Israel and the family line will become Jewish. Nicholas wants to marry a rabbinically (matrilineally) Jewish woman, explaining, "I feel like I want to get my name restored in Israel, because rabbinically I'm not Jewish, according to rabbinic laws and stuff. And I would like to give my children that heritage."

In attempting to unearth a Jewish connection, many Gentiles find a link to the Sephardic tradition. One congregant told me that in her 50s, she had spent time in Israel because she wanted to understand her Jewish background better. She was raised in the United States as a Catholic; her parents were Mexican, descended from the Spanish conquistadores. Their history, combined with her mother's name (a name "similar to Cohen"), suggested to her that her ancestors were *marranos* (crypto-Jews), Spanish Jews who converted to Catholicism during the Inquisition.

Harry, an older man who brings his granddaughter to services, told me that he grew up Italian Catholic but discovered recently that he was Jewish. He read that in 1492, when the Jews were expelled from the Iberian peninsula, there was not a single family in Spain without Jewish blood. Although Harry's family lived in Italy in the 15th century, they came from a part of Italy that was predominantly Spanish. Growing up in the United States, Harry remembered that his grandmother unknowingly did "Jewish things," such as following kosher ritual when cooking. She always soaked chicken in salt water for two to three hours before cooking it; she also boiled meat before cooking it; she butchered chickens according to rabbinic tradition, cutting their throats rather than

strangling them. She also made "those Italian biscotti which are basically *kamish* . . . with anise even, like the Sephardic Jews." These practices, along with his grandmother's maiden name Leonbruni (which
Harry translates as "the Lion of Judah"), indicate to Harry that his grandmother came from a *marrano* family.

Other congregants, however, are not sure of their Jewish background
but continue to question it and consider it a possibility. One woman,
who has an Italian natal name, thinks her family might be Jewish. The
Italian Jewish connection intrigued yet another woman, a Messianic
Jew married to a Gentile of Italian descent. He has ancestors in a "Jewish town" in Italy, and the family shield bears a six-pointed star. She
and her husband cannot discuss the possibility of Jewish ancestry with
members of his family, however, because such talk upsets them. Other
Messianics said that their family surnames (especially maternal names
that have been lost in the lineage) sounded Jewish, an indication that
they themselves may be Jewish.

By using elements of traditional Jewish culture, Messianics seek to
reach traditional Jews in a framework that the Jewish community can
understand. In doing so, they hope to distinguish themselves from Christians who try unsuccessfully to share Jesus with the Jewish people.

Drawing the Line on the Jewish Community

In many ways, Messianic Believers seem to spend as much time and
effort in distancing themselves from the traditional Jewish community
as in aligning themselves with it. Although the congregants hold the
Jewish community in high regard, they find aspects of traditional
Judaism obsolete and absurd. Messianics reject what they view as
the legalism, the lack of spirituality, and the elitist separatism of
Judaism.

Messianic Believers do not accept what they perceive to be the empty
ritual of Judaism. They emphasize the importance of keeping the spirit
rather than the letter of the law. One baby boomer said that before she
became a Believer she felt that the more she did, the more God would
love her. As a result, she started lighting shabbat candles every Friday
night. Rabbi Jason, hearing this comment, added that the emphasis on
doing is a common misunderstanding among those Jews who do not
realize that law was fulfilled in *Yshua*. After all, he said, one can do all
one wants, but it is to no avail if the heart is not right with God: "We can
fool people, [but] we can't fool God."

Rabbi Jason insists that "Torah is instruction, not law. . . . We're not under the Torah, but too often Believers say 'Throw it out.'" He agrees with mainstream Protestant evangelicals that legalism does not earn points with God and that believers, including Messianic Believers, should fear legalism. Rabbi Jason maintains that faith is a matter of the heart, not of wearing *tallit* and other observances; therefore, when Messianics perform rituals, they should do so voluntarily.

The dietary laws present the most salient example of Messianic Believers' disdain for legalism. As Mary Douglas (1970) points out, these dietary restrictions function as signs inspiring meditation on the oneness, purity, and completeness of God. Such laws remind members of the Jewish community of the connection whenever they refuse bacon and ham. Although some Messianic Believers observe kosher dietary laws, they stress that they adhere to biblically kosher rules rather than the stricter rabbinically kosher rules.[19] The Flynns, for example, keep kosher unless it offends their host. When Kathy Flynn goes to her mother-in-law's house, she picks the pork sausage out of the Italian dishes, but because she and her husband are not legalistic, she eats the sauce in which the sausage cooked. In some situations, they have found themselves eating ham because not eating it would have offended their hosts so deeply that they "wouldn't be receptive to the Lord." This comment reveals both the focus on Jewishness (the kosher law) and the self-distancing from the Jewish community; the Flynns take pride in their ability to break down the fences of the traditional community in order to eat with Gentiles.

As Rabbi Jason has said from the pulpit, *kashrut* (kosher dietary laws) serves as a reminder that "we're a people set apart. You're not saved if you [keep kosher], nor are you better, just different. You serve as a reminder." Biblical *kashrut* gives Messianic Believers a private, symbolic ethnicity:[20] they abstain from forbidden foods such as pork and shellfish, but eat at Gentile homes. This position is peculiar to the Messianic community. Harris-Shapiro points out that for those unsaved Jews who do keep kosher, biblical *kashrut* is not acceptable; for Jews who do not keep kosher, eating pork and shellfish is acceptable (1992:293). Thus, the Messianics' attempts to strike a balance become an internal contradiction. In seeking to offend no one, they potentially offend everyone. Rabbi Jason told me

If you keep rabbinically kosher . . . you can't even go out and eat with someone . . . or go to their house or whatever. So I think the Messianic

realm to us is a good balance . . . it's like we can have our convictions
but . . . if someone's not kosher, that's their choice.

The reverse side of empty ritual or legalism is the lack of spirituality.
Many Messianics are confused by the Jewish community's unwillingness to consider *Yshua* the son of God. Often I heard the refrain "Don't
they [the Jewish community] see it? If only they'd open their eyes and
read." Many were baffled by my own lack of acceptance; often I was
taken aside and asked where I stood in my beliefs, given my long exposure to the Word. Nonetheless, Messianics hold the traditional Jewish
community in high regard. After all, they note, Jews are the chosen
people, even if they are unable to see the Truth.

A more pervasive sign of this sentiment is the Jewish community's
seeming disregard for God. Ethan recalls a Reconstructionist wedding
at which he performed the music. Confused about a translation during
the ceremony, Ethan later approached the rabbi. The two men talked
about Ethan's beliefs, and Ethan told the rabbi that he believed the Bible
to be divinely inspired and inerrant. The rabbi asked incredulously, "Really? Honestly? What about the miracles?" Ethan explained that he believed they had happened as explained in the Bible. Again the rabbi
replied, "Really? Honestly?" and added, "So what's to stop you from
believing that guy Jesus really is the Messiah?" "Exactly," Ethan countered. He tells the story humorously, hoping that I can reveal to him
how Jews—especially rabbis—are distanced from God and their Jewish spiritual roots.

Celia, too, finds that American Jews have a superficial cultural identity, not a real concern about understanding what it means to be Jewish:

For Americans, being Jewish is like being Irish. . . . They might even do
the *bruchas* [blessings] on Friday night, but they don't really care what
the Bible has to say. And then they come to the Lord, and all of a sudden
they are just hungry. . . . Their spiritual self has been awakened.

Both Ethan's and Celia's remarks are consistent with Harris-Shapiro's
finding that the Messianics' most widespread criticism of the Jewish
community is the gap between the spiritual and the cultural—that traditional Jews in general have not found God in the synagogue (1992:130).

Messianics claim to be especially confused by the fact that the Jewish community can accept those Jews who do not believe in God or who
do not have a strong relationship with Judaism, but reject Messianic

Judaism. One congregant's sister underwent a Reform conversion after marrying a Jewish man. This conversion, he explained, is absolutely meaningless to everyone but Reform Jews. His sister sends her daughters to a Hebrew day school, although her husband "couldn't care less about God." Ethan surmised, "I guess [being Jewish] means eating *challah* and telling funny jokes." Thus, it is unlike Messianic Judaism, which is about God and spirituality (as well as eating *challah* and telling funny jokes.)

Messianic Believers keep their distance from the Jewish community in part as a response to the alienation they feel when the Jewish community holds Messianic Judaism at arm's length. The Messianic movement has internalized this experience and uses it to protect—and distance—itself from the parent community. The greatest pain in Adam's life is the chasm between Messianics and traditional Jews. Although he points out that Orthodox Jews do not seem to care either way about Messianic Believers, the rest of the traditional Jewish community is hostile. A music teacher, Adam faces this hostility each time he loses a student after his faith has become evident. His pain was not eased by the awareness that the loss of a few dozen students is the price of his belief. Adam would like to go to Chabad house[21] and become bar mitzvah, but he points out that this is impossible because, as far as traditional Jews are concerned, he is a *meshumed* (traitor).

Rabbi Jason's wife Becky wishes that she did not have to explain her faith continually. However, she thinks even well-meaning people do not understand that Jews can believe in Jesus and still be Jewish: "I don't like that the Jewish community just thinks that we're a bunch of *meshugenehs*, that we're crazy, or that we're traitors." She knows she would encounter this reaction more often if she spent more time among Jews. As it is, when she runs into Jewish people at the park, she immediately explains, "I'm Jewish also, but I also happen to be a Jew that believes in the entire Bible, including the New Testament, and I have come to believe that the Messiah was Jesus, and I call him *Yshua*. I give 'em a whole paragraph."

When people see one member's star of David, *kippah*, or other trappings and remark on his being Jewish, he answers, "Yes, and I'm a Messianic Jew." He notes, "It doesn't take long before Jewish non-believers get it, [that] there's something weird here. . . . You find yourself dropping subtle hints too, just to get into dialogue about it. . . . You might say, 'Yeah, I just can't wait for the Messiah to come back.' *Back* [speaker's emphasis], yeah, back."

For Tammy, a Jew by birth, being a Messianic Jew means having to do a lot of explaining, both to her Gentile-believing friends and her nonbelieving friends. Her Gentile-believing friends ask her, "Why don't you marry someone who's non-Jewish?" or "What's the big deal about being Jewish, now that you're a Believer?" She finds it difficult to explain what it is like to "love your Jewish people and them not love you back." Similarly, Kay says

> It grieves me that they [the Jewish community] desire that separation. That a Messianic Jew cannot make *aliyah* to Israel when they are born Jewish and they love the Jewish God of Israel. . . . I feel that separation. Because I don't think it's good for Jews in general to fight amongst each other . . . even if we don't all agree who the Messiah was.

Messianic Believers' Alignment with the Evangelical Christian Community

Doctrinally and politically, Messianic Judaism is aligned very closely with evangelical Christianity, an extremely powerful religious group in membership, material resources, and in other resources such as media opportunities that give it an influential public voice (Harris-Shapiro 1992:351). Messianic Believers make this alignment clear in three ways: their children's education, the devotional texts they use, and their political alignment. Like many other evangelicals, Messianics identify with Christianity in general by creating historical continuity with the first-century Christian Church.

The majority of Adat haRuach congregants want to give their children a Believing education—one with a basis in evangelical Christianity. Many fulfill this desire through home schooling. Others send their children to Christian schools; only a few support secular public or private schools. The Northrops are trying to start a Messianic school, but, meanwhile, their eldest daughter attends a Christian school associated with a local evangelical church. They want her to receive a godly and spiritual foundation, which they doubt the public school system will provide.

Many congregants fear that the public school system brainwashes their children—for example, by promoting certain views, such as evolution over creation. By presenting evolution as fact to the exclusion of creationism, Diana says, "they're brainwashing kids into believing that. I think that kids should be able to choose for themselves." Most parents also share a concern about violence in public schools. Public education, they feel, is unsafe for their children because of the weapons all too frequently found in school facilities and because of the dangerous values the system teaches.

Although many Messianic parents do not support the public school system, they also believe that Christian schools ignore the Jewish heritage. Home schooling is common among those who feel that Christian schools do not give their children all the training they need. These parents meet occasionally with other Messianic Believers who home school and join evangelical home-schooling networks. Messianic Believers feel that a godly foundation is most important in their children's schooling and that this foundation is best imparted at home.

Adat haRuach also connects with the Christian community through Christian devotional literature and popular culture. The men's ministry, women's ministry, and singles' ministry use study guides produced by Christian publishers such as Bethany House, Living Books (Tyndale House), and NavPress. The women, in particular, read Christian novels, including Christian romances. Celia Eisenstadt, for example, used to read romantic novels, the kind "where people are jumping in and out of bed with each other." Today, she reads only novels that have a Christian foundation. Celia's husband, Izzy, once read "the boys' equivalent" of the romantic novel genre: *Playboy*, *Sports Illustrated*, and the like. Now, when he reads, he reads the Bible, which he affectionately calls his "Basic Instruction Before Leaving Earth" (B.I.B.L.E.).

All of the people to whom I spoke listen to Christian music or talk shows on the radio (KPRAISE and KWAVE). Adat haRuach congregants also frequently join other Christians for various events, including Harvest (a music outreach conducted by Calvary Chapel, a new evangelical denomination), March for Jesus, Christian poetry seminars, Christian marriage workshops, joint activities with Christian singles groups, and pro-life human chains (blockading entrances to abortion clinics).

Messianic Believers align politically with the evangelical Christian community; their political conservatism is reflected in their social and voting patterns. Like most of their fellow congregants at Adat haRuach, the Flynns identify with the causes of the religious right. Harry says, "If we could get back to that [the religious right's causes], it would be good for the country from a sociological aspect. I think that the country, since the 60s has degenerated and . . . they've gotten away from God's law and his concept of family that we, as a society, have done everything to destroy."

For some, becoming a Believer has meant a rethinking of political stances. Sara, for instance, embraces the politics of the pro-life movement and disapproves of premarital sex, a dramatic change from her early adult years. She attributes her earlier political beliefs to her self-centered life style. For Sara, being a Messianic Believer is less offensive to her Jewish family than is her new understanding of certain political issues. Another congregant explains how her political views have shifted since she has gone from "being of the world" to "being in the world": "All I wanted was just my own life, my own way, and that really perpetrated that type of life style." When she was self-involved, she was more liberal. Now that she understands the importance of being in the world but not sharing its values, her politics have become more conservative.

Although Messianic Believers accept Jesus, they reject what they term "bumper sticker Christianity," a term they use to describe superficial Christianity. Even so, the cars in Adat haRuach's parking lot sport bumper stickers. Indeed, as Balmer (1989) pointed out, the bumper stickers in the parking lot may be the best indicator of a congregation's politics and values. At Adat haRuach, the stickers express politically conservative and Christian (*Yshua*)-oriented views. Examples include "Found *Yshua*" (by far the most popular), "I Believe in Jesus," "Pornography Destroys," "Rush Is Right," "Pray for the Peace of Jerusalem," "Harvest Crusade," "Say No to Drugs," "I Support Our Troops," "Real Men Love *Yshua*," and numerous fish or Holy Spirit symbols.

Messianic Judaism emphasizes continuity, community, and comfort (also see Cannadine 1983). They use the early church as a controlling metaphor to reconcile Jewish and Christian symbols and to create a sense of historical continuity. Messianic Jews have looked toward the past to create a new form of tradition (also see Morgan 1983). They use early texts, read the Gospels and other first-century works, and trace Jewish Christians through the centuries to establish a symbolic social cohesion through their roots in antiquity (also see Hobsbawm 1983).

Hobsbawm coined the phrase "invented tradition" to describe communities that create or maintain themselves by developing narratives that relate them to the past. Hobsbawm (1983) discusses invented tradition in terms similar to Douglas's (1970) work on ritual. Like Douglas, Hobsbawm finds that symbolic practices, through repetition, inculcate certain values and norms of behavior. In invented tradition, however, these values and norms imply continuity with the past. "The peculiarity of 'invented' traditions is that the continuity is largely factitious. In short, they are responses to novel situations which take the form of reference to old situations" (Hobsbawm 1983:2). Cannadine suggests that (perhaps paradoxically) it is the continuity that imparts the attributes of uniqueness, tradition, and permanence (1983:150).

Messianic Believers have invented tradition by attempting to "establish continuity with a suitable historic past" (Hobsbawm 1983:1). For Messianics, this historical past is the first-century Christian church. For instance, they observe all seven feasts listed in Leviticus 23, because these observances are consistent with the practice of *Yshua* and the early church. These seven feasts—Passover, the Feast of Unleavened Bread, the Sheaf of First Fruits, Pentecost, the Feast of Trumpets, the Day of Atonement, and the Feast of Tabernacles[22]—are mentioned in the New Testament as well as the Pentateuch. Therefore, these feasts are thought to have both symbolic and prophetic significance for the Messianic community.

Likening themselves to the early Hebrew followers of Jesus, congregants observe many of the Jewish holidays, albeit with a twist. They keep many of these holy days primarily because they believe that the early Christians did, that "this is how *Yshua* worshiped, the custom He followed." Rabbi Jason negotiates uncomfortable practices, such as meeting on Saturday rather than Sunday mornings for worship, with variations on the statement "This is how *Yshua* did it." For example, because congregants observe the traditional ritual of reading the Torah portion, Rabbi Jason states that "this is how *Yshua* worshiped, the custom He followed. . . . Periodically it's important to bring out the Torah and affirm our faith." Messianic Believers emphasize that their rendition of Jewish ritual is a matter of tradition and choice, not legalism. When evangelical peers point out that the Old Testament feasts are full of legalisms such as restrictions on what one eats (as for Passover), where one eats (as for Tabernacles), and whether one is allowed to eat at all (as for Atonement), Messianic Believers respond with "The feasts symbolize the freedom in Messiah" and "The law is a blessing rather than a burden."

Messianic Believers, then, have created a sense of continuity in two ways. First, they claim to practice rituals inherited from the early church. Second, they believe that the practice of these rituals has continued unbroken through the centuries because of the persistence of a "saving remnant" of which they are a part. Together these strategies anchor the evangelical pole of their combined identity.

Drawing the Line on the Evangelical Christian Community

As in their relations with the Jewish community, Messianic Believers' relationship with the Christian community is ambivalent. Frustrated by the church's failure to recognize *Yshua*'s Jewishness, Believers attempt to model themselves after the first-century church rather than their Christian contemporaries. They distance themselves from the contemporary Christian church in two ways: invalidation of the anglicized church and the rhetoric of misguidedness.

Language is one way in which the Messianic movement simulates the early church. Messianic Jews work to purge their ritual and interpretation of Hellenistic Christian terms. By claiming identity with the earliest church, they disavow connection with the Gentile church that succeeded it (Harris-Shapiro 1992:210). Adat haRuach congregants do not deny that they are Christians, but they prefer to label themselves Believers. Whenever the word "Christian" appears in a study guide text, they replace it with "Believer." Believers call Jesus by his Hebrew name, *Yshua*. Similarly, they avoid terms such as convert, New Testament, and cross; instead they use completed (or fulfilled) Jew, New Covenant, and tree. In Bible study and *Havorah*, Rabbi Jason gently reminds readers who use Greek terms that he prefers using "the Messianic terms." Quickly trying to remedy her mistake when she mentioned Jesus Christ, one reader responded, "Sorry—*Adonai*!"[23]

Messianic Believers are frustrated and intolerant of Christians' lack of Jewish understanding and their anglicization of the church. To those who speak as if *Jehovah* is God's name, Rabbi Jason responds in a sermon by asking, "When did you study Hebrew? There's no *J* in Hebrew. It's not *Yahweh* either. I don't mind saying it because I know it's not the right name;[24] there's no *W* in Hebrew. It's clear if you take Hebrew 101."

In the same vein, Rabbi Jason speaks about the cultural aspects of modern-day Christianity. "You want to celebrate Easter? Fine! Where's your Easter in the Bible? These are all cultural shadows. We [our western culture] threw out biblical shadows . . . threw out shabbat and replaced it with what? [The] shadow of Sunday. But don't get mad at me because I use biblical shadows, the shadows spoken by God."

Most Messianics do not initiate Christmas celebration in their own homes. When they do join a Christmas gathering at their families' homes, they acknowledge that it is not a biblical holiday but rather, as Abby says, "one of those things that's tradition and family." Adat haRuach's congregants regard the cultural tradition as just that. As Harry pointed out, "It's amazing how history's been anglicized and changed. . . . I treasure that [Jewishness] in the Messianic congregation, how that's been brought back."

Adat haRuach congregants share a common rhetoric about paganism and the increased importance, over time, of biblical holidays. All of the respondents, regardless of the extent of their involvement in the holidays, use one of these rhetorics. The first rhetoric is the overshadowing of the biblical holidays. This rhetoric is exemplified by Nicholas, who celebrates Christmas with his mother because it is important to her. Even so, he finds more fulfillment in celebrating the Jewish holidays (Hanukkah, Passover, and the High Holy Days) because they have provided his life with more richness than the Gentile holidays and have made him feel closer to God.

The second rhetoric, paganism, is often overlaid with the rhetoric of overshadowed biblical holidays. Wiley reported that he changed his focus because of his knowledge of the pagan origins of Christmas: "I don't believe Christ was born in the middle of winter on the birth date of Mithras, the sun god, and I don't think Jesus was born that time of year. And I don't like as commercialized as it's gotten. It seems to have left Christ out of the whole picture." The Slaters, as well, do not celebrate Christmas because it is a pagan holiday, not a biblical one. Both the Northrops and the Ruettgers celebrate Christmas, but, since they became involved with Adat haRuach, they have tried to emphasize the Jewish celebrations and minimize those based on pagan ritual. The Ruettgers say that they try to disregard the pagan elements of Christmas, which is difficult because "even the tree has pagan roots." Messianic Believers seem to use pagan to signify a despised "other." Believers consider paganism a corrupting element within Christianity (but not within Judaism, its predecessor). As a group seeking to build bridges between Jews and Christians, they find common ground in their opposition to pagans and paganism.

Messianic Jews' disdain for the anglicized church evolves, in part, from their feeling that the Christian church is largely misguided. Believers feel that modern-day Christians, by not understanding the "Jewishness of *Yshua*," practice a version of Christianity gone awry. For example, Messianic Jews are repelled by Christian groups that believe in the "spiritual Israel." Spiritual Israel refers to the idea that Jews offended God by rejecting Jesus and that God then transferred His holy covenant to the Gentiles—at which point, Gentiles became the spiritual

Israel. Christians who hold this belief are in direct opposition to Messianic Believers.

Messianic Believers also take issue with Christians who refuse to believe that Jesus was Jewish. Congregants report that when some of these Christians are reminded of their savior's heritage, they reply, "No, God wouldn't do that to us." Diana recalled, "Somebody told me that Jesus spoke Aramaic, [so] he was an Arab." Her husband, Ethan, laughed and added, "And I speak English. Therefore we're Teutons, right?" Missy remarked, "I'm not saying that [Christians] are any less of a Believer, but I do believe that God's gonna call them on the carpet for discarding all the Jewish [aspects]." She said, "I just feel very firmly that Adat haRuach has the best grip on God's choice for a true belief. I'm not disputing any other belief. . . . But you can have a deeper understanding. You can be more closely related to the true form." Nicholas would be satisfied if more Gentiles understood and did not "downgrade and persecute Jewish people."

Everybody with whom I spoke at Adat haRuach reported a long-standing disillusionment with the Christian church. Adam was drawn to Adat haRuach because its congregants were living as he had read they were supposed to live. He had never before witnessed such consistency between faith and action, and he found it encouraging. Unlike the Christian denominations he had encountered previously, Adat haRuach was not a "bunch of hypocrites." Shelly was similarly disillusioned with the Baptist church, which she has since left. She did not like the way her Baptist congregation disregarded the Old Testament and ignored Jesus' Jewishness and the Jewish underpinnings of the apostles' lives.

Congregants cite the electronic churches and megachurches as the extreme examples of everything Adat haRuach is not. Billy Graham, Jimmy Swaggart, and other well-known preachers are favorite targets of disdain. At a *Havorah* meeting, Rabbi Jason said in disbelief, "I can't believe Jimmy Swaggart still has his congregation. What's worse—the shyster who leads or the sheep that follow?"

Messianic Believers make clear that they are separated from Christians by their lack of interest in the trappings of a church. The leader of the women's ministry group spoke about "Billy Graham and others like him," remarking that the size of the church becomes important and "you have to talk the talk, walk the walk." She pointed out that in such a situation, the church, not God, prescribes excellence in the same way that the outside world dictates signs of excellence.

Negotiating the Boundaries of Messianic Judaism

For communities that are defined territorially, boundaries are easy to identify. Boundaries for Messianics are problematic, however, because their community is demarcated socially, not territorially or even ethnically. To examine social boundaries, one must analyze interactions within the group, as well as the interactions occurring between group members and nonmembers. These interactions measure membership as well as exclusion (Barth 1969; Douglas 1970; Waters 1990). Community is an interactive process, shaped by its members just as its members are molded by it (Markowitz 1993).

Just how Messianic Believers draw social boundaries is revealed in the Jewish-Gentile relations within the group. The Messianic community's constant work to form its identity entails an ongoing negotiation between Jewish and Gentile cultures, and thus results in ambiguities, dilemmas, and hierarchies. Messianic Believers define themselves as having a unique identity, in some ways linked to the Jewish and Christian communities and in other ways opposed to both. Their constructed identity and their doctrine of exclusivity result from their rejection by both parent communities. This sense of rejection is also a source of strength to Believers who derive pleasure in being different. Glad to be neither Christian nor Jew, Messianic Believers consider themselves an exclusive group (see also Nippert-Eng 1996). Tammy, for example, stated that her favorite aspect of the Messianic way of life was "the *mishpocheh*, being a part of the true family of God," which does not include Gentile Believers or traditional Jews.

For Rabbi Jason, Messianic Judaism is the best of both worlds: "We're still Jews and we can live this way. . . . Some Christians disagree with us, they don't understand it, but it's really a worldwide family. . . . We go to any major city . . . and it's a special connection because of our faith and our heritage." Rabbi Jason believes that this special connection is promoted among Messianic Jews more strongly than within most Christian or Jewish denominations. His wife Becky added that Messianic Jews are "the subset of the subset, the intersection of both." The people I talked to described this sense of exclusivity in a variety of ways. One congregant said, "You get comfortable with the fact that, well, we are a little different . . . but it's a blessing . . . in the Messianic understanding, . . . we really embrace and can have friendship and fellowship with a lot of different people, but at the same time maintain our identity." For Messianics, their faith is the best of all possible worlds.

They can claim uniqueness while simultaneously finding the community and conformity with others that they also crave (also see Waters 1990).

Dynamic boundaries produce a cultural tradition that is ever changing, "an ongoing dialogue among people and traditions" (Markowitz 1993:6). According to Nippert-Eng, boundary work is "enacted and enhanced through a visible collection of activities that help reinforce distinctions" (1996:6). Messianic Believers draw on such things as clothes, foods, language, and memories. These tangible resources also point to the ethnic-cultural hierarchy of the Messianic movement. As such, the production of boundaries, as with their ethnic identities, is an elective construction.

The Messianic Believers' reconstruction and readjustment of identity is not surprising in light of previous findings by Waters (1990). She notes that the essential contradiction in American culture is between individual and community. Individuals struggle between these two poles and demand a flexible ethnicity. Jews are attracted to Messianic Judaism via the Messianic Judaization of traditional proselytizing rhetoric, which makes a Christian message more palatable to them. Gentiles, on the other hand, are attracted by the opportunity simultaneously to adopt a new ethnic and a new religious identity, thereby achieving a special ethnic status that otherwise would have eluded them. Being ethnic makes Believers feel unique and special while giving them a sense of belonging to a collectivity. Being Jewish, or having a Jewish heart symbolizes a permanence that cannot be severed, that cannot eradicate their Jewish identity (Markowitz 1993).[25] The symbolic ethnicity of Messianic Judaism, therefore, gives individuals the sense of conformity, but with the element of choice.

Constructing such a community enables Messianic Believers to define the boundaries of collective identity, establish membership criteria, generate a shared symbolic vocabulary, and define a common purpose (Nagel 1994:163; also see Nippert-Eng 1996). This work is particularly clear in Adat haRuach's emphasis on Jews as their primary mission. Congregants will witness to anyone, Rabbi Jason says, "but we're not trying to reach the Hispanic community or the Vietnamese community." Rabbi Jason also compared Jewish Christians to members of the Korean, African American, and Japanese churches, explaining that the Bible-believing (evangelical) churches are the same, even if "they eat sushi and we eat bagels." Like all of these cultural groups, Messianic Believers view themselves simultaneously as a separate group (in this case, a Jewish ethnic group) and as part of the larger body of Christ.

Messianic Believers' attempt to combine Christianity and Judaism is contested at every level. Their identification with Jews and Christians binds them to both communities ("We keep kosher"; "We're not legalistic") but also alienates them from both groups ("How can you keep kosher if you mix meat and milk?" "Why won't you eat a pepperoni pizza?"). In constructing their identity in the way they do, Messianic Believers systematically highlight certain contradictions and systematically ignore others.

In response to the parent communities—which draw sharp distinctions between themselves—Messianic Believers have tried to blur the distinctions. Yet their fluidity and fuzziness does not reach past the evangelical and Jewish cultures. Vis-à-vis secular society, Messianic Judaism is firmly bound, absolutely clear about who is within the group and who are nonmembers. Their sense of order relies on a literal interpretation of the Bible. Messianics make this a point of distinction between themselves and those who do not incorporate a pure reading of the Bible, including both nominal Christians and the traditional Jewish community.

According to Zerubavel, those who have the ability to be both rigid and fuzzy are flexible. By recognizing structure and feeling comfortable destroying it, the flexible mind appreciates that any entity can be situated in more than one context. Flexibility implies that the symbols and meanings of a cultural group are dynamic. While they still carve up the world into categories (Believers versus nonbelievers), Messianic Believer's religious expression is dynamic, always in flux and open to negotiation at the level of the individual and at the level of the movement itself (Zerubavel 1991).

Culturally, Messianics struggle for recognition in ways that normative Jews and evangelicals do not. They aim to identify with evangelicals, with Israel, and with Jews. They draw responses ranging from tepid to overtly hostile. Blessing their Manischewitz wine in the name of the Father (*Abba*), the Son (*Yshua*), and the Holy Spirit (*Ruach ha-Kodesh*), they succeed in offending Jewish and Christian sensibilities alike. Although some branches of the evangelical Christian community distance themselves from the Messianic movement, most evangelicals accept them. Messianics' relationship with the traditional Jewish community is different, however, because of that community's perception of the Messianics. Messianic Believers are very aware of this perception and find it painful. Yet, even the effort to break down barriers creates new ones, enclosing their community more tightly while distancing them from their parent communities.

NOTES

1. This work was funded in part by the National Science Foundation, the Society for the Scientific Study of Religion, and the Religious Research Association. The author would like to thank the following people for their suggestions on earlier drafts of this chapter: John Sutton, Valerie Jenness, Geoffrey Sternlieb, and Elsa Feher.

2. Yiddish for immediate and extended family.

3. Happy Holidays.

4. Hebrew name for Jesus.

5. The name of the Messianic synagogue is a pseudonym.

6. I have changed the names and identifying characteristics of the Messianic Believers I mention.

7. The Messianic movement is made up of ethnic Jews and ethnic Gentiles. Together, Messianic Jews and Messianic Gentiles are Messianic Believers. Among Messianics, the term "Believer" is considered better to reflect their relationship than "Christian." They view the latter as a Hellenistic term and, therefore, not Messianic.

8. Hebrew name for Jesus the Messiah, or Jesus Christ.

9. At the Last Supper, the rabbi told us, *Yshua* (Jesus) took a portion of the bitter herbs and told John that the person he gave it to was the one who would betray him; he then handed it to Judas.

10. Traditionally, the unleavened bread commemorates the Israelites' exodus from Egypt. They were so rushed that they could not wait for the yeast to rise in the bread they were baking.

11. To ensure that we realize that the traditional matzoh—which "even" the mainstream Jewish community eats—is also pierced and striped, Rabbi Jason said, "I remind you, this is not Messianic matzoh. This is out of the Jewish caterer's stove."

12. Many of the visitors were family members of Adat haRuach congregants, who invited relatives to the seder in the hope that they would come to understand Messianic Judaism better and, perhaps, even join them in their belief.

13. Blessed be God (literally, Blessed be the Name).

14. God is the Father.

15. Thumma (1991) discusses how religious identity is negotiated with respect to sexuality in situations where the two identities are considered mutually exclusive.

16. Of the 77 families and individuals listed in the congregation's roster, 19 are Latino, African American, or Asian American; three of the families are ethnically mixed. The single members include comparable numbers of men and women. Almost all age groups are represented, from small children to

grandparents, but the majority is families of the baby-boom generation. All but two of my 30 interviewees were between 30 and 40 years old.

17. The other half attended Adat haRuach regularly but had not officially joined.

18. This role always struck me as simultaneously humorous and embarassing. I have never considered myself particularly informed on matters of Judaism or Yiddishkeit, but Messianics looked to me for explanations. My role as "Jewish informant" did ease my acceptance at Adat haRauch and engendered trust.

19. Messianic Believers distinguish between practices that are prescribed in the Bible (biblically based) and regulations that are based on the Talmud (called "rabbinically based" because they were put into practice on the advice of rabbis).

20. In other words, keeping kosher is a way of being identified with Judaism without the support of organizational or cultural structures of Jewish culture. For more detail on symbolic ethnicity, see Alba (1990); Gans (1994); Gans (1979); and Waters (1990).

21. A Lubavitch outreach center. The Lubavitch Hasidim are a sectarian group of ultra-Orthodox Jews. They are active in outreach to fellow Jews.

22. For a comprehensive description of the feasts, see Fischer ([1978] 1983); Kasdan (1993); Liberman (1976); Schiffman (1992); and Zimmerman (1981).

23. Hebrew for God.

24. A reference to the Jewish taboo against saying God's name.

25. See Markowitz (1993) for a discussion of the biological inalterability of Jewish identity among Russian/Soviet Jews.

References

Alba, Richard D. 1990. *Ethnic Identity: The Transformation of White America.* New Haven: Yale University Press.

Balmer, Randall. 1989. *Mine Eyes Have Seen the Glory: A Journey into the Evangelical Subculture in America.* New York: Oxford University Press.

Barth, Fredrick. 1969. "Introduction." Pp. 9–38 in *Ethnic Group and Boundaries*, edited by Fredrik Barth. London: George Allen and Unwin.

Becker, Penny. 1994. "Mining the Tradition: Social Change and Culture Work in Two Religious Organizations." Presented at the annual meetings of the Society for the Scientific Study of Religion, Albuquerque, NM.

Cannadine, David. 1983. "The Context, Performance, and Meaning of Ritual: The British Monarchy and the 'Invention of Tradition,' c. 1820–1977." Pp. 101–64 in *The Invention of Tradition*, edited by Eric Hobsbawm and Terence Ranger. Cambridge: Cambridge University Press.

Douglas, Mary. 1970. *Natural Symbols*. New York: Pantheon Books.

Gans, Herbert J. 1979. "Symbolic Ethnicity." *Ethnic and Racial Studies* 2(1):1–20.

————. 1994. "Symbolic Ethnicity and Symbolic Religiosity." *Ethnic and Racial Studies* 17(4): 577–92.

Fischer, John. [1978] 1983. *The Olive Tree Connection*. Palm Harbor, FL: Menorah Ministries.

Harris-Shapiro, Carol. 1992. "Syncretism or Struggle: The Case of Messianic Judaism." Ph.D. Dissertation, Religion Department, Temple University, Philadelphia, PA.

Hobsbawm, Eric. 1983. "Inventing Tradition." Pp. 1–14 in *The Invention of Tradition*, edited by Eric Hobsbawm and Terence Ranger. Cambridge: Cambridge University Press.

Kasdan, Barney. 1993. *God's Appointed Times: A Practical Guide for Understanding and Celebrating the Biblical Holidays*. Baltimore, MD: Lederer Messianic Publications.

Liberman, Paul. 1976. *The Fig Tree Blossoms: Messianic Judaism Emerges*. Indianola, IA: Fountain Press.

Markowitz, Fran. 1993. *A Community In Spite of Itself: Soviet Jewish Emigres in NY*. Washington, DC: Smithsonian Institution.

Morgan, Prys. 1983. "From a Death to a View: The Hunt for the Welsh Past in the Romantic Period." Pp. 43–100 in *The Invention of Tradition*, edited by Eric Hobsbawm and Terence Ranger. Cambridge: Cambridge University Press.

Nagel, Joanne. 1994. "Constructing Ethnicity: Creating and Recreating Ethnic Identity and Culture." *Social Problems* 41:152–73.

Nippert-Eng, Christena. 1996. *Home and Work: Negotiating Boundaries through Everyday Life*. Chicago: University of Chicago Press.

Royce, Anya Peterson. 1982. *Ethnic Identity: Strategies of Diversity*. Bloomington: Indiana University Press.

Schiffman, Michael. 1992. *The Return of the Remnant*. Baltimore, MD: Lederer Publications.

Thumma, Scott. 1991. "Negotiating a Religious Identity: The Case of the Gay Evangelical." *Sociological Analysis* 52:333–47.

Waters, Mary C. 1990. *Ethnic Options: Choosing Identities in America*. Berkeley and Los Angeles: University of California Press.

Zerubavel, Eviatar. 1991. *The Fine Line: Making Distinctions in Everyday Life*. New York: Free Press.

Zimmerman, Martha. 1981. *Celebrate the Feasts*. Minneapolis: Bethany House Publishers.

Chapter 2

STRUGGLES FOR MUTUAL REVERENCE

Social Strategies and Religious Stories

MATTHEW P. LAWSON

Religion is first and foremost a system of ideas by means of which individuals imagine the society of which they are members and the obscure yet intimate relations they have with it. Such is its paramount role. And although this representation is symbolic and metaphorical, it is not unfaithful.

Emile Durkheim

What role do religious symbols play in everyday life? In this chapter, I propose a Durkheimian answer: that religious symbols give individuals normative ways of interpreting society. By guiding individuals' thinking, symbols may also come to guide social action. "Society" as Durkheim uses it, however, is too vague. To specify where and how religious symbols apply to social experiences, I analyze life-history narratives in which transformations in a narrator's relationship with symbolic others are related to transformations in relationships with specific social others. Society is thus translated down to structures of phenomenological experience in personal relationships.

I analyze the life-history narratives of four women in the same family, the O'Douls of Sycamore Grove outside of Chicago. To protect their anonymity, I have changed names and identifying details. I interviewed the O'Douls as part of an ethnographic study of the Faithful Servants prayer group, a Catholic charismatic congregation in Chicago. The

O'Douls fell into a snowball sample of 30 current and former members of this prayer group with whom I conducted extensive, semistructured, audiotaped life-history interviews. Across the entire sample, interviews averaged slightly more than three hours. On the four O'Doul women, I have about 21 hours of taped, transcribed interview material. I spent the least time with Janese (three hours) and the most with Anne (seven hours over three sessions).

The O'Douls offer revealing cases because, as members of a single alcoholic family, they share a great deal of life experience, including exposure to a particular configuration of religious symbols (see Figure 1). Yet they responded to this exposure differently. Anne and Laura, who are charismatic, told sin-to-salvation narratives; while Harriet and Janese, who are not charismatic, constructed more idiosyncratic narratives. Looking at their life trajectories helps us understand why Anne and Laura converted while Harriet and Janese did not. Delving more deeply into the stories of the two who converted helps us to understand how religious symbols transformed their lives. Before taking up either of these tasks, however, I explain charismatic symbolism and how the O'Doul women differ in regard to it.

Symbols and Stories

If religion represents social relations in a manner that is "symbolic and metaphorical," then we must develop some method for showing analogic similarities between the sacred and profane domains of action. Most scholars who have followed Durkheim have looked for categorical parallels between these domains, equating God the father, for instance, with human fathers (see, for example, Parsons 1979, McLoughlin 1978, Neitz 1987). For Neitz (1987), the significance of the God symbol for the Catholic Charismatic Renewal is its stress on a warm and caring "daddy" God. This new way of conceiving God for American Catholics evolved, Neitz suggests, because upwardly mobile Catholic fathers in the post–World War II era must have become more warm and responsive parents. She drew this conclusion from her respondents' status characteristics, not their talk about their relationships with their fathers.

In contrast, my approach is more structuralist. Rather than look for correspondences between sacred and profane categories, I focused on correspondences in the relations among categories in each domain. Wuthnow (1987) and Bourdieu (1990) argue for such structural analysis, but we may arrive at it from another angle. Freud (1965) interpreted dreaming as an object world in which social-relational problems are symbolically represented and worked through (cf. Parsons 1967). I would contend that religious symbolism constitutes an idealized object domain in which individuals practice normative interaction sequences, which may then be generalized to nonritual object domains (see Rizzuto 1979, Jones 1991, cf. Greeley 1981). Attention to object relations led me to focus less on the level of discourse and narrative than on the structures of interpersonal relationships referred to and encoded within it. Similarly, I stressed the more inclusive analysis of religious symbolism rather than of religious discourse because, while religious "objects" (like Jesus) are figured in discourse, they are also figured iconically (as in crucifixes) and indexically (as in tongues and other charismatic gifts).

I examined the lives of individuals because it is they who create the structures of relations in the sacred and the profane and who are the points of articulation between the two domains. In the domain of the sacred, that is, of religious ritual and discourse, charismatic Catholics express a relationship with God of obedience and responsiveness. This relation appears in their beliefs about the charismatic gifts of tongues and prophecy and in how they manifest these gifts. These individuals freely and willingly subject themselves to the promptings of an other who controls their very thoughts and bodily movements. They become "dodos for Jesus," according to Mother Angelica, a charismatic nun with a weekly show on the Catholic cable channel. In charismatic rituals, Catholics willingly act in ways that other people might consider signs of mental illness. Those who display charismatic gifts in public ritual demonstrate their obedience and responsiveness to God's will, but the public ritual is organized to move all participants into a state of deeper obedience and responsiveness to God, to move them from sin to salvation.[1]

This transformative process serves as a structural principle that organizes many aspects of charismatic experience, not just the two-hour prayer meetings. It also operates during weekend retreats and the seven-session Life in the Spirit seminars, which culminate in baptism in the Holy Spirit. For the individual, opening oneself to prophesy or to speak in tongues at prayer meetings is a process of coming into attentiveness and submission to God's will. Personal testimony in prayer meetings also refers to this transformative process in the individual's everyday life. Testimonies typically recount some blessing or answer to prayer given by God in return for obedience. These statements are shared to encourage others to submit to God's will. This motive for telling conversion stories also operated in the interview setting, where converts thought that my research might help propagate their stories, and so convince my readers of the transformative power of faith. It is in testimonies, especially, that the relations between the domains of ritual and nonritual, sacred and profane, are mapped and remapped.

For Anne and Laura O'Doul, the content of their personal testimonies is a sin-to-salvation narrative. Both of them talked about lives of "sex, drugs, and rock and roll" before conversion, about abortions, broken relationships, and unstable career aspirations. After conversion—which is a difficult, ongoing process as they describe it—many of their behavior patterns changed. They shaped up their moral lives to strive for committed, long-term relationships and disciplined themselves to achieve long-term career aspirations.

Critics of the use of self-narratives argue that they are unreliable records of experience precisely because converts describe past history as sinful and their present life as striving for the good (e.g., Snow and Machalek 1985, Neitz 1987). Converts thus appear to revise their biographies to characterize themselves as the religious group says they should (cf. Berger and Luckmann 1966). This argument has merit, especially when considering formal public testimonies such as the ones upon which Snow (1993) based his analysis. But many of my respondents were willing to tell their stories from other perspectives and to fill out the elliptical or opaque summaries that might appear in a "three-minute testimony" with gritty detail.[2] To be sure, religious genres and symbolism affected how individuals referred to past experience, but their struggle seemed to be to interpret that experience, not to invent it.[3] With Wallis and Bruce (1983), I would argue that it is more likely that people comply with a narrative genre because it fits their experience than that they invent experience *ex nihilo* to comply with the prescriptions of a genre. I can be more confident of this with the O'Douls because I have multiple accounts about some events and circumstances and about the transformations that individuals underwent.[4]

Harriet and Janese O'Doul do not tell sin-to-salvation stories, and I do not classify them as charismatics. But Janese talked about what a pain her sisters became at family gatherings after their conversion. Though their mother Harriet scorns anyone who acts on the belief that they have heard God speaking to them, she holds the charismatic renewal in very high regard: "I saw a change in my girls' lives. Drastically. I think that too [pushed me toward the renewal]: I saw what it was doing for them."

Figure 1: The O'Doul Family in 1990

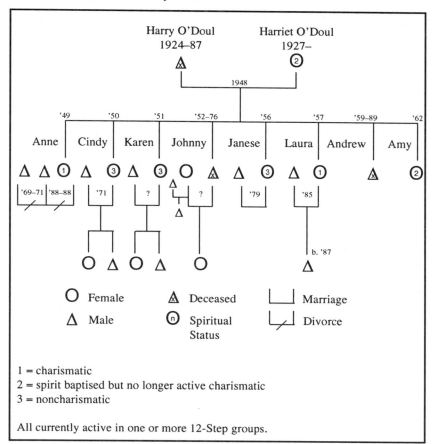

That the O'Doul women share a great deal of experience is evident not only in their stories of particular events, but in the discursive traditions they incorporate into their accounts. Well versed in the alcoholism and codependency literature, they all use its concepts to interpret their experience. Anne and Laura also incorporate charismatic language, and, to a degree, Harriet does too. Following Anne and Laura's conversions, their mother too underwent baptism in the Holy Spirit, regularly participated in prayer meetings for a time, and continued to profess support for the spiritual healing available in the charismatic renewal. However, Harriet does not claim any charismatic gifts for herself and explicitly rejects a relationship with God in prayer. From this, and from her remarks on biblical criticism and on her favorite theologians (Theillard de Chardin and Matthew Fox), her theology is more transcendental and mystical than charismatic. For Janese, the situation is more clear-cut. By idiosyncratically combining elements of Buddhist, Christian, and 12-Step religiosity, Janese seems to be a classic case of Bellah and colleagues' (1985) Sheilaism or, in this case, Janese-ism. She asserts that no one has the right to tell her what to do in the sphere of religion, or in any other for that matter.

Three intersecting factors, then, allow me to designate Anne and Laura as charismatic and Harriet and Janese as not. First, Anne and Laura's stories involve moments of radical breaks with the past, in contrast to the others' stories of spiritual evolution. Second, in this evolution, the locus of control and the ground for moral authority remain firmly in Harriet's and Janese's own hands. They critically assess various theological positions and take what they like, accepting none completely. Anne and Laura, on the other hand, submit to the authority of a God who speaks to them personally. This difference is quantitatively evident in their interview transcripts. Neither Harriet nor Janese ever used the words "obedience" or "submission" (Harriet carefully avoided it when pressed), while Anne and Laura each used obedience five times, and talked specifically about wives' duty to submit to their husbands.

This language points to the third difference, the characteristics of their intimate social relationships. As Anne put it

> [The Bible] says the husband is to love the wife as Christ loved the church—[speaking softly] he gave his life—and the woman is supposed to submit. And what woman isn't going to submit to a man who loves 'em like that! Give me a break! It's not a war zone, this is like mutual reverence, mutual laying down lives.[5]

For Janese and Harriet, marriage appeared to be more of a war zone. Janese talked about "control battles" over finances and her struggles over household chores:

> In his opinion he supports me, and therefore I should be his nigger—not that he uses that word—that I should be his wife. I won't be his nigger. I tried it. I did. You know, you try everything for a marriage. I tried everything, but I don't respond well to being a nigger.

Harriet described ongoing struggles with her husband about his drinking and about his being more responsible, and Laura and Janese agreed that Harriet was the dominant parent in the household when they were growing up. When Harriet adopted Al-Anon's injunction simply to accept Harry's drinking, this apparently meant just trying to ignore it as another strategy to beat it, rather than acknowledging that he was in any way controlling her. Ignored during his binges, Harry eventually "died of alcoholism on the bedroom floor," Harriet said.

I interpret these interlocking differences between the two sets of women to reflect charismatic attentiveness and responsiveness (obedience or submission), in the cases of Anne and Laura, and the sort of self-centeredness or self-directedness that charismatics identify with worldliness, in the cases of Janese and Harriet. The question is: why? Through the evangelizing efforts of Anne and through similar experiences with 12-Step symbolism, all of them were exposed to the notion of a relationship of attentiveness and responsiveness to God, but choose to get into it, or not, in different ways. What differences in their life experiences contribute to this?

The Irish Virus

Harry O'Doul's alcoholic career, his struggle with the "Irish virus," profoundly affected the lives of his family members, including their spiritual lives. More than half the respondents in my larger sample reported that they were raised in families that suffered from alcoholism; among those I categorize as most charismatic, like Anne and Laura, the proportion is two-thirds (cf. Fichter 1976). The unique temporal and structural position of each O'Doul family member, combined with conjunctions of events in adult life, resulted in idiosyncratic narratives in our interviews. Let me first combine them to point out some features of family interaction patterns as Anne and her sisters grew up, then turn to differences in how their individual trajectories developed.

Harriet said that her Irish Catholic father was alcoholic, as were many of his relatives. Her mother's parents were German Baptists—"fundamentalists," Harriet called them. Her family never went to church, but when they moved to Chicago during the Great Depression of the 1930s, Harriet was sent to Catholic grammar school. At 21, she married Irish Catholic Harry O'Doul, and they immediately started contributing to the postwar baby boom. By their fifth anniversary, they had their first four children (Anne, Cindy, Karen, Johnny). When the youngest was three, they began raising four more (Janese, Laura, Andrew, and Amy), bringing eight healthy children into the world in 13 years.

Table 1: O'Doul Chronologies

Year	Harry	Harriet	Anne	Laura	Janese
1966		leaves church	grad. HS, lv. home	to public school	to public school
1967	43 y.o.	40 y.o.	19 y.o.	10 y.o.	11 y.o.
1968					plans suicide
1969		starts Al-Anon	marr. Vietnam vet.		
1970		starts Bible study			
1971			divorced		
1972				dates 28 y.o.	
1973	cirrhosis & dry		move nearer home/		dates fut. husband
1974			begin status quest	lives w/ boyfriend	grad. HS
1975	drinks again			grad. HS	
1976	[Johnny dies]	threatens divorce	break w/ boyfriend	break w/ boyfriend	Fs in coll. classes
1977		daily mass	year of celibacy	school new salvation	
1978			beg. spir. quest		Bible study
1979	dry again: into AA		physical breakdown	dates med. student	marries
1980		last child leaves	"born again" to Faithful Servants		
1981	drinks again			breakup-home-conv	
1982	30 year confession	Spirit baptism	confronts Father		
1983	chronic drinking		evangelizes family	into Al-Anon	
1984			quits prayer group		to California
1985				to Steuben-ville	
1986			to Steuben-ville	marries	
1987	dies			son born	
1988			married & divorced	confronts husband	
1989	[Andy dies]		ret. to Chicago		ret. to Chicago

In the early years of their marriage, Harriet drank with Harry. But by the early 1960s, they were in conflict over alcohol. Janese remembered when she was "a little kid," her mother dragged all of them out of bed in the middle of the night to tell their father that he had a drinking problem. Harriet said she did "everything" that alcoholics' wives do: "throwing out his bottles, marking his bottles," even quitting a job so he could not spend her money on alcohol. Laura said her father was "not your weekend drunk, he was the skid-row type" who went to the bar every day after work, even when he was working back-to-back shifts. Laura said that, in some ways, the four older kids grew up in a different family than she and Janese did, because Anne and the older ones remembered their father as a "happy drunk." Laura and Janese remembered him depressed, mumbling and gesturing while drinking alone at the kitchen table and blowing up if the kids made any noise.

The family lived in a three-bedroom house under intense financial pressure. Harry never went to church when the kids were young, perhaps because he worked two full-time jobs during the week. Harriet, however, went with the kids until they were transferred to public school, when the whole family left the church. Laura remembered the transfer was precipitated by an increase in the cost of school uniforms. Anne was unaffected because she graduated from Catholic high school that year, but she recalled that Harriet had asked her to move out after graduation to relieve financial stress. Janese associated leaving Catholic school with the end of family picnics, which had been continuous from the time Harry and Harriet were courting. Although no one mentioned it, I wonder about the impact of the Vatican II reforms, announced in Chicago the year the family left the church. McGoldrick and Pearce (1981:233) say that Vatican II was "stressful for many Irish-Catholics raised with the security that there was a clear, definite source of authority in their lives. Once anything about the Church could change, the whole foundation was shaken." This change would help make sense of Anne attributing her mother's scorn of "followers" to the consequences of having been a follower of the Catholic life-plan of marriage and many babies.

All of the O'Doul daughters claimed their family was dysfunctional. Anne said, "I always heard that I was Daddy's girl," and later dropped a reference to participating in a sexual abuse recovery group. Laura talked about spiritual healings for the wounds of sexual molestation by her father and brothers. Their father also verbally and physically abused their younger brother and made Anne complicit in the abuse by giving her, not Harriet, the authority to tell him when he was being "too hard" on Andrew. Janese did not talk about being abused, but she also played a different role in the family. Laura said she and Janese, born only 18 months apart, differentiated from each other in competition for parental affection. Janese "was more masculine looking," with her mother's black hair and stocky frame, while Laura was cute, with curly blond hair— "and what is cute unless you get a man." Anne explicitly talked about later using sex and seduction to get what she wanted from men, and Laura seemed to have done so too. If Janese did this, she did so to a much lesser extent.

Anne said she felt her mother's "wrath, from the earliest time I can remember. I didn't know where it came from, but certainly she wouldn't allow any relationship with my father." Laura also talked about spiritual healing for "lack of mother's love," but she did not attribute this to her mother's hatred or jealousy. She said, "my mother had very, very strict parenting techniques." Janese concurred. Harriet was "iron fisted. Absolutely. A general. She had to. She had eight kids and an alcoholic husband. She had to be that way to survive."

Given this constellation of family tensions and the family's poverty, which prevented financial support for the children's college and professional careers, it is not surprising that "getting a man" was quite important. Janese said, "boyfriends [were] the most important thing in the world" for her in high school. Laura said, "boys were going to be my salvation." When I asked why, she said, "First of all, I guess I was trying to get Daddy's love and never got it. But also, they were gonna rescue me from poverty." Janese simply said, "It's like, the big thing, you're supposed to get a man. This is it. That's what you're supposed to do." Anne, for her part, was wary of marriage and babies because, "I had it up to here with babies." Yet she married less than two years after leaving home.

Divergent Trajectories

If the stories of these four women have some common themes, they differ most in regard to the trajectories of their relationships with men and in what I view as related occupational trajectories. All of them worked as secretaries after high school. Harriet quit work when she became pregnant with Anne. Janese reacted violently against the "makeup and nylons," then worked a variety of odd jobs, especially house cleaning, where she could be her "own boss." Both of them organized their work lives around their marriages, which were secure and relatively stable, despite their struggles to get their husbands to reform and better meet their own needs. Anne and Laura, on the other hand, had disastrous experiences with their first major relationships. Afterwards, they had trouble committing to a relationship and dedicated themselves to career advancement through higher education. A series of personal and family crises later led them to feel that they were not in control of their lives. These feelings made it easier for them to turn control over to God.

The trajectory of Harriet's relationship seems fairly straightforward. After marriage, she and Harry hardly had time to establish their relationship before Anne and the other children started coming along. Harriet and Harry fought over his drinking and the fact that it precluded his helping with other family and household responsibilities. Harry, however, managed work well enough—holding two jobs when necessary, one of them a good union job he kept for more than 25 years. Harriet could struggle with him over his drinking, but with eight kids she could not afford to lose him altogether. When the youngest was in school, a priest who was a family friend convinced her to start Al-Anon. The first few times she attended, Harriet thought that Al-Anon was ridiculous to be telling her to accept Harry's drinking, that she was part of the problem. Even so, she persisted. The next year, she joined a weekly neighborhood Bible study group run by fundamentalists. She objected to some of their interpretations, but she enjoyed figuring out "the meaning of the Bible, as to where it fit in my life." It was with this Bible study, not Al-Anon, that she began her narrative of spiritual development in our first interview.

She continued with Al-Anon and Bible study for several years, and this may have influenced Harry's going on the wagon for almost two years. Harriet attributed his abstinance to the terror of a hospital stay for cirrhosis of the liver. This change, and other developments in Harry's career as an alcoholic, had an impact on his daughters, so I will keep coming back to Harry and Harriet's story. Harry and Harriet had a troubled relationship but one in which they had worked out patterns of struggle that allowed them to go on as a couple.

Janese's relationship trajectory is more like Harriet's than Laura's or Anne's. She dated an "acid head" from high school and lived with him later when he became a computer programmer. The family crisis that ensued when her father started drinking again set her on a spiritual quest, which involved studying the Bible with a fundamentalist group, like Harriet. Janese too was turned off by their dogmatism, but the experience may have helped her commit to marriage with her boyfriend. When

I interviewed her 11 years after their marriage, they still had no children, and, perhaps like Harriet and Harry early in their relationship, Janese and her husband still partied together, though she had been struggling for change. Rather than shatter the relationship, Janese sought marital therapy. There, the couple worked out a detailed set of contracts that allow them each the greatest amount of relative happiness. (His agreeing to stop "stealing" her cigarette lighter indicates the level of contractual detail.) In short, like Harriet, Janese was able to "get a man" who would give her financial security and enough commitment to the relationship that it was worth continuing, despite serious dissatisfactions and conflicts.

In contrast, Anne and Laura both had disastrous initial adult relationships with men who were significantly older than they were. The age difference seems significant to me, especially in light of their talk about sexual abuse. After Anne moved out, she worked as a secretary and lived with high school girlfriends. They convinced her to join the party scene she had avoided till then. The Vietnam veteran she soon began dating loved her family, and Harriet thought he was "a peach." But the clincher, Anne said, was her guilt about having had premarital sex with him. After they married, it quickly became apparent that he got along better with Harriet than with Anne ("she never had to live with him"). They divorced two years later. Anne partied and dated after her divorce. An abortion, however, and seeing her father discipline himself to stop drinking, caused Anne to change her ways. She disciplined herself, too, quit partying, and got on the promotion ladder at work by taking advantage of her employer's college tuition policy. Men were still important, though, and she was living with a man she thought was "the one" when another family crisis challenged her sense of control and set her on a spiritual quest.

Janese said, "I had boyfriends [in high school], so I was cool." Laura, 18 months younger, considered herself even more cool when, as a high school sophomore, she began dating the 28-year-old brother of a school friend. When he moved out of town, she was glad to break up but then started dating his 29-year-old friend. She left home her senior year to live with him. When she was 19, he stayed home all day while she worked to pay the rent. She realized "these bozos are not gonna come through." She moved out and thought, "now school was going to be my salvation."

Janese, Laura, and Anne did not correlate their own turning points with family crisis, but matching up the chronologies of their stories makes these relationships clear (see Table 1). After almost two years on the wagon, Harry started drinking again. Harriet spent several months trying to follow Al-Anon's advice about accepting Harry's binges but, eventually, told Harry she would divorce him if he kept drinking. This ultimatum spurred him to undergo a 28-day treatment program, but he was drunk again a week later. The following Tuesday their older son Johnny, the family hero, visited on his new motorcycle. Returning home to his own wife and child later that evening, he took his first corner too fast and died instantly when he slammed head-first into a tree.

Johnny's death had a profound impact on the family. Harry's depression over it became an excuse to continue drinking. His periodic hospitalizations also continued. Harriet was "back in church the next day" and thereafter attended mass daily. Janese flunked out of her second semester of college as family tension rose over Harry's drinking. Following Johnny's death, she began Bible study with the fundamentalists. It was in this year that Laura decided "these bozos are not gonna come through" and broke up with her boyfriend. Anne too broke up with the man she was living with and began a spiritual quest that landed her in the charismatic renewal. She experimented eclectically for a while, then went back to her roots in the Catholic church, attending daily mass with Harriet. Together, they attended a charismatic Life in the Spirit seminar at their home parish. At its culmination, Harriet refused baptism in the Holy Spirit. Anne did not and, thereafter, dove deeper and deeper into the charismatic renewal.

Three years of alcoholic binges later and after all the children had left home, Harry got out of the hospital and began seriously "working" an AA group. Harriet said "the best three years" of their marriage followed, and then Harry started drinking again. "He just thought he could drink again," Harriet said. Again, Harry's resumption of drinking had a big impact on the family. Laura broke up with a boyfriend. She said she was "suicidally depressed, like six of the eight kids in my family" and decided that her life was a "total ruin." She moved back home. "And it was just horrible to be back there and watch my father drink himself to death. . . . It was just *such* [speaker's emphasis] a nightmare."

Anne convinced Laura that if they went to the full weekend of the annual national conference of the Catholic Charismatic Renewal at Notre Dame, then God might heal their father's alcoholism. While there, Laura was "convicted" of the sin in her life and resolved to change. Several months later, Anne visited her father, hospitalized yet again, and expressed concern over the state of his soul. Encouraged by his response, she came back the next day with a priest, who heard Harry's first confession in 30 years. Out of the hospital, Harry went to weekday masses with Harriet. Harriet never mentioned Harry's change of heart as influencing her decision soon thereafter to participate in charismatic prayer meetings and undergo Spirit baptism. She talked only about the transformation she saw in her daughters' lives. Harriet's omission may be due to Harry's continued drinking, which for her made a sham of any supposed spiritual change.

Five years after Laura's conversion and just before the holiday family gatherings, Harry lost his battle with the bottle and died. Bateson (1972) and Denzin (1987) present a model of alcoholic interaction patterns that fits Harry's trajectory. Alcoholics, they propose, turn to drink to prove to others that they are in control of themselves, not controlled by others. The drinking itself expresses the paradoxes of control in relationships. Like his or her relationships with other humans, an alcoholic begins a relationship with the bottle (here expressions such as "married to the bottle" suggest object-relational dynamics) as an act of mastery and control, but that very act of commitment involves the loss of a degree of control. Each drink is a further assertion of control, coupled with a further challenge to it. This dynamic of assertion and challenge governs the escalating cycle of binges. Most alcoholics bottom out and admit defeat before losing as decisively as Harry did.

Two years after Harry's death, again before the holidays, Harriet and Harry's son Andrew shot himself in the head. Andrew was failing two required classes in his senior year of college, and thus would fail to graduate on time, even with a scholarship and the financial assistance that his parents had offered to none of the other children. Andrew's suicide was less of a blow to family members than Johnny's death, but for all the O'Doul women, it forcefully reiterated, as Anne put it, that "there are serious problems in our family system." For Laura and Janese, talk of Andrew's suicide sparked discussions of eschatology. Building on the concept of Christian heaven, Laura imagined that Andrew and her father were living their lives over again in truly loving family relationships, still with the same individuals, but now blessedly free of the abuses and hurts that caused their lives to turn out the way they did. Fitting with her eclecticism, Janese's eschatology involved repeated reincarnation into the same family, again with all the same individuals, working out relational issues over many lives "until you can like, be harmonious in your spirits." It is worth noting that not only is the afterlife a model of perfected family relationships for these women, but also that spirituality and spiritual development are so linked with patterns of interaction with significant others.

What these women wanted to be saved from, and the perfection toward which they were struggling, had to do with day-to-day social interaction. Congruent with 12-Step ideology, they all associated freedom from the bondage of past interaction patterns with increasing personal happiness. Harriet and Janese seemed to have pursued this freedom as a means of multiplying strategies to influence significant others to respond in ways they desired, that is, as a means of gaining more control in relationships. Anne and Laura, on the other hand, gave up trying to control others to get what they wanted. In AA terms, they "let go and let God." They gave control to God with the trust that He would lead them into relationships that would work to their greater happiness.

At one level, this synthetic history of the family allows us to understand why Anne and Laura embraced charismatic symbolism when they were exposed to it and why Janese and Harriet did not. Even though all of them learned basic patterns of interaction in alcoholic households, Anne and Laura were led by family crises and unsatisfying relationships with others to conclude that they were not in control of their lives. They gave up seeking control, feeling that such a course of action would ultimately lead to greater unhappiness. Harriet and Janese still sought control for the enhancement of their own happiness, personally defined.

Social Ills and Spiritual Healings

Anne and Laura embraced charismatic symbolism because they felt their lives were out of control. Consequently, they struggled to change with the help of charismatic symbolism. I consider Anne's story in detail, because she was most explicit about the interconnections between early family interaction patterns, later relationship crises, and the healing power of her relationship with God. The main points of Laura's story show similar connections. Anne and Laura both illustrate that their experience of conversion changed not only their beliefs, but also their patterns of social action—particularly their interactions with intimate partners and their pursuit of jobs and job security.

At the national charismatic conference at Notre Dame, Laura was convicted of leading a life of sin. But "it was a long road to giving up the drugs, giving up the sex." Four months after the conference, Laura told her new boyfriend "no more sex." He left her. She suffered combined bladder and yeast infections. Drug therapy for one infection left her vulnerable to the other, she explained, so her only hope was to change her body chemistry through a strict macrobiotic diet. The diet allowed her to heal 15 months later, but, to stay on it, she said she had to be spiritually healed of her addictions to food, drugs, and sex.

She told me she experienced the spiritual healing in therapeutic encounters with a female charismatic healer in Chicago (cf. Csordas 1994) and with a young priest who taught at the Franciscan University of Steubenville, Ohio. With the former, Laura was healed of "lack of mother's love" by coming to realize that Jesus' mother Mary loved her unconditionally. At the hands of the young priest, she obtained a healing of "father's love, brother's love, totally nonsexual male love. . . . I felt like he was the first man who ever loved me nonsexually." He was "so compassionate, so tender, I felt like it was Jesus standing there." In both instances, the reorganization of her relationships with symbolic others affected her conception of her relationships with real social others, allowing her to forgive them for the injuries she felt they had done her.

After these healings, Laura accepted a standing proposal of marriage from her boyfriend at Faithful Servants. She had known he was "aggressive." Even so, she thought that he would "be my knight in shining armor, but his aggression turned on me." The change came after a leadership crisis at Faithful Servants challenged the legitimacy of his claim of charismatic gifts. His withering criticism of charismatic spirituality kept the couple away from prayer meetings, but Laura kept up attendance at Al-Anon. She also started counseling again with a leader in another prayer group:

> So I spent about two years in [counseling], getting the courage to leave. And in that time, I had my son, which was not too clear thinking on my part. And when I finally had the nerve to leave, my husband said he would do anything that I wouldn't leave, you know. And so [I said], "well then, I want to go to marriage counseling." So then we started in marriage counseling. And we did that for six, seven months, and then he got into individual counseling.

Laura's husband also began attending AA meetings and told her he got more out of them spiritually than he got from charismatic prayer meetings. Laura concluded

> I think without God the marriage would've been finished. God was able to work with both of us, because we were both trying to walk with God.

All of a sudden, we looked at each other and kinda laughed. And I've become more assertive, and he's become Mr. Psychology, I call him. . . . You come to receive each other's gifts. You turn into the people you live with, don't you? Sometimes their bad habits. But sometimes there are good things.

Laura seemed hopeful that the marriage would continue to improve.

Religious symbolism here appears to offer new options in Laura's relationships with significant others. In her relationship with God, Laura had experimented with commitment to a relationship without being able to predict or control the outcome of her decision. The immediate result had been personal suffering and self-abnegation, but the longer-term benefits seemed clear. By admitting that she could not control the outcomes of her actions, that such control was in the hands of a loving God, Laura was free to act in new ways. Her trust in the unconditional love of a symbolized significant other allowed her to commit to marriage. But beyond simply trust, her relationship with God gave her a new model to be applied in her relationship with her husband. When he failed to reciprocate with the responsiveness she had come to expect in her relationship with God, her trust in God gave her the security to threaten divorce. Rather than losing control by giving it up to God, Laura paradoxically gained it.

Laura's story generally conforms to the charismatic conversion testimony genre. She led a life of sin ("sex, drugs, and rock and roll"), was convicted of sin, repented, and was rewarded by God with a relatively happy marriage. The rewards did not come without suffering, but the story ended on a positive note. Though Anne also led a life of "sex, drugs, and rock and roll" and used seduction as a relationship strategy as Laura seemed to do, her walk with God has left her less in the warm glow of loving relationships than in the valley of the shadow of death.

Anne associated the start of her spiritual quest with what she called a "God dream" dated to the year that Harry resumed his drinking and Johnny had his motorcycle accident: "I was crossing the tracks and this train hit me head on. Head on. This huge locomotion [sic] and I was splattered in little pieces everywhere." With this dream Anne began to feel drawn toward spirituality. Unfortunately the man who was living with her—not a "bozo" but a respectable young professional ("I thought this guy was gonna be the one")—was not so drawn. Relational conflicts that were already becoming apparent to Anne subsequently increased. He left her. In the interview, I asked her, "So that ending of the relationship was the train hitting you and blowing you apart?" Her reply illustrates the themes of control and submission and how these are intertwined with both spiritual and relationship issues:

> It was the beginning of the train hitting me. *It was the beginning of the breaking that happened that let me see that I no longer lived in the illusion that I had control over everything* [author's emphasis]. Because I could usually pick the guy I wanted or I could pick whatever I wanted, or I could work my way into things. I'd use my talents as if they were out of a grocery bag—and try to control and manipulate. And that was the beginning of me seeing that there was another control [i.e., God].
>
> I mean in those days, seduction was really helpful in getting my needs met, because uh . . . because men are easy to control through seduction. And if I want to go to certain restaurants—I mean it was just stupid. But it's almost like how our society lives, you know. Men want to be seduced, and women want to seduce so that they can control, and the men think that they're controlling them, and everyone is controlling each other, and it's all false. It's all false. It's not really reverence. And what Christ calls us to is mutual reverence.

After her boyfriend left her, Anne decided to refrain from using seduction to manipulate men. She spent a year "white knuckling" in celibacy, then a couple of years engaging in periodic flings. Her next crisis occurred at work where she supervised a clerical pool of 100 women and was a step away from promotion into corporate management. This crisis too was announced by a spiritual sign. A telephone repairman (her first husband's occupation) stopped her at work and said, "Selling your soul for business, huh?" She told me

> I mean, he pierced through everything. What I was doing was not good. I looked at all that objectively and said, "This isn't me. This is who I've become for them. It's not what I wanted to become. I want something else, but I don't know what it is."

In subsequent months Anne began to suffer from chronic insomnia and confused thinking such that "a 15-minute report might take me a couple of hours." She struggled to keep up the facade of competence until forced to take a leave of absence for health reasons. To survive on leave, she provided private day care and took short-term, part-time jobs. She also devoted time to her relationship with God by taking theology classes, reading avidly, and attending mass. Several months into her leave of absence, she had what she called a "born-again" experience at a weekend Catholic singles' retreat. She then began the Life in the Spirit seminar with her mother that led to her Spirit baptism and initiated her continuing career in the charismatic renewal.

In these crises—one concerning a potential marital relationship, the other concerning her occupational identity—Anne was close to attaining personal goals when the relationship crumbled. To say that "he left" and "I got sick" relieves Anne from personal responsibility, but she also indicated to me that she bore some responsibility for the outcomes. She implied that her effort to push her potential mate toward a deeper spirituality was part of the reason that he left her. And she partly accounted for the crisis at work by referring to personal dysfunctions generated by her dysfunctional family.

We talked about the illness that followed her crisis at work for more than an hour one day. Her symptoms included blurred vision and a burning sensation on her skin. "But mostly I get this spaciness," she offered. "It's like, where was I going, what was I doing? Just complete memory loss." In this interview we also discussed one of her deepest issues: the contradiction between her mother's injunction not to be a follower and her father's injunction not to be a leader. In talking about the injunction against leading, Anne mentioned reactions like the symptoms from her illness. She told me

> I can logically look at [the potential] consequences [of my actions], but I get to a certain spot emotionally and I can't see, I can't think. And that's where I'm afraid of leadership. Because of my brokenness, because of my dysfunctionalism. I feel like I can't trust myself at certain levels. Because when it touches some of those emotional unhealed areas I can't see clearly and I can't think. I get blocked, just like I did with my marriages. I get completely blocked.

I asked her, "What do you mean 'blocked,' what happens?" and she replied

> It's almost like it takes over. It's like the emotional deprivation, or fears, or anger, or enclosed rage, it takes over, and I just make a decision. And I know darn well that I'm not thinking it through but I can't get there from here. . . . There was no room for mistakes [in my family], so the thought of making a mistake in public was [she giggles] was too scary. Too scary. So I couldn't cope.

Anne seems to follow a consistent family pattern here. Her father dealt with the burden of leadership by escaping into the bottle. When her brother Johnny, who Anne called the family hero, confronted Harry, Johnny was probably cursed and humiliated, after which he had his fatal accident. When the younger brother Andy was on the verge of becoming the new family hero, he flunked critical classes and killed himself. When Anne's success at work made her parents proud, her environmental illness did not kill her, fortunately, but it forced her into the solitude of a highly controlled environment.

Her relationship with God fit squarely into this complex of identity problems and offered a road to healing:

> I find that the only time I'm any good is if I spend three hours a day in prayer. That's when I'm at my most steady, that's when I'm my most consistent and unscathed. Or not easily give my identity to other people.

When I asked her what that meant, "not give your identity to other people," she went on to say

> Yeah. As dysfunctional people, we often let other people define us. If you're an authority or you're, and when you let other people define you, you're consistently fitting into their mold. And finding out what pleases them and living out that. Or else trying to break out of it, but either way, it's got you. But just to be able to stand in who you are, not being for or against them, just stand in that, hold fast. And the other things just kind of wash away. They're not an issue. . . .
>
> You know how you delight in a child, and all this love pours out? And the child looks at you and just drinks in your love? When I stay with that meditation, of who God is as my creator, then I see how He really wants to look at me and take delight in me. I go, Lord, you delight in *me*? [speaker's emphasis] Woah. OK, I'll meditate on that, I'll stay there for a while, and then truth lives. And then truth lives. And the lies go away, all the lies: that I don't measure up because I don't look like this person on TV, or I don't have this degree, or whatever. My identity is only in Christ and in love and in my identity. And then what you do is born out of who you are, not the other way around.

What Anne finds in this relationship of mutual reverence with God is the security of unconditional love. This differs considerably from her previous relationships, in which, to ensure reciprocal commitment and positive valuation, she had to mold herself to the desires of the other, she had to "give [her] identity to other people." She expressed this in her discussion of controlling men through seduction, and of "playing a game" and becoming someone else "for them." When I pressed about who the "them" is, Anne mentioned "most of the men in my life," her parents, her bosses at work, and the women at work for whom she was the vanguard on the road into management. The heart of the matter seems to be trying to control another person or persons by responding to them with behaviors they desire. She desperately wanted secure love, but long-term commitments may have been too scary for her because offering the gift of herself to another is not sufficient to guarantee that same gift in response. Sennett and Cobb's (1972) analysis of the economy and shortcomings of personal sacrifice in working-class life offers a similar analysis of the roots of relationship dissatisfaction. The gift of oneself cannot coerce but only influence the other to desire to respond in kind. Admitting that one is not in control is thus more true to the reality of interactional dynamics than an insistence on personal control (Bateson 1972).

As Anne describes it, this dysfunctional pattern fits neatly with Beattie's (1987:31) definition of codependence: "a co-dependent person is one who has let another person's behavior affect him or her, and who is obsessed with controlling that person's behavior." Anne also appears to follow the prescription for healing in the codependency and 12-Step literature. Grounding her identity in her relationship with God allows her to develop her "true self" (Bradshaw 1988), to "detach with love" and "act, not react" in interaction with others (Beattie 1987). Anne detaches to the extreme of almost total social isolation, apparently because she demands in her social relationships the same mutual reverence she experiences in her relationship with God.

In contrast, Laura and other people in my larger sample who were immersed in codependence issues usually remained in unsatisfying relationships after conversion. They differed from Anne in that they saw these relationships as created by God and willed by God for them personally, and thus necessary to endure. The security of their relationship with God often, as in Laura's case, allowed them to take risks and experiment with new modes of interacting in relationships. In most of these cases, the risks and experiments paid off. Laura's marriage got better. Anne was not so fortunate.

Trusting in her new relationship with God, Anne began to lead others into a similar relationship. She heard about the vibrant worship at Faithful Servants and joined it. She brought many other people to worship there. She brought her father to confession and repentance where Johnny had failed. Confident that God was leading her aright, she and Laura demanded an end to cursing, drinking, and rock music at family gatherings. They were rebuked, and both then cut off family ties.

Turning to her new "spiritual family" at Faithful Servants, Anne offered the recently reformed leadership her gift of spiritual leadership—evident to her in her evangelical successes. They rejected her, telling her that, with their God-given gifts of wisdom and discernment, they did not see the gift of leadership in her. She was crushed. She continued going to prayer meetings anyway and, in the spirit of Christian forgiveness, prayed for them. She stopped both when she heard from God in prayer, "withdraw your prayer from this place." The following fall, Laura moved to Steubenville. The next winter, Anne followed. Laura accepted an invitation of marriage from a charismatic man. Two years later Anne did the same. Laura said her marriage was "a disaster." Anne's was a tragedy.

Probably because it was so painful to her, and so challenging to her faith in God, Anne volunteered nothing about her second marriage, except a single use of the plural "marriages," which I failed to catch on first hearing. Harriet told me that Anne had married a man she met in the prayer group at Steubenville; "a priest had told him he should never marry," she explained. Anne soon found herself pregnant, at which point her husband fled back to live with his parents. Anne miscarried and was completely debilitated by a new attack of the symptoms that had driven her from her career. A doctor finally diagnosed her ailment as environmental illness (EI), or multiple chemical sensitivities, brought on originally by new formaldehyde-treated carpets at work and pesticide sprayings in her old apartment (cf. Roueche 1988). By eating nothing for 30 days, she began to recover the faculties she had lost so many years before, "but I was so lonely, and so alone in this town that I was in, [that] I came to Chicago. I gave up my health because of loneliness."

At the time of our interviews, lacking the ability to hold a job, refusing to request support from her family, and ineligible for disability payments from the state, Anne and another EI victim were being sheltered and cared for by a recovered EI victim. Anne said

> The world is hostile. Everything has been taken from me. Everything. . . .
> When this process all ends, which I believe it will, I think I will be restored
> and healthy. But what I am going through in between has extremely

strengthened my faith, has tested it to the limit. . . . All I know is that I have been as faithful as I can be to God, and it has caused . . . it's caused me a lot of thinking and a lot of commitment, and there's nowhere else to go.

My conversations with Anne troubled me as a researcher. She was desperate for help and was then in two therapy groups. But I felt that my role was to gather information and analyze it, not to be a therapist or to force my own sociological understandings on those I interviewed. I have not talked to any of the O'Douls since the interviews, but I hope that Anne has passed through her most troubled time, that she has taken new risks and initiated relationships that give her at least some of the mutual reverence she holds as an ideal. I also hope that now she might see my sociological translation and interpretation of her story as one that does justice to her own experiences and feelings.

Conclusion

"Healing" and "inner healing" are centrally important elements of the Catholic Charismatic Renewal (McGuire 1982, Neitz 1987, Csordas 1994). This transformative process may occur as a result of contact with charismatic symbolism. In this essay, I have tried to show not only how this transformative process works, but also why some people open themselves to it and others do not. The core of the healing process is constructing and entering into an imagined relationship with a significant other, entering into, in native terms, a "personal relationship with Jesus." In charismatic ritual, symbolism, and discourse, this process involves abandoning the struggle to enhance one's personal happiness by exerting personal control in relationships and ceding control to God in return for whatever happiness God may see fit to give. The content of this symbolized relationship may then become a pattern that is transferred onto real social relationships, as a Durkheimian perspective might lead us to expect.

Laura, for example, committed to marriage and to transforming herself to the demands of the relationship, just as she had committed herself to obeying God. The parallel goes further though. Submission did not make all things well for Laura, because her husband did not respond to it with the reciprocal responsiveness or mutual reverence that her relationship with God led her to expect. Her trust in God's love ultimately allowed her to demand her husband's responsiveness under threat of divorce. Her relationship with God set up normative expectations that she demanded of human relationships. Anne's story shows the same dynamic at work. The difference is that the commitments she risked after conversion repeatedly failed her. These failures challenged her faith in God, but she is convinced that "there's nowhere else to go."

Anne and Laura turned their lives over to God. Harriet and Janese did not. The reason for this difference seems to be that the former had experiences, including tenacious physical ailments, which convinced them that their control was tenuous at best. Both of them, probably as a result of abuses in their family, tried to control others by offering sexual gratification. This is a codependent pattern, where, by giving the other pleasure, they seek to manipulate the other to reciprocally fulfill their own desires. For Anne, this codependent pattern was generalized beyond sexual relationships. The strength of Harriet's and Janese's commitment to Al-Anon and other 12-Step programs suggests that they too struggled with codependent patterns in their primary relationships. Their relationship trajectories showed a different pattern, in which they made lasting marital commitments relatively early in adult life. These different trajectories indicate that their strategies were more effective and, thus, that Janese and Harriet actually did have more control in their relationships. Alternatively, they may not have had the insecurities that generated such a great need for control. Certainly, they did not feel so out of control that they wanted to turn their lives over to God. On the contrary, both scorned people who did.

Restricting myself to the analysis of the stories of four women in the same family poses obvious problems of generalization. Their stories seem to depend, idiosyncratically, on early socialization and accidents of fate that determined with whom they formed relationships. In other work (Lawson 1996), where I include the stories of 27 other people socialized in different families, I show a variety of common patterns in stories and relationship strategies. Codependence and alcoholism are just two of them, though important ones. I also analyze how these patterns arise not only from common features of mid-20th-century American families, but also from the logic of market relationships and from economic and demographic dynamics of the last few decades.

Ultimately the stories of these four women are suggestive rather than conclusive. Andrew Greeley (1981), among others (Jones 1991, Rizzuto 1979), has already pointed out the connection between the character of people's relationship with God and their experiences in social relationships. What these stories mainly suggest is that we have not exhausted the uses of self-narratives for understanding how structures of symbols and structures of social relationships influence one another.

NOTES

1. My focus here is only on charismatic symbolism, though I think my findings could be generalized to other sectarian Christian groups. Ammerman's (1987) fundamentalists, for example, also emphasize characteristics that distinguish them from secular society and that indicate their obedience to God's will. Their worship services, like charismatic prayer meetings, are based on the revival service, building toward an altar call or call to repentance.

2. There is no doubt a standard formula for charismatic conversion accounts. In a citywide Catholic charismatic conference in 1989, one session was devoted to instruction and drill in one-minute and three-minute testimonies. Mansfield (1987) also provides guidelines.

3. It seems reasonable to conclude that the O'Doul women were referring in their testimony to actual experiences and that the interview methods used provide some window not only into standard conversion narratives but also into these women's own experience.

4. See Stromberg (1994) for a sensitive treatment of how the referential ideology in contemporary Western culture affects how converts use metaphors to describe their experience. See Searle (1995) for a philosophical argument that language use makes no sense unless we assume that people are really trying to refer to events and experience. Briggs (1986) provides a primer on context-sensitive interviewing and interpretive techniques, and Denzin (1987) suggests verification of narrative data by triangulating among various accounts.

5. This interpretation of wifely submission is quite similar to that taught in the nondenominational charismatic congregation in Stacey's (1990) study. In this respect, Anne and Laura echo the Lutheran charismatic Larry Christianson's (1970) interpretation of Ephesians 5:22–33 more than than of the Catholic charismatic Therese Cirner (1985).

References

Ammerman, Nancy Tatom. 1987. *Bible Believers*. New Brunswick: Rutgers University Press.

Bateson, Gregory. 1972. "The Cybernetics of 'Self': A Theory of Alcoholism." Pp. 309–37 in *Steps to an Ecology of Mind*. New York: Ballantine.

Beattie, Melody. 1987. *Codependent No More*. Center City, MN: Hazelden Foundation.

Bellah, Robert N., Richard Madsen, William M. Sullivan, Anne Swidler, and Steven M. Tipton. 1985. *Habits of the Heart: Individualism and Commitment in American Life*. New York: Harper and Row.

Berger, Peter L. and Thomas Luckmann. 1966. *The Social Construction of Reality: A Treatise in the Sociology of Knowledge*. Garden City, NY: Anchor Doubleday.

Bradshaw, John. 1988. *Bradshaw on the Family: A Revolutionary Way of Self-Discovery*. Deerfield Beach, FL: Health Communications Inc.

Briggs, Charles L. 1986. *Learning How to Ask: The Role of the Interview in Social Science Research*. Cambridge: Cambridge University Press.

Christenson, Larry. 1970. *The Christian Family*. Minneapolis: Bethany Fellowship.

Cirner, Randall and Therese Cirner. 1985. *10 Weeks to a Better Marriage*. Ann Arbor, MI: Servant Books.

Csordas, Thomas. 1994. *The Sacred Self: A Cultural Phenomenology of Charismatic Healing*. Berkeley and Los Angeles: University of California Press.

Denzin, Norman. 1987. *The Alcoholic Self*. Newbury Park, CA: Sage.

———. 1989. *The Research Act, Third Edition*. Englewood Cliffs, NJ: Prentice Hall.

Durkheim, Emile. 1995 [1912]. *The Elementary Forms of the Religious Life*. Translated by Karen E. Fields. New York: Free Press.

Fichter, Joseph. 1976. "Parallel Conversions: Charismatics and Recovered Alcoholics." *Christian Century* 93:148–50.

Freud, Sigmund. 1965. *The Interpretation of Dreams*. Translated by J. Strachey. New York: Avon.

Greeley, Andrew. 1981. *Religion: A Secular Theory*. New York: Free Press.

Jones, James. 1991. *Contemporary Psychoanalysis and Religion: Transference and Transcendence*. New Haven: Yale University Press.

Lawson, Matthew. 1996. *The Structure of Charismatic Moral Action*. Ph.D. Dissertation, Department of Sociology, Princeton University, Princeton, NJ.

Mansfield, Patti Gallagher. 1987. *Proclaim His Marvelous Deeds: How to Give a Personal Testimony*. Steubenville: Franciscan University Press.

McGoldrick, Monica M. and John K. Pearce. 1981. "Family Therapy with Irish Americans." *Family Process* 20(3):223–41.

McGuire, Meredith B. 1982. *Pentecostal Catholics: Power, Charisma, and Order in a Religious Movement*. Philadelphia: Temple University Press.

McLoughlin, William G. 1978. *Revivals, Awakenings, and Reform: An Essay on Religion and Social Change in America, 1607–1977*. Chicago: University of Chicago Press.

Neitz, Mary Jo. 1987. *Charisma and Community: A Study of Religious Commitment within the Charismatic Renewal.* New Brunswick, NJ: Transaction.

Parsons, Talcott. 1967. "Social Structure and the Development of Personality: Freud's Contribution to the Integration of Psychology and Sociology." Pp. 269–73 in *Culture and Consciousness*, edited by G. B. Levitas. New York: George Braziller.

———. 1979. "Religious and Economic Symbolism in the Western World." *Sociological Inquiry* 49:1–48.

Rizzuto, Ana-Marie. 1979. *The Birth of the Living God: A Psychoanalytic Study.* Chicago: University of Chicago Press.

Roueche, Berton. 1988. "The Fumigation Chamber." *The New Yorker Magazine* 63(January 4):59–66.

Searle, John. 1995. *The Construction of Social Reality.* New York: Free Press.

Sennett, Richard and Jonathan Cobb. 1972. *The Hidden Injuries of Class.* New York: Vintage Books.

Snow, David A. and Richard Machalek. 1984. "The Sociology of Conversion." *Annual Review of Sociology* 10:167–90.

Snow, David. 1993. *Shakabuku: A Study of the Nichiren Shoshu Buddhist Movement in America, 1960–1975.* New York: Garland Publishing.

Stacey, Judith. 1990. *Brave New Families: Stories of Domestic Upheaval in late Twentieth Century America.* New York: Basic Books.

Stromberg, Peter. 1994. *Narrative and Self-Transformation: A Study of the Christian Conversion Narrative.* Cambridge: Cambridge University Press.

Wallis, Roy and Steve Bruce. 1983. "Accounting for Action: Defending the Common Sense Heresy." *Sociology* 17(1):97–111.

Chapter 3

The Gospel Hour

*Liminality, Identity,
and Religion in a Gay Bar*

Edward R. Gray and Scott L. Thumma

We squeeze through a crowd filled with gay men.[1] Some ignore us; others greet us with smiles. Everyone is animated. Bartenders race back and forth, opening bottles of beer and mixing drinks for the hot and thirsty assembly. Dance music plays at a high volume. Suddenly, the music changes to a stirring orchestral version of the "Hallelujah" chorus. This is Morticia DeVille's cue. Unnoticed in the rear of the darkened room, Morticia starts to move slowly toward the dance floor. The crowd begins to applaud. A spotlight—after what seems a long moment—strikes her sequined gown, perfectly made-up face, and blond wig. As she takes the stage, she looks the perfect southern gospel singer on a televised revival hour. With all eyes on her, Morticia begins to sing "Living in the Presence of the King," a popular contemporary Christian hymn. The Gospel Hour at this midtown Atlanta gay bar has begun.

Morticia is a gay man in drag in her early 30s. As a member of the Gospel Girls, she sings with a popular African American drag queen and a straight African American woman. Each week, the Gospel Girls and their audience create a unique gay gospel cabaret, The Gospel Hour. It is a two-hour long gospel performance and sing-along. Performers sing or lip-sync traditional gospel hymns and contemporary numbers. Morticia and the Gospel Girls perform for a mostly white gay male audience. Many in this audience come from evangelical backgrounds, and many remain Christian.

Morticia DeVille is the founder and star of the Gospel Hour. She is also a make-believe character, an identity created by a man we call

Paul.[2] As Morticia, Paul combines religious sensibilities and songs learned as a child in the mountains of North Georgia with the art of high drag learned as a gay man in the bars of Atlanta. Even as a child, Paul was drawn to both drag and religion. He told us how he would sneak into his grandmother's bedroom to steal her lipstick. Afterwards, he retreated to the relative safety of an empty mountain hollow. Robed in a bed sheet, he preached to the winds, pretending he was Billy Graham. Paul has exchanged bed sheets and covert lipstick wearing in rural Georgia for sequined frocks and the public identity of a drag queen in Atlanta.

The Gospel Hour is a fascinating institution on the Atlanta gay scene. It is also an event well suited to ethnographic study. A weekly occurence, the Gospel Hour lends itself to repeated participant observation to determine regular and deep patterns. In our examination, we identified, approached, and interviewed regular participants in addition to the principals. We also talked to others more casually and overheard many equally revealing conversations. The Gospel Hour is a multilayered, symbolic event, and ethnographic methods uncover these levels of symbolic meaning. Is it a religious event or mere spectacle? Is Paul still pretending to be someone else at the Gospel Hour, presiding over gay men likewise pretending to belong to a church? Or does the Gospel Hour's ritual generate new but not make-believe identities and models for being both gay and Christian?

At the Gospel Hour, evangelical gospel music blends with drag, not for parody but for purpose. The performance challenges everyday categories of experience by absorbing these categories and transforming them. The Gospel Hour merges gospel performance models with high drag. It also blends southern evangelical Christian sensibilities and cultural norms with those of urban gays. Its audience of gays, straights, African Americans, and whites have different encounters with the Gospel Hour, shaped by individual and shared experiences. For the performers, and for the segment of the audience that we observed, the Gospel Hour is a ritual of identity negotiation. Using Christian symbols and songs, southern gay men reconcile their more recently achieved modern urban gay identity with their childhood and young-adult evangelical Christian formation. The Gospel Hour—a drag show—is the setting for this identity work. Its product is a model that defies dominant cultural norms and establishes new ways to organize social relations.

The Gospel Hour generates what Victor Turner (1969) has called "templates" or "models" that reclassify social relationships. These templates provide motives and guide actions. We examine how the model or template of gay drag gospel performance allows participants to reclassify ordinary, taken-for-granted social relationships and cultural categories framing Christianity and gay sexuality. Turner described modern social life as "a type of dialectical process involving successive experiences of high and low, *communitas* and structure, homogeneity and differentiation, equality and inequality" (Turner 1969:96). Our investigation employs Turner's insight to show how culturally marginal groups create new cultural forms and practices through ritual. His theory illuminates how our informants use the ritual template generated by the Gospel Hour to negotiate their identity as southern gay Christian men. The performance is a liminal time and space set apart from the everyday. It is betwixt and between dominant cultural and subcultural norms. Being gay and Christian, within this liminal moment, is not exceptional or odd; it is normal.

Singing gospel songs in a gay bar led by men in drag defies most norms and experiences of both urban gay culture and evangelical Christianity. Because it is a drag show in a gay bar, the Gospel Hour is alien to the evangelical world. Because it is a Christian gospel music performance, it falls outside the expected parameters of gay drag. Yet the Gospel Hour is both—a gay drag show and a gospel music performance. Morticia DeVille is a gospel singer and a drag queen. Singing gospel hymns in drag is a ritual act redefining everyday classifications of experience and creating a new model for identity.

This model or template has a normative function. It reconciles being gay and Christian. "All rituals have this exemplary, model displaying character," according to Turner. Rituals create society "in much the same way as Oscar Wilde held life to be 'an imitation of art'" (Turner 1969:117). A young man, a former Christian charismatic, may have said it best to us one night after the Gospel Hour:

> It's hard [to get used to at first] because you grow up and you believe that these are praises to God and you see this big drag queen camping it up, and you are thinking, "Oh no, something is really wrong here, and we can't let this go on." It clashes with all the preconceived ideas you have. . . . Later on, you realize that it can be this way too.[3]

Ethnography beyond the Local Congregation

The Gospel Hour is the longest running drag show in Atlanta. Our first encounter occurred in 1992, its seventh year. One author's sporadic but enthusiastic attendance led to this formal investigation in the spring and summer of 1994. The Gospel Hour had just moved from the bar that had been its home for more than four years. During our study, the Gospel Girls increased the frequency of new numbers, rehearsed more often, and wore the occasional coordinated costume. Our regular presence as identified researchers may have prodded these changes. We cannot determine, however, if our observation had any direct effect. Nevertheless, the Gospel Hour remained basically unchanged during the course of our study.

Using participant observation, we collected our data over 12 evenings, or 24 services. We interviewed informally, chatted with, and eavesdropped on participants, including the owner and several bartenders. We also formally interviewed Morticia DeVille and Ramona Dugger and 13 participants, including several who were regular guest performers. The audience members volunteered to talk with us after a general announcement by Morticia. She encouraged "her flock" to help us in our research. Of those we formally interviewed, all but one was male. Seven interviewees reported that they were born and raised in the South. Two others were reared in the northeast and central regions of the country. Four interviewees did not provide this information. They were all white, middle class, and in their 20s and 30s, and the majority had at least some college education. They gave us a less than fully representative picture. We spoke informally, however, with many African Americans and older participants.

Our informants, although not a randomly selected sample, are part of an important segment of the participants—those who identify themselves as gay and Christian. These sons of the church have creatively reappropriated cultural forms they once thought off limits. They—like other members of modern fragmented urban society—ritually negotiate religious and social identities in a multiplicity of settings, many of them contested. They choose from a repertoire of ritually created and sustained forms of identity.

The Gospel Hour As Ritual: Fully Gay and Altogether Southern Evangelical

Twice each Sunday, the Gospel Girls conduct what they call "services" for their "congregation." During the first half of the nearly two-hour performance, they sing solo numbers. Some of these are signature pieces.

Also during this time, special guests often sing from a repertoire of classic and contemporary gospel music. The songs differ at each service, but they are selected from a circumscribed range of a few dozen pieces. The quality of performance, nonetheless, is uniformly high each week. "That's the good thing about us," Morticia told us one day in a slow drawl. "The music is so powerful. It's so good. And southern."

Morticia is sweet and warm—grandmotherly in a Sunday-school-teacher sort of way. She can stir the audience with her singing. For some songs, like "Standing in the Presence of the King," she lip-syncs to a recording. Most often, however, she sings well-known hymns in her own strong and beautiful voice. Audience members place dollar bills in her hands and kiss her on the cheek.

After her opening segment, Morticia introduces Ramona Dugger. Ramona, the number-two Gospel Girl, has a remarkable vocal range. When she sings "Amazing Grace"—a signature number for her—patrons begin to fear for the glassware in the bar. Her songs are emotional and passionate. Ramona is straight, young, and African American. She favors contemporary gospel music. Her background is Episcopalian. Many songs in her Gospel Hour repertoire, therefore, were unfamiliar to listeners. When she does sing traditional evangelical hymns, she favors the classics like "Amazing Grace" and "How Great Thou Art." Sometimes, she sings "If You're Happy and You Know it, Clap your Hands" changing the words to, "If you're happy and gay, clap your hands!"

Ramona became a Gospel Girl in 1994. She had been a regular guest performer for five years, most of the ensemble's career. When Morticia announced that Ramona would become "official," one owner of the bar objected. He said that bartenders were getting complaints about the explicitly religious nature of Ramona's on-stage comments. The barkeep's description of Ramona's remarks—explicitly Christian—struck us as accurate. Soon after, the Gospel Hour moved. We asked Ramona about proselytizing during her performance. She said

> We're treading a fine line as it is. You know, it's a very fine line. And I quite frankly identify with it probably most strongly, more than anyone else in the show on a higher spiritual level. And because of that, I probably step over that line. Tish never says "God." She never says "Jesus." I will. I don't do it on a regular basis because I don't want people to feel like "I'm coming into a bar and I'm just getting preached at," because I'm not preaching to anybody. But I do think there are so many people who are so hungry to know that God does love them, you know, and that they're under so much stress and so

much trouble in their lives that they need to be reminded that it's just not all here and now. There's more to that. You got to look up and know you are not alone in all this. . . . And try to give them some comfort. So I do, I admit, I do cross that line a bit.

After her initial song—usually "Friends are Friends Forever," sung powerfully and warmly with Morticia—Ramona invites an American Sign Language interpreter to the stage. He reported to us that deaf people come regularly. As he signs, Ramona moves to the rear. Under the spotlight, his hands sing gracefully and energetically for the deaf. The beauty and grace of the signing captures the audience.

Alicia Kelly is the most recent Gospel Girl. She is a young muscular black man. Ramona and others report she does an amazingly realistic Patti LaBelle. She lip-syncs her numbers but everything else about her performance is authentic. She pours a fantastic amount of energy into her dancing, or "shouting," imitating a Pentecostal devotee possessed by the Holy Spirit. The congregation watches her transport herself acrobatically across the stage, and they respond with loud applause. Many toss crumpled bills onto the stage, and shout "Amen, Sister!" Alicia dramatically concludes by throwing her wig into the crowd and dousing herself with a bottle of beer or mineral water grabbed from a startled member of the audience. They roar.

Alicia, Ramona told us, "is doing the style she grew up with. They're the women that she saw in church. Often she will say, 'Well, this is Sister so-and-so,' and she'll become Sister so-and-so." The manager of the group, echoing an assessment that could have come from anyone in the audience, said, "If [Alicia Kelly] doesn't light your fire, your wood's wet!" Her electrifying performance concludes the first half of the hour.

Immediately, Morticia introduces the greeting portion of the service, a time for the congregation to meet and greet one another. Like the gospel songs, a greeting time is a traditional part of evangelical Christian worship services, transposed here to the Gospel Hour setting. She invites strangers to introduce themselves. Morticia leads the way and begins to mingle with the crowd. Most people do not follow her example, but some do. Romances have started at the Gospel Hour, including some lasting ones. Morticia takes this portion of the service seriously:

I really want them to meet each other. The greeting portion, I mean, it's very difficult for them to talk to each other. Nobody will go up and speak to a stranger. And at Drakes,[4] I'd make a point to go all the way around the entire room. I don't do that so much anymore. I really do try to push. . . .

Gospel music continues to play during the 15-minute break. The service resumes with the crowd eagerly anticipating the "High Church Sing-Along," the highlight of the performance. Morticia, Ramona, Alicia, and guest singers sit on bar stools. They lead the crowd in favorite hymns like "When the Roll is Called Up Yonder," "Because He Lives, I Can Face Tomorrow," and "There is Power in the Blood of the Lamb." The volume, quality, and passion of the singing would be the envy of any church. During these hymns, participants occasionally close their eyes; some bow their heads. A few others raise their hands in praise. "I really missed gospel music," Gary, a tall, handsome son of a famous Pentecostal minister told us. "There is a part of me that likes to sing," he continued, "so now I sing gospel music in a gay bar." Like so many at the Gospel Hour, Gary loves to sing, and he loves to sing familiar songs.

The Gospel Girls then invite individual members of the audience to sing a verse of "Amazing Grace." The ability of the audience participants covers a wide range. On Easter Sunday in 1995, a young man in a wheelchair sang. He chose the verse including the line "I once was lost but now I'm found, was blind but now I see." The bar fell silent straining to hear his weak voice. Later, Morticia DeVille confided that she wanted to cry because she found the young man's singing so sweet.

Although weeping is not supposed to happen in a gay bar, tears are no strangers at these services. We have seen men cry openly during the Gospel Hour, caught up in the music and the emotion of the evening. One Sunday, a young man began to sob after a mention of the many who had died of AIDS, sometimes abandoned by family at their deaths but often surrounded by friends. The man, whom we assumed was mourning the loss of a loved one, was embraced and comforted by his circle of friends. He did not hide his tears. No one made any move to the door. The emotion was very public, and so were the comforting embraces of friends, like at a revival meeting.

Participants have reacted emotionally ever since Morticia began to sing gospel songs in the gay bars of Atlanta. She recalled how her first audience responded in 1984: "I did a show at Doug's. And it was just me and this piano player. And, it just went so well. All those leather men like, had tears, they were all singing, they were crying. It was, it was really moving. . . ."

Each Gospel Hour concludes in the same fashion. Perched on a row of bar stools, the Gospel Girls lip-sync a rousing version of "Looking for a City." Members of the audience grab cocktail napkins and wave them like hankies in rhythm with the music. The Gospel Girls mirror the movements of the enthusiastic crowd. "See You in the Rapture," a contemporary song, follows immediately and is the grand finale. More than a dozen men take the stage with no prompting to form a chorus line. Some participate every week. New people also join the line which is several columns deep. The dancing, like the napkin waving, is campy.

The theology behind the lyrics of "See You in the Rapture" and "Looking for a City" is explicitly eschatological. The heavenly city is a place where residents will never die, where they "will be with Jesus and their loved ones too. Where the Holy Spirit all [their] hopes renew." Both songs promise an imminent new order marked by what Turner called *communitas* (Turner 1969:94–129). The eternal home that "Looking for a City" envisions and the bliss that "See You in the Rapture" promises are there for the taking. The songs describe an eternity of acceptance. Despite "all we have been through," participants await the day they will see Jesus and each other, including those taken by age, accident, and disease, "in the air some sweet day." These hymns anticipate a time and space of spontaneous relations among equals and contrast with participants' current experiences.

We do not know the choreographic origins or theological referents of the hankie waving during "Looking for a City" or the line dancing during "See You in the Rapture." Neither was planned by the performers. When asked about them, Morticia admitted, "I don't understand the napkins. The napkins were way before our time. There were other queens who did 'Looking for a City' [in their drag shows], and they always waved napkins. I don't know where that came from."

She shed no more light on the line dancing but did volunteer that she was "just a little offended by the dance." Recalling the enthusiastic participation of the audience the previous Sunday, however, she began to soften. "But it is OK." Then, coming further around, she admitted to perhaps a guilty pleasure in her audience's enthusiastic participation. "I mean . . . Sunday, there was just an incredible amount of people up there!" Morticia and the Gospel Girls are not the only creators of the rituals of the Gospel Hour.

Morticia and Ramona explicitly address the crowd as they might in a church service. One often hears, "Say Amen, congregation!" and "Hang around for the next service." Morticia carries on a relaxed banter with insider references. Playing on her weight, she jokes about where she has eaten that day or how hard it is to find clothes. The Gospel Girls relate an ongoing joke about their old Gospel Bus: sadly, it was lost in a fire; during a tour, one of the original Gospel Girls started the blaze while frying chicken in the rear of the bus; and they plan a fund raiser in order to replace it. In reality, the bus never existed.

Yet some "churchly" accouterments do. These have included faux stained-glass windows, choir robes, bulletins, and guest choirs. The Gospel Girls are respectful of clergy, regularly recognizing ministers in the crowd. Several Metropolitan Community Church (MCC) pastors are regulars. The choir of a local MCC church sings once each month. They pass the plate to collect for their church building fund. On Palm Sunday, the bar was decorated with fronds. Finally, of course, there are the hymns. The Gospel Girls go right up to the line of creating an explicitly religious environment. On occasion, they call the bar a cathedral. "If I had my way," Morticia told us, "when we moved to Prism from Drake's, we would have had furniture, you know, church furniture. I thought I could make it myself. Spray paint it white."

The Gospel Girls and participants behave themselves during the hour. Ramona and Morticia sometimes openly enforce a standard of conduct on the audience. Morticia once chastised some rowdy participants with the rebuke, "As my Mamma used to say to me, 'Girl, you can give one hour a week back [to God]!'" They avoid the kind of bawdy sexual remarks typical of drag performances. Morticia, however, can be sexually suggestive in a more subtle way. The hour never seems so sexually charged as when Alicia Kelly dances her ecstatic African American Pentecostal shouts. Yet none of this sexuality is overt. Like church, there may be undertones of sexuality, but the worship service is not the place to act on these feelings, or even to acknowledge them explicitly. One Sunday, a male stripper danced between services. The bar scene before, between, and after each Gospel Girls' performance is indistinguishable from any other drag show. In this regard, a male stripper was not out of place. However, Morticia said that while there is nothing wrong with strippers, they are inappropriate as part of the Gospel Hour or in proximity with it. She explained this to the crowd. The stripper never returned.

Restrained sexual expression is just one of the several informal rules at the Gospel Hour. The Gospel Girls never charge a cover. They never make fun of religious personalities. When the audience chooses to, however, they do not object. One recording popular with the audience captures Jimmy Swaggert giving a warm welcome to some unidentified religious group. He encourages them to hug, embrace, and show how they love each other. Participants enjoy the irony, or perhaps the ambiguity, of the liminal setting. Although they perform almost exclusively in bars, the Gospel Girls are careful not to drink in public. Seeing anyone drunk during the performance itself is rare, although the bar does a brisk business. Almost no one cruises overtly. Audience members, however, do pick each other up on occasion.

The two other bars in the immediate area attract their own crowds. One fills when the Gospel Hour ends. Many participants move on to this other bar rather than stay at Prism after singing "See You in the Rapture." The transition from the Gospel Hour's concluding notes to the familiar gay bar dance music is abrupt. After the hour, most regulars prefer to go elsewhere to dance. They maintain the distinction between sacred time and secular entertainment. One comment summarized a common attitude: "I don't normally do here what I do in a bar. I just feel funny about doing it. . . . I don't chase men when I come to the Gospel Girls. That's not the purpose of coming here." Participants separate themselves from the straight world by coming to the gay bar. They actively set themselves apart from norms of the gay world too—especially the gay bar scene. They do this by making the choice to listen to and sing gospel music.

The "ritual subject," according to Turner (1969:95), has an ambiguous social role as he negotiates a new identity. We found no one with a more ambiguous identity than Morticia DeVille. Our interview was the first time we had seen Morticia-Paul away from the Gospel Hour, out of role, as a man. It was a startling sight. It was only dimly, however, that we could see him. One small kitchen light illumined our way through Paul's darkened home. We talked out on the enclosed porch. We sat on the floor among potted plants, exercise equipment, and shadows.

Gone were the sequined gowns, blond wigs and makeup, stained-glass windows, and stage lights. During our interview, Morticia-Paul described Paul as a bitch, Morticia as sweet and grandmotherly. Paul—not in drag, away from the bright lights of the stage—struck us as shy, almost withdrawn. Where, we wondered, was the bitchy queen? Part of our confusion may have stemmed from Morticia DeVille's sexual ambiguity and Paul's ambivalence about the religious nature of the event, as we discuss below. This ambiguity shapes the liminal nature of the entire Gospel Hour.

The Participants: Identity Negotiation in a Modern, Fragmented World

At the Gospel Hour, the phases of ritual are not only multilayered and ambiguous, they are also more flexible and open than one might expect from Turner's theory. Plenty of nonreligious activity takes place. People come and go constantly. Many participants are out with their friends, having a good time. The performance dominates, but it does not monopolize. Both participants and singers combine behaviors learned in church and in bars. They have created a new model or template of identity mixing evangelical and gay forms seamlessly.

The first-time visitor to the Gospel Hour immediately notices the predominantly young white crowd. A second glance, however, uncovers the approximate ten percent who are African Americans, along with a few Hispanics and Asians. On any given night, ten to 15 women attend. Perhaps 20 percent are more than 55 years of age. Several of those we interviewed attested to this unexpected diversity. One person claimed that Gospel Hour participants were "not your normal S and M gays . . . you know 'Stand and Model' gays." One-fourth of our informants insisted they were not "bar people." Not only was this an older and more mature group, most did not have gym-perfected bodies. Many, in fact, were overweight, short, bald, or unattractive by conventional standards. The youngest, most handsome participants who might be seen in any popular gay bar often gather in small groups hugging the railing around the large stage. Directly in front, a group of regulars, many of them members of the MCC, enthusiastically sing along. Most of the audience crams into the space behind these clusters. A middle-aged mother of a gay man or a sympathetic minister may sit at the few small tables to one side of the bar. Morticia is careful to greet and introduce them and other special guests each week. When she does, the audience receives the newcomers warmly.

Variety in participants' familiarity, interest, and motives, of course, is common to most groups, and the Gospel Hour is no exception. Many in the crowd are regulars. Some come, we suspect, because they want to be in a bar full of gay men. Some are visitors from out-of-town. More unusual are those attracted by the beehive of activity who enter and become confused. A few are further drawn in by the spectacle and stay. Others remain because of the familiarity of the music or a fascination with the setting.

Some participate to reconcile Christian belief and practice with modern urban gay identity in the safety of the gay bar, a sort of cultural womb of the urban gay community. Donald, a former Southern Baptist and middle-aged man with no current church affiliation, reported that "at the Gospel Hour we can feel safe, like we won't be condemned." Regular participation allows him and others to identify more openly as Christian to gay friends. "We can say, 'Come go to the Gospel Hour.' We could never say 'Come go to church,'" he explained. "The Gospel Hour is fine because it's in a bar."

"Going here I now can realize that I can be gay and still be with God," Mark, another regular participant, said. "God can reach out and say, 'I love you!'" For him, a man in his 20s from South Carolina, this was a significant realization. Mark, like many of those who spoke with us, was raised as a Southen Baptist. He grew up knowing that he "couldn't be both gay and Christian at the same time." By the time he came out, he had been an ordained minister for five years. Since that time, Mark has left institutional religion. "I was very fearful of incorporating the two concepts together," he confided. "I was told by most organized religion that I was wrong and damned to Hell."

Mark was not the only one to believe and fear the message of rejection and condemnation from American religious institutions (Roof and McKinney 1987:212ff). Most Gospel Hour participants know all too well the historical incompatibility of Christianity and homosexuality. Their childhood and adult experiences with the church, its ministers, and—through these—with the Christian God, are ample proof. The Gospel Hour provides a model for the place of gay people in the church contrary to dominant Christian practices and beliefs.

For gays and lesbians of evangelical Christian heritage, religious support and advocacy have been nearly nonexistent. For the most part, gay evangelical and Pentecostal Christians face hard choices. They must remain closeted in their conservative churches, switch into more liberal denominations, or leave organized Christianity all together (Thumma 1987:125). With the two latter options, the gay evangelical southern man must leave behind the symbols, rituals, hymns, and religious culture in which he was raised. The Gospel Hour is another option. It offers a setting in which participants can be openly gay and openly Christian. High drag, an art form to which urban gay men have become acculturated, combines with the familiar and cherished worship style of participants' early religious formation.

Our informants reported considerable early religious formation as evangelical Christians. Six were raised as Southern Baptists; two, Methodist; three, Pentecostal or charismatic; one, Presbyterian. Evangelical churches and institutions educated and employed these men. Three attended Christian colleges; and three, seminaries or Bible schools. Four spoke of being called to the ministry. Ben sang in choirs at Jerry Falwell's Liberty University. Gary sang at Church of God congregations throughout the South. One person was currently a minister. Mark and another man were former ministers; a third was a former Southern Baptist missionary. The remainder reported their earliest religious formation in moderate and liberal Protestant churches. We encountered few who were Catholics, Jews, non-Christians, or not religiously identified at all.

The MCC dominated informants' current church affiliation. The Universal Fellowship of the Metropolitan Community Churches is an independent denomination of approximately 290 congregations and 30,000 members. Gay Christians created the denomination to fill a religious void for gay (and heterosexual) believers. MCC's founder Troy Perry was raised and served as a minister in a conservative Pentecostal church. The MCC as a whole reflects some of Perry's theological heritage and early religious formation. Of the three MCC congregations in Atlanta, one borrows predominantly from Baptist worship, one from Methodist, and the eclectic third congregation from high Episcopal to low Methodist (Cotton 1996:295). However, unfamiliar or high church rituals or even the overt gay emphasis of MCC worship can deter gays from evangelical backgrounds from participation and membership (Perry 1972; Warner 1994; Bauer 1976).

Six of those we interviewed claimed the MCC to be "their church"— including an MCC associate pastor. Three others had attended an MCC congregation but no longer did. Two of these said they "didn't connect" with the church, and one complained that it was "too ritualistic." Two other informants attended Presbyterian and Episcopal churches where they were organists. Except the six active MCC members and two organists, all informants reported little current involvement in local congregations.

Almost every person acknowledged that religious groups generally do not accept gays and lesbians. Many said they had experienced animosity from religious persons. Our informants believe that gays have been, as one said, "shut off from Christianity." "If you are gay, you are going to hell!" said another, summarizing the prevailing message of the church of his youth. This older message sharply contrasts with what gay men see, hear, and do at the Gospel Hour.

"I realized that the God that the Baptists preached hated me," Shannon, a former missionary, said one Sunday between services. "I was told for so long that [as a gay man] I was hated by God." Many told us of their personal experiences of exclusion and alienation. "I always thought that God completely hated me. I was told, 'You are gay and you are going to hell.'" Another told of his church friends' reactions after he shared his sexual orientation with them. "My best friends in the world turned their backs on me," he remembered. In the face of overt rejection by Christian communities, many gays have exited. Gary described his response plainly but with some of the cadence of an evangelical preacher. "I jumped out of the closet and slammed the door right behind me. I left in the closet my family, my religion, and my God."

The Gospel Hour participants' views of American Protestant and Catholic attitudes toward their life style are supported by survey data. Nearly three-quarters of the respondents to the 1984 General Social Survey considered same-sex relations to be always or almost always wrong (Roof and McKinney 1987:213). Surveys of Christians from every denomination, from the most liberal to the most conservative, confirm the responses of rejection that our informants mentioned. Gallup and Castelli found only 19 percent of evangelicals and 42 percent of mainline Protestants favor legalizing homosexual acts (1989:190). Likewise, Roof and McKinney (1989) reported that an average of 64 percent of those surveyed from liberal denominations, 77 percent of those from moderate denominations, 79 percent from historically African American denominations, and 89 percent from conservative denominations thought homosexuality was always or almost always wrong (cf. Ellison 1993). Sixty-nine percent of the Catholics surveyed agreed (Roof and McKinney 1989:211, 212). In a 1990 study of Southern Baptists, only two percent of the respondents thought homosexuality was a "viable" Christian life style (Ammerman 1990:109).

It is not surprising that nearly every study of gays and lesbians shows very little participation in organized religion. In one study, more than 50 percent of the respondents noted that they were not religious in the conventional sense at all (Bell and Weinberg 1978). In various studies, on the other hand, many gays and lesbians described powerful childhood religious influences and their own desires for spiritual meaning (Thumma 1987, 1991; Greenberg 1988; Boswell 1980; McNeill 1976).

In spite of almost always negative, frequently hostile, and occasionally violent responses to homosexuality in and outside the church, many at the Gospel Hour are still Christian, when construed in broad, cultural terms, although they do not regularly participate in organized church activities. For many southern gay men, evangelical churches provided important models of identity. Many Gospel Hour attendants continue as the members of a choir, as the participants in testifying and witnessing lay members, and even as the clerical leaders that they were in the evangelical churches of their youth and young adult lives. As children and youths, many gays learned their religious identity and prepared to be Christian men in the South in these churches. In the more diverse cultural spaces of the city where they have learned to be gay, they are negotiating new Christian identities.

Some of our informants reported feeling hostile, ambiguous, or conflicted about Christianity the first time they attended the Gospel Hour. Others still respect the church or cherish a childhood memory of it. For six of the 13 interviewed, the Gospel Girls' performance initially seemed wrong, even disgusting. Ben, a former fundamentalist Southern Baptist who attended Jerry Falwell's University, recalled his first impression. "I thought it was hypocritical and blasphemous." Guy, deeply involved in the charismatic movement, left after his initial visit and did not return for six years. "The first time I came, I was just totally disgusted. I thought, 'How could they be doing this in a gay place—singing gospel music and trying to be religious?'" Gregory recalled for us his reaction to the Gospel Hour. "At first I was appalled. I just knew the ground was going to open up and we'd be sucked straight into hell . . . *but,* [speaker's emphasis] after a while, I began to notice the look of joy on people's faces."

These participants no longer find the Gospel Hour appalling or hypocritical. To the contrary, they spoke of feeling the presence of God. "I do, many times, sense the presence of the Spirit," one said. Another commented, "I never feel like I leave here without getting something out of this." The message of the Gospel Hour contradicts the view that gay life and Christianity are irreconcilable, but the Gospel Hour does more than send countervailing information. It enacts in a specific time and space a new model of gay Christian identity and a new template for cultural and social relations between evangelicalism and gay life.

Many participants in the Gospel Hour are faithful attendants. Half of those we interviewed attended the drag show regularly for several years. One person missed only four times in three years. We estimated that almost half of each Sunday's crowd are regulars. Another 20 to 30 percent attend occasionally, about once each month. And, an additional 20 to 30 percent are marginal. This group attends infrequently, only once, or to cruise the crowd. A minority of these men undoubtedly view the Gospel Hour as pure entertainment, an oddity, or even disturbing. One of us overheard the conversation of three first-timers who walked in during the middle of the performance. After looking confused and uncomfortable, one fellow turned to his friends and implored, "Let's get out of here!"

For the regular attendants, however, the drag show is a moving spiritual experience. "Everybody gets something out of [the Gospel Hour]," Gregory said in his smooth southern accent, "even if it is just that God doesn't hate them. It is a good and positive outlet." "It is a form of ministry," another maintained. Paul, however, is reluctant to talk about his work as Morticia DeVille as anything approximating a religious calling. In fact, he explicitly denies it. Paul, who earns his living as Morticia, speaks of her as a different person, someone apart and different from himself. Morticia is "jovial and funny and loving and trying to be grandmotherish" in Paul's description. He acknowledges that the character of Morticia DeVille might be ministerial, but not the person we call Paul. Other Gospel Girls and regular participants, however, are not hesitant to claim that Paul is following his calling. One Sunday, Morticia read a card from an MCC minister, a regular at the services. "You wear makeup and a wig," he wrote to her. "I wear a robe. But we both serve the same person."

That Morticia does wear a dress, however, is essential to the ritual. Drag is an ambiguous art. The drag performer embodies a picture of the gay man as the feminine, a picture rejected by many gays. Drag erases symbolically in a particular subcultural setting the gender lines created and maintained symbolically and socially in the dominant culture. Urban gay men must rehearse these gender norms daily in some segments of their lives. They are increasingly free in the American urban milieu, however, to ignore dominant gender lines in other segments.

The Gospel Hour functions differently for each person, and sometimes on multiple levels. For core participants, it is their church. One said, "I always call it 'coming to church'. . . my friends and I call it 'coming to services.'" Another participant stated, "It is just an extension of church." Some participants have attended the Gospel Hour regularly for years but have not stepped foot in a church.

For others, the Gospel Hour represents an opportunity for spiritual reconnection and restoration. Shannon (the former missionary) said, "Many [gays] are scared to go back to church because [it] turned them away. This is their one touch with God." James, a Presbyterian from New Jersey who serves as the organist for an Episcopal church, stated, "Gay anger against God is dealt with here." The pain of rejection is also displayed and addressed. A gay man visiting from Minnesota broke down during the singing. Regaining some composure, he confessed, "I can still identify with God, there is hope for me, a backslidden Christian. . . . I really want to get involved in church again," he tearily told Ramona. The comments of other participants echoed this sentiment. One participant told us, "The Gospel Hour has helped me find an outlet to develop my spirituality." Another explained to us, "It showed me a void. A need in my life . . . it created a hunger for [church] again." Yet another offered, "The Gospel Hour made me aware of the longing I had for a relationship with God that I had turned away from."

For these and other informants, the Gospel Hour offers fellowship and a sense of community. James, the organist, stated plainly, "It's a time of fellowship, that is what it is all about." Ben, the former fundamentalist, added, "I look forward to this as much as I do Sunday morning. . . . This is the fellowship portion." Mark, the former Southern Baptist preacher, found intimacy and an acceptance of his spirituality. "I could talk to others about what I feel, and it was at the deepest, most intimate spiritual level." At the Gospel Hour, new norms and new classifications of social relations take hold.

The Gospel Hour is most overtly a structured time for singing the old gospel songs. The act of singing these hymns has its own power, fulfilling a deep need created during our informants' early years of church life (Clark 1993:105,6). One regular attested that "music communicates in a way that words cannot." Some missed gospel music because singing it reminded them of home and family. Singing gospel music, Shannon said, is "my way of showing my religion, my relationship to God." Singing these songs, he continued, "is when I feel closest to God." Guy, the former charismatic, told us that "the music makes you feel real good about yourself."

Almost every informant found the combination of gay and Christian cultural templates the most compelling feature of the Gospel Hour. It is a time and space in which they can be fully gay and altogether evangelical on their own terms. Informants saw it as "our own place," a place of security and divine acceptance. Mark exclaimed, "I am able to be myself . . . I can do both [be gay and Christian] and be happy!" Shannon, his friend, explained,

> Here were people who knew "the songs" . . . knew what I had been raised with. I could identify all of a sudden. I was in a bar and it was not a sexual thing, not a social thing, it was a spiritual thing. . . . I could talk

to others about what I feel and it was at the deepest and most intimate spiritual level.

Conclusion: Gay Liminality and Christian Identity

This ethnography has described how, each week, an urban gay bar becomes a religious space. The Gospel Hour transforms the bar into a liminal setting. High drag blends with southern evangelical Christian music and song to create a new model or template for the relationship between being Christian and being gay. Some embrace the exemplary template enacted ritually at this gay drag gospel cabaret to negotiate their identity as Christian and gay. Others find familiar cultural symbols that remind them of a past repudiated or simply left behind. Still others discover an amusing or disconcerting southern gay curiosity.

The Gospel Hour provides a model of identity and a template for social relations. But the liminal space it creates is not a simple egalitarian *communitas*. It is a structured social setting, an institution with its own norms. Its ritual enactments of liminal identities and social roles are contingent on a wider social and institutional context. In modern cities like Atlanta, residents have the opportunity to create and sustain liminal rituals and to choose among them. Liminality may comprise an entire ritual event. It may involve an entire segment of an audience. The models and templates created may be more durable than fleeting *communitas*. Such durability makes ritual a richer source for normative, exemplary behaviors and practices. It also demonstrates that liminality, although ritually generated, is institutionally sustained in wider settings. The Gospel Hour ritually creates a make-believe picture of gay and Christian social relations and turns the make-believe into reality by replacing and institutionalizing dominant norms with new ones.

The Gospel Hour provides a safe haven for gays coming from evangelical and other conservative Christian traditions. The songs remind them of the comfort they once found in their faith, while drag performance marks the space and time as uniquely gay. Using cultural models extant in gay and evangelical subcultures as tools to negotiate a new identity and a new set of relationships with Christianity, gay culture, and even God, participants at the Gospel Hour fuse both gay and evangelical realities. They can be gay and Christian at the Gospel Hour, a cabaret and revival.

At the Gospel Hour, life imitates art.

NOTES

1. An earlier version of this study, "Amazing Grace! How Sweet the Sound! Southern Evangelical Religion and Gay Drag in Atlanta," appears in *Gay Men's Issues in Religious Studies*, (Dallas, Monument Press, 1996, pp. 33–55), which is Volume 7 of the series "A Rainbow of Religious Studies," edited by J. Michael Clark and Robert E. Goss. We thank our colleagues at Emory University for numerous discussions of some of the ideas in this study.

2. The stage names of all the performers, unless otherwise noted, are accurate. Personal names and the names of the taverns and clubs have been changed.

3. All quotations of informants' comments are from our transcribed interviews conducted in Atlanta in 1995.

4. The bar where the Gospel Hour was previously held.

References

Ammerman, Nancy T. 1990. *Baptist Battles: Social Change and Religious Conflict in the Southern Baptist Convention*. New Brunswick, NJ: Rutgers University Press.

Bauer, Paul. 1976. "The Homosexual Subculture at Worship: A Participant Observation Study." *Pastoral Psychology* 25:115–27.

Bell, Alan and Martin S. Weinberg. 1978. *Homosexualities: A Study of Diversity among Men and Women*. New York: Simon and Schuster.

Boswell, John. 1980. *Christianity, Social Tolerance, and Homosexuality*. Chicago: University of Chicago Press.

Clark, Linda J. 1993. "Songs My Mother Taught Me: Hymns as Transmitters of Faith." Pp. 99–114 in *Beyond Establishment*, edited by Jackson Carroll and Wade Clark Roof. Louisville, KY: Westminister/John Knox Press.

Cotton, Angela. 1996. "Religion in Atlanta's Queer Community." Pp. 291-310 in *Religions in Atlanta: Religious Diversity in the Centennial Olympic City*, edited by Gary Laderman. Atlanta: Scholars Press.

Ellison, Marvin M. 1993. "Homosexuality and Protestantism." Pp. 149–79 in *Homosexuality and World Religions*, edited by Arlene Swidler. Valley Forge, PA: Trinity Press.

Gallup, George, Jr. and Jim Castelli. 1989. *The People's Religion: American Faith in the 90s*. New York: Macmillan.

Greenberg, David F. 1988. *The Construction of Homosexuality*. Chicago: University of Chicago Press.

McNeill, John. 1976. *The Church and the Homosexual*. Mission, KS: St. Andrews and McMeel.

Perry, Troy. 1972. *The Lord Is My Shepherd and He Knows I'm Gay.* Los Angeles: Nash.

Roof, Wade Clark and William McKinney. 1987. *American Mainline Religion: Its Changing Shape and Future.* New Brunswick, NJ: Rutgers University Press.

Thumma, Scott. 1987. "Straightening Identities: Evangelical Approaches to Homosexuality." Masters thesis, Candler School of Theology, Emory University, Atlanta, GA.

———. 1991. "Negotiating a Religious Identity: The Case of the Gay Evangelical." *Sociological Analysis* 52:333–47.

Turner, Victor. 1969. *The Ritual Process: Structure and Anti-Structure.* Ithaca: Cornell University Press.

Warner, R. Stephen. 1994. "The Place of the Congregation in the Contemporary American Religious Configuration." Pp. 54–99 in *American Congregations: New Perspectives in the Study of Congregations,* edited by James P. Wind and James W. Lewis. Chicago: University of Chicago Press.

Chapter 4

TO STAY OR TO LEAVE?

Organizational Legitimacy in the Struggle for Change among Evangelical Feminists

JANET STOCKS

Grace, a woman in her early 50s who has been an active church member in her small, evangelical denomination her whole life,[1] has been threatened with excommunication because of the feminist ideas she is attempting to introduce into church discussions. Robin, Grace's niece, who shares many of Grace's feminist ideas, has chosen to leave this church and join another because she does not believe she can influence the denomination's stance on the position of women.

Sara, a leader within her evangelical community, exhibits a great deal of patience with the group's male leader who has not given her the range of authority many members believe she deserves. Kate has lost patience with the same male leader and has left the community to form a new group without a hierarchical leadership structure.

Although the circumstances surrounding each woman's decision are unique, these four women's experiences represent the dilemma that many evangelical Christian feminists face today: whether to remain within their churches and work to correct what they see as a departure from the original intent of Christ's teachings, to leave and join other churches that already embrace their feminist beliefs, or to start new groups that will meet their needs. Such decisions involve basic judgments about the meaning of group membership and organizational legitimacy. Drawn from in-depth, open-ended interviews with a variety of women and men, this essay explores how feminists in two small evangelical groups frame the decisions they make, what is at stake for them, how they maintain—or fail to maintain—faith in the legitimacy of their group, and how they see the issues being resolved.

Women and Conservative Religion

How can some evangelical women embrace a conservative theology that has traditionally limited women's roles and simultaneously challenge the gender norms of their evangelical groups? I was initially surprised to find active feminists within the groups I studied. Later, as I came to know these evangelical feminists, I was curious about how they reconciled a belief in the legitimacy of their churches' authority structures with the teachings and practices that placed real limits on their power in the very same churches. Many secular feminists share these questions about women's participation in conservative religion. On the other hand, many Christians wonder how Bible-believing women can identify themselves with feminism, a secular movement they hold responsible for the downfall of the family and other social ills.

In scholarly circles, women's involvement in conservative religious organizations has been the topic of some excellent studies in the past several years.[2] Most of these studies sought to explain why women in the United States today choose to participate in conservative religions that limit their freedom. In addition, much has been written by feminist theologians and Bible scholars.[3] This literature analyzes the continued patriarchy of church teaching and practice. Much of this literature argues for a different interpretation of biblical passages that limit women's roles. In addition, some of these scholars suggest new and alternative forms of religious expression for women, some squarely inside Christian and Jewish traditions and some that stretch these boundaries or clearly leave these traditions behind.

My study differs from previous sociological studies and from feminist theological writings in that it focuses on feminists who intentionally and self-consciously challenge evangelical teaching and practice and who attempt to change the institutions to which they belong. When a society offers myriad options for religious and spiritual expression and when privatization of religious authority is the dominant trend, we must wonder why these women stay, women who admit their discontent with the restrictions of evangelical religion (see Bellah et al. 1985; Wuthnow 1988). Why do women who are not content with their church's stance on the role of women remain within these churches instead of seeking a religious organization that is more friendly to their feminist ideas? For those who depart, what caused them to leave their religious organizations when other feminists have found a way to stay? What is the trigger that makes some questioners leave while other questioners do not?

Organizational Legitimacy, Group Loyalty, and Individual Identity

Albert O. Hirschman (1970) identified two factors that influence a group member's decision to remain in a group and voice her dissatisfaction or to exit the group. The first factor involves the extent to which customer-members are willing to trade the certainty of exit against the uncertainties of an improvement in the deteriorated product. The second factor requires customer-members to assess their ability to influence the organization.

The first factor clearly relates to the special attachment to an organization known as loyalty. Thus, even with a given estimate of one's influence, the likelihood of voice increases with the degree of loyalty. In addition, the two factors are far from independent. A member with a considerable attachment to a product or organization will often search for ways to make herself influential, especially when the organization moves in what she believes is the wrong direction. Conversely, a member who wields, or thinks he wields, considerable power in an organization and is therefore convinced that he can get it "back on the track" is likely to develop a strong affection for the organization in which he is powerful (Hirschman 1970:77–78).

For the women who spoke with me, the possibility of influencing the group by staying and voicing their discontent has been a major factor in the decision to stay or to leave. Though they realized that the organization did constrain their choices and opportunities for leadership, some chose to stay to continue their struggle. For other feminists, however, questioning their group's teachings and practices unraveled their commitment to the entire structure. For these women, the group lost its legitimacy. Women who could no longer believe in the legitimacy of their organization chose to leave and put their energies elsewhere. Additionally, some evangelical feminists articulated organizational ideals and priorities, apart from their concerns about gender issues, that were central to their decisions. Though the opportunities available for women's leadership were important, this issue alone did not determine their decision to stay or to leave.

Women Who Stay and Women Who Leave: The Reformed Protestants

The Reformed Protestants are a small denomination whose membership has become increasingly conservative on women's issues in the past half century. Most of the approximately 4,000 members of the Reformed Protestants reside in the Northeast and Midwest. The denominational seminary is located in a medium-sized midwestern city around which many flagship congregations are concentrated. The nation's abolitionist controversy in the 1800s marked the early years of the denomination and precipitated the secession of many southern congregations.

During the early 1900s, the denomination was more liberal than it is today on the "woman question." Many older members recall women being very active in the church of their youth. Grace reported

> In my congregation, women, my aunt, my grandmother's sister went to China as a single woman missionary. I just remembered her visits in the home and her speaking from the pulpit and talking about this, that, and the other thing. And there wasn't anything women couldn't do in the Church. . . . We had city missionaries that were women. In the city of Philadelphia, they would go around and bring people in. You couldn't do that now in the church. That would be a big no-no.

Growing up, Grace experienced a church in which women could be active and perform a wide range of roles. Many long-time Reformed Protestant members recalled aunts who had been single women missionaries in the early 1900s.

Insiders trace the denomination's more conservative stance to an influx of new members and congregations during the past 40 years. Newer members were refugees from main-line churches and sought a more conservative theology than they had experienced previously. This rightward shift has altered women's roles in the church and denominational teachings about gender roles in the home.

Grace

Grace and her husband trace their family roots through many generations of Reformed Protestants. In describing her denomination's theology and practice, she says: "We're a mixture. We're our own little unique blend. So sometimes we feel like we don't fit anywhere." Like many long-time members, Grace knows well the denomination's history. She recalls with pride that her denomination took an abolitionist stand early in the 19th century, and that people in the church fought for the end of slavery. She is proud that her church was one of the first to ordain women as deacons beginning in 1888—even though her great, great grandfather opposed the move. "[He] was really indignant about it. Because he saw that the theology that permitted women deacons would also permit women elders. And he just was horrified."

Grace was reared in a loving home centered on Christianity and its positive message. Women were active in her church. When Grace married, she expected to use her considerable intelligence and energy in service to her church.

But her congregation's young conservative pastor began to limit the possibilities for women's service. Grace had served as chair of the social committee, but the pastor believed that women should not chair committees, especially ones that included men. His rationale was biblical: women should not have authority over men. Women were also prohibited from teaching adult Sunday school classes. Again, the pastor opposed placing women in any position in which they had authority over men. Grace recalls, "The whole time we were [in Philadelphia], I taught the adult class. And [when we came back home], I was asked to teach the high school class, and I did for a couple months. And by then the new minister came. Pretty soon women were not to teach any class older than sixth grade."

In her hometown, Grace immersed herself in her role as the mother of three boys, but she remained frustrated with her limited role in the church. Eventually she was asked to sit on the Reformed Protestant retirement home's board of directors—composed entirely of women. Grace welcomed the opportunity to work with the elderly and spent much of her time working on a building project for the home. As president of the board, she bore primary responsibility for a $4-million building program. Through this work, she met women from other congregations within the denomination and discovered that some pastors had not made the dramatic changes concerning women's roles that her pastor had made.

The inconsistency between the church's willingness for her to manage a $4-million building project and its reluctance for her to lead an adult Sunday school class caused Grace to wonder about the scriptural basis for these conservative changes. As she told me

> We campaigned and raised a million dollars from the church. In other words, we were making tremendous decisions as women. And we were overseeing the work of men. Individually, they'd come and say, "This is a wonderful work you're doing here." And I thought, you know, last week I wrote my name to a check for $4,129,000. And yet, when I go to church on Sunday, I can't pray. It's a shame if I pray out loud. I cannot chair the social committee. And I thought, this is really strange. When the minister said, "You shouldn't be doing this," I wasn't at all certain that he was right. And here I was doing this work [at the home] in the Lord's name, exactly what they said I couldn't be doing in the church. I felt it wasn't right, which was right.

When the building project for the retirement home was finished and the responsibilities handed over to the administrator of the home, Grace wondered what to do next. She had spent 50 hours a week at the home. Her three boys were all in school, and she wanted a challenge. It was time, she decided, to look carefully at the question, "May women have authority?" She researched this matter for three years, even taking a semester of Greek at the denomination's seminary. After completing her research, she wrote and published a book that questioned the denomination's stance on the role of women. In the process of investigating and writing this book, Grace came to identify herself as a feminist.

Ironically, the denomination's growing conservativism prompted Grace's identification as a feminist. "Up until that time I had considered feminism, what I had watched of it, [as] something interesting and a societal problem, but I could never tie it in with what it meant to my faith." In researching and publishing her book, Grace was motivated by pressing questions about the authenticity of her faith:

> Was the faith I had been brought up in naive? Had we neglected that teaching, as the conservatives were trying to say? Or was the faith that I had been given the true faith? So I, maybe it sounds like I've just gone and studied and found what I feel comfortable with, but I do believe that it was the Christian faith that was handed to me as a child that I'm kind of reclaiming.

Near the completion of her research and writing, Grace formed a study group of 15 people. The group, mostly women but also a few men, met at her house for six weeks to study the question of the role of women in the church. Some women from the study group went on to form another group which has published and distributed a quarterly evangelical feminist newsletter since 1987. The offshoot group today numbers approximately 12 women.

Grace has come under fire both for her book and for her involvement with the feminist newsletter. Several men opposed to Grace's work have introduced censorship motions at various levels of the church's courts. These motions also led to the formation of the denomination's Committee on the Role and Service of Women. This committee met for two years and wrote a report that neither supported nor directly opposed the work of Grace and other feminists in the denomination. Recent action taken by the demonination's ecclesiastical courts responded directly to issues raised in Grace's book and the feminist newsletter. These courts articulated the denominational position that men alone have authority in the church and that, in the home, husbands have authority over their wives. Additionally, the courts told Grace and other feminists in the denomination to submit to the authority of their pastors and elders in publishing their newsletter.

Grace has not been excommunicated even though she is considered a heretic by some in her denomination; nor has she left of her own accord. She contends that she is engaging in the historical process of the church, similar to a century-long debate that occurred prior to the church taking a stand on abolition. The Reformed Protestant church is her church, too, she contends. She maintains that she has as much right to it as the more conservative men who are trying to limit women's participation. She asserts

> I'd say [I'm] in it for the long run, unless I had no choice. Before I started this, that was a part of the cost we counted. Could we go to another denomination if we were kicked out? And we said yes, we'd be willing to do that. I say we, because that was something [Frank] and I talked about. My heart would be broken if I did have to, but my commitment was such that I wouldn't back down. I mean, I couldn't. It is so wrapped up in my belief in what it means to be a Christian.

Grace stays within the Reformed Protestant church because she feels it is where she belongs. Her religious heritage means a great deal to her, and church membership is central to Grace's identity. Although she maintains that the denomination's current practice and teaching on the role of women is wrong, she agrees with many other aspects of the church. Change takes time, she argues, and the woman question might take a century to resolve, just as the slavery question did.

Her tolerance for the slow process of change enables Grace to maintain her allegiance to the Reformed Protestant church as a legitimate organization even as she struggles against the denomination's errant teachings. Her commitment to her family's legacy in the denomination, the centrality of the church in her daily life, and her occasional successes in countering the denomination's conservative tide bolster Grace's resolve to stay and seek change. She is optimistic that history is on her side.

Robin

Mary, Grace's friend and collaborator on the evangelical feminist newsletter, expresses a concern shared by many older feminists within the denomination:

> I've heard from others the fear that younger women will leave the church and go elsewhere. Well, why not? I think that's something to be confronted. They can't use their gifts in our church the way it is now very much. Men can go all the way for Jesus Christ. Women come up here and we're stopped with church doctrine.

The fear that young women will leave the church is well founded. According to older feminists, few younger women engage in the struggle. Instead, many simply leave the denomination to find religious options more friendly to their ideas of a woman's place.

Robin, Grace's niece, is one such young woman. Robin's paternal family traces its roots back many generations in the Reformed Protestant church. Her mother, though unchurched as a child, attended the Reformed Protestant undergraduate college where she became a member of the denomination. Robin was reared in a home with strict religious practice. She recalls

> My dad was very "God and rule," and my mom sort of took it all with a grain of salt. But they were very strict about everything. They kept the sabbath on Sunday. You couldn't watch any TV or listen to the radio, or

even just read a book that wasn't a religious book or listen to music that wasn't religious.

Despite maintaining conservative religious norms in the home, Robin's parents also encouraged her independence. She maintains that she was always a feminist, a stance her parents supported:

> My parents have a very traditional marriage where Dad makes all the rules and Mom follows them. But he always told us not to put up with that, and he always pushed us too, you know. If you said, "I want to be a nurse," he'd say, "No, you want to be a doctor." When I said I wanted to be a teacher: "No, you want to be a college professor. Don't sell yourself short."

Robin belonged to the same congregation as Grace. She, too, responded negatively to the arrival of the young, conservative pastor. She recalls the changes vividly

> I remember one sermon that he preached about headship or something. And, in fact, we were sitting right behind Aunt [Grace], as we often did, and he said something like all men are head over all women. And I remember Aunt [Grace] and my mom were furiously scribbling notes back and forth with just steam coming out of their ears.

For Robin that sermon was the beginning of the end of her commitment to the church, though her decision to leave did not come for several years. "I think [the pastor] pressing such a ridiculous issue was a big part of me unraveling a lot of the theology that I was all caught up in. It was like the first string to pull on, and it all sort of started coming apart."

During her early years in college, Robin felt called to be a preacher—a dream she could not realize in the Reformed Protestant church. When Robin announced her decision to her parents, they were surprised but did not discourage her. "I remember when I called home and told them I was going to go to preseminary, my mom was really startled. 'Well, how can you say that when it says this and that?' But my dad said, 'Well, you picked a tough row to hoe, but go for it.'"

Robin went to Calvin Seminary, which is associated with the Christian Reformed Church (CRC) and which is close to the Reformed Protestants in its theological conservatism. While women were allowed to attend seminary, the CRC does not ordain women pastors (although this position is now debated in the denomination). The CRC's prohibition against women's ordination meant Robin was barred from taking courses in preaching, because this was the preserve of those destined for ordained ministry. Robin graduated with a master's degree in theological studies, intending to attend another seminary to complete courses she would need for ordination. Robin, however, did not continue her schooling. Now, several years after graduation, Robin is a teacher and a former member of the Reformed Protestant church.

For Robin, careful analysis of the denomination's stance on the woman question resulted in a questioning of her Christian faith in general. "Looking into these passages on biblical interpretation, in order to reinterpret and understand what these feminist Christians were saying about Christianity, opened up a whole lot of issues. The more you study them, the more you realize that there's not that easy certainty." Though her conservative pastor was quoting directly from the Bible, Robin had learned that biblical passages cannot always be interpreted straightforwardly. Questioning led to doubt, and doubt, to decreased commitment.

Robin has not rejected Christianity altogether, but she has separated from the church in which she was reared. Once she questioned its teachings on the place of women, she considered the possibility that none of the Reformed Protestant positions were infallible. She could not find a place to stop her questions. Robin does not share the feelings of belonging and optimism that hold her Aunt Grace to the church. For Robin, the woman question became the defining issue in her struggle with the church. Church teachings on women blocked her vocational goals. Educational institutions reinforced her second-class status in the denomination. Despite strong family ties to the Reformed Protestant church, Robin came to believe the "ridiculous" teachings on women were characteristic of a deeper flaw in the denomination itself. Leaving the denomination and rejecting it as a legitimate authority, Robin determined that her energies were best directed elsewhere.

Women Who Stay and Women Who Leave: The Seekers

The Seekers are a small evangelical community in a northeastern city. The core group consists of a dozen people who live within a block of each other in a low-income neighborhood. During regular worship services, the group swells by an additional ten to 100 members, depending on the season. The Seekers also operate two ministries: a Christian peace-and-justice magazine with a national distribution and a neighborhood center which provides after-school tutoring and a summer camp for children, a food-distribution program, and adult education activities.

Formed during the social ferment of the late 1960s and early 1970s, the Seekers originated at a small evangelical seminary in the Midwest. The founding members, like the seminary from which they organized, were exclusively male. Although many founding members are no longer with the group, Joseph, the group's leader and visionary, has been around from the beginning. Even though the group has long embraced the equality of women, including the use of inclusive language for God, gender issues have caused tension throughout the history of the group. In 1990, about two-thirds of the community's core membership, approximately 40 people, left the group. The causes for the schism are multiple and complex. However, sources on both sides of the split named feminist issues as central to the division.

Sara

Sara has been with the Seekers community since 1984 when she began working for the group's outreach magazine. She became a member of the core community in 1986. Only one woman has been with the Seekers longer. Sara currently serves as managing editor of the magazine and one of a group of six people who make up the leadership team in the worship community.

Reared in the Methodist church by parents who were active church members, Sara has maintained a consistent pattern of church attendance. During her college years, she became interested in social justice issues and joined an evangelical group within the United Methodist Church. Although she embraced the new evangelical theology, she was disappointed by its inattention to social issues. In the Seekers, Sara found a felicitous combination of evangelical theology and social consciousness. She recalls

Mainstream Protestantism seemed to me a little bit too loose, a little bit too relative. If you want to believe it, believe it; if you don't, just ignore it, kind of. And that meant then that people could get off the hook on social justice issues, just like they could get off the hook on a lot of other things. So there was an attraction for me at [the Seekers] of taking the Bible seriously—reading the Bible, but also, of course, all of the social justice concerns.

Like Robin, Sara was reared by parents who encouraged their daughters "to be independent and confident, so I just headed into life that way." Despite encounters with individuals who expected her to stay silent and in her place, she maintains that she has been a life-long feminist. During college, Sara chose a community leadership and development major, a field that had few women. Through her classroom and social experiences, Sara came to identify with feminism as a political issue. She defines feminism in terms of power-sharing:

> What feminism means to me is an approach towards power which is a power-sharing approach. It's not that I want to learn to operate in a world like the worst of the men have. It's that I want to promote a power-sharing approach in work or in community or in relationships and that we figure out who it is that God calls us to be, to *be* [speaker's emphasis] all of who God calls us to be, and then to be able to meet other people in the middle without having to give up your identity or take something away from theirs. And that's a feminist model today.

Sara was attracted to the Seekers because of its support for women and women's issues. "I felt as though women were empowered to participate more than what I had seen elsewhere. And, also in those days, there was a concern even about inclusive language, much more so than other places, much more so even than the United Methodist Church."

Despite these positive experiences with the Seekers, Sara has also felt tension in the community, especially concerning the way power is shared. While she holds a responsible position at the magazine, she is troubled by unresolved issues about power and gender in the community. Nonetheless, Sara did not leave the community during the big split of 1990. She felt that God was not calling her to another community; so she stayed put with a community in crisis. Sara draws on this calling in her struggle to improve the community's power sharing. She is confident that the Christian social justice work of the community is important locally and nationally.

Particularly difficult for Sara are dynamics of leadership and power at the magazine. Her position as managing editor makes her second in command on editorial decision making. Joseph, the Seeker's leader, maintains final control. Joseph's leadership style has been described by many as authoritarian. Sara contends that Joseph is wary of relinquishing command. She finds much of the day-to-day operations at the magazine frustrating. Nevertheless, she remains strongly identified with the goals and priorities of the community.

Peter, a Franciscan priest who worked with the community for three years before his departure, agrees with Sara that the community's power sharing is not what it should be. He believes that Sara deserves to be given a lot more power and authority within the organization. He admires her dedication to the community. Peter notes, "She has a high quotient of acceptance of this vision. She's a [Seekers] type—that sustains her. She's the one I think who probably takes it the most because she's the one called on to make this *work* [speaker's emphasis] every month. This magazine comes out because [Sara's] here."

Sara sustains a hope that eventually the organization will share power more equally. She sees change as an ongoing process and will keep pushing for it. Her willingness to continue the struggle comes from a strong sense of calling to the Seekers' vision. Despite occasional dissatisfaction, Sara remains committed to the legitimacy of the organization and its overarching goals. Like Grace, Sara's participation in her religious organization is central to her identity and sustains her commitment to its goals. Thus she is willing to stay and struggle for change rather than leave for an organization that comes closer to her ideal.

Kate

Kate grew up in a working-class family and describes her parents as antireligious. While an adolescent she was influenced by a neighbor who invited her to attend Bible school. In high school, she was involved in the Young Life program, an ecumenical religious group for high school students that stressed the connection between religion and social justice.

During the early years of her marriage, Kate and her husband spent time "exploring values" and reading the Bible and came to identify themselves as Christians. When they began looking for a faith community, they were surprised by the different beliefs they found among Christians. Kate recalls

I think when I first became a Christian I thought all Christians agreed on everything, and if you heard a preacher say something, that was the truth. So the first couple years were pretty tumultuous—realizing how much of a range of opinions and beliefs and differences in theology and doctrine and all of that were in the church, and just kind of trying to find our way with that.

Prior to becoming a Christian, Kate had thought little about feminism. The mix of ideas she encountered in Christian teaching and practice prompted her to reflect on gender roles and customs:

> I experienced the paradox of, for the first time, believing that my life had meaning and value—kind of hearing the message: God loves you; there's a plan for your life; what you do is significant; and, you can make a contribution. And then also really hearing the message that because I was a woman there were definite constraints and limitations on how I could express that and how I should grow and develop.

Kate attended the first Evangelical Women's Caucus in 1976 which she described as a turning point in her life. Feminist theologian Virginia Mollencott gave the keynote address. Mollencott drew together gender analysis and liberation theology in a way that helped Kate make sense of her own theological and social justice commitments. Kate recalls her excitement

> [I]t was just an incredible night. I didn't go to sleep after her address. She got done speaking about 10:00, and I sat in the lobby of this hotel, with my mind just racing, until 6:00 in the morning, because it was like: I'm not a crazy person, you know? Somebody else thinks these things; somebody else has put all this together. And it was a really revolutionary experience for me.

After the conference, Kate studied the Gospels and came to believe that Jesus was a feminist. According to her, Jesus related to women in ways that sought to undermine the sexist attitudes of his day. Christianity and feminism are hewn from the same cornerstone.

As Kate came to see the coincidence between Christianity and feminism, she and her husband Reese felt that their lives were too fragmented. On the one hand, they worked on social justice issues among secular folks who had little use for their Christianity; and on the other hand, they worshiped with people who were not especially concerned with social justice issues. Their decision to move to the Seekers community was their effort to reconcile their two passions:

We'd been reading [the Seekers' magazine] since it started, since the first year they published, and it had been a significant shaper of our thoughts. And we thought, "Well, why are we trying to do something here that's already happening there? Why not just go hook ourselves up to a group that seems like they've already gone some way towards putting this all together?"

Kate and Reese were part of the Seekers community for ten years. Kate counts their years in the community as good ones. Each worked for the magazine during their decade of involvement. Reese also worked for the Seekers' neighborhood center. They correlated their work schedules to permit each parent to spend equal time raising their children. They believed that they had finally found a community where they could bring together their political convictions and their faith.

Kate characterizes their time with the Seekers community as a season of exploration and experimentation. Much of that exploration for Kate concerned her feminism and how it fit within her evangelical Christian faith. She organized a women's group within the community and led several feminist liturgies that, for some in the group, bordered on heresy. She began to realize that her feminism was causing problems within the community. As time went on, Kate began to believe that the union of Christianity and feminism that she wanted could not be satisfied within the Seekers community.

She maintains that leaders within the community resisted some of the feminist challenges, which they called unorthodox. Particularly troublesome for Kate were the roles assigned men and women in the community and its leadership structure:

I was the one always kind of saying, "I'm uncomfortable with this community being where it's predominantly men in leadership" or, "I'm uncomfortable that the women are the ones who are heading up the child care." That no matter what we talked about, we'd end up falling into what were the more traditional roles.

Kate also began to see Joseph's leadership as a hindrance to justice in the community. "I wondered sometimes whether he was willing to step down and not be in charge of things in order to embody his beliefs about empowerment; not just with women, but also with black people and with low-income people and that kind of stuff. I wondered if he was willing to take a back seat." For Kate, the Seekers was failing to live by the standards of Christian love and justice that it upheld as God's mission in the world.

Kate and Reese left the Seekers community during the split in 1990. The couple helped to organize a new worship community, composed of many schismatic members. Named the Circle Community Church, this group formed on the basis of a rotating, shared leadership, and it concerns itself less with theological orthodoxy than the Seekers community does. Kate contends that honoring her religious journey takes priority over her holding to evangelical tenets. Despite her willingness to explore, Kate remains rooted in Christianity:

> My own salvation journey has been through Christianity. . . . It sort of gave me everything that has sent me on this journey. So I couldn't say I'm a Buddhist, or I couldn't say I'm a New Age thinker. Even though I feel like I've incorporated aspects of those other kinds of thought into my understanding of faith, Christianity is my foundation really, because that's my home. And I think a lot of really exciting things happen in the Church, and a lot of really exciting things happen among Christian people, and I think I don't want to let go, I guess, of my hold in there, even if it might look tenuous.

While Kate feels at home within Christianity in general, her sense of belonging to the Seekers was affected by her desire to explore and, when possible, to incorporate other exciting ideas that did not necessarily fit within the community's theological framework. Her faith in the authority structures of the community suffered when she began to question the group's practices and beliefs regarding gender. Her distrust led to more questions about the group's ability to affect change in other domains of social justice that were important to her. Her sense of identity was Christian, in a larger sense, and she preferred to start a new group that more closely fit her ideal, rather than remain and struggle with a community from which she felt increasingly estranged.

"Jesus Was the First Feminist"

I began my study wondering how women who called themselves both Christian and feminist negotiated the contradictions between these two systems of belief. I soon realized that these women see no contradiction between Christianity and feminism. In fact, they believe that Christianity, when deliberately modeled on the teachings and practices of Jesus, is completely consistent with feminism. Many evangelical feminists expressed this belief in their contention that "Jesus was the first feminist." The struggles of the evangelical feminists in my study centered on their religious institutions, largely governed by men, and the practices that they felt departed from Jesus' teachings. These women believe that in adopting more feminist practices, their churches would also come closer to true Christianity.

Despite differences in size, structure, and gender norms between the two groups in this study, women in both groups expressed similar questions, frustrations, doubts, and feelings of efficacy. Evangelical feminists who attempt to reconcile their feminist beliefs with their church's teachings and practices regarding women face a complex challenge. Should they stay within an organization that may not give them equal authority with men? Do they trust the process of negotiation, engaging in a struggle that may take years, stretching even beyond their lifetimes? Do they abandon an organization that has been meaningful to them when the situation goes from bad to worse? Do they set out on new terrain to join or help build an organization that will more clearly meet their needs?

Hirschman (1970) writes that one reason a member may be reluctant to leave is the fear that in doing so, the organization may deteriorate further. Such fear explains Grace's experience, who stayed in her church because she felt she was its voice of conscience, urging it to "do the right thing" on the woman question just as it had on the question of slavery. But, clearly, Grace accepted the fact that her influence might not have any effect in her own lifetime, or might not convince the denomination to change its stance on women. For Sara, staying with the Seekers depended not so much on a belief in her ability to change the group quickly, nor on a generalized fear that the organization would fall apart without her. Rather, she stayed because it was a venue in which she could continue to do the work she valued. Grace and Sara stayed, in short, because of loyalty, not because they hoped for immediate change.

It is harder to explain why Robin and Kate left because, in their own accounts, the loss of loyalty and the loss of confidence in change are intertwined. These two women no longer felt their churches offered them enough to justify any efforts to effect change. Robin and Kate lost interest in their churches' direction. In addition, they both came to doubt that change was possible. It was not their perceptions of their influence, but their judgments concerning the legitimacy of the organizations that made the biggest difference for them.

So the question becomes, what factors lead to the loss of loyalty? To put it another way, how did Kate and Robin cease to value their membership in their group and cease to regard the teachings as valid and legitimate? Several factors affected the decisions these four feminists made. The strength of their identification with their groups helped to determine the ease or difficulty in separating from them. The perceived distance between their feminist ideals and the teachings and practices of their groups influenced the decision to exit or stay. The estimation of the likelihood that they would be able to bring about change within their group contributed to their decision making.

Yet, consistently, the most important factor was their ability or inability to maintain a belief in the legitimacy of their group in the face of dissatisfaction. Grace and Sara hold serious questions about their organizations' treatment of women. Even so, they believe that the groups are valuable and legitimate. Grace and Sara both bolstered their flagging optimism with the long view of their communities' history. Change, in these particular groups, was slow coming, but come it would; of this they were hopeful. Robin and Kate lost faith in their organizations. As they pursued questions that arose from their growing feminism, the legitimacy of the authority structures of their churches began to unravel. They began to question teachings and practices not only about women but also about other issues. Their commitment to these organizations waned, and they refused to expend the energy necessary for a protracted struggle. For them, finding another outlet for their religious expression that did not clash as directly with their feminist ideals became their objective.

In short, the question of loyalty can be understood as the question of whether or not a group or activity remains valued for its own sake, on its own account. When such is the case, members may engage in a variety of strategies to maintain their commitment, including taking a long view of history that minimizes the importance of their own immediate influence. When loyalty is lost, influence seems irrelevant because there is no commitment to put in the time and energy it would take to bring change about. Loss of hope for change can lead some women to the process of questioning that ultimately undermines legitimacy. For evangelical groups like the Seekers and the Reformed Protestant Church, maintaining the loyalty of younger feminists, who have not experienced the excitement of the group's founding (like Sara) and who do not feel the connection with the heyday of women's participation (like Grace), may grow more and more difficult.

NOTES

1. I have used pseudonyms for the names of all individuals and the names of the two groups in this study.

2. For example, see Ammerman (1987); Neitz (1987); Klatch (1987); Warner (1988); Stacey (1990); DeBerg (1990); Davidman (1991); Kaufman (1991); Bendroth (1993); Riesebrodt (1993). These studies cover women's participation in conservative Protestantism, charismatic Catholicism, and Orthodox Judaism in the United States.

3. See Daly (1973, 1985); Ruether (1974, 1984, 1986); Christ and Plaskow (1979); Evans (1983); Fiorenza (1985, 1986, 1992, 1993); Kolbenschlag (1987); Mollencott (1987); Martin (1988); Plaskow and Christ (1989); Van Leeuwen (1990); Thistlewaite and Engel (1990); Anderson and Hopkins (1991).

References

Ammerman, Nancy Tatom. 1987. *Bible Believers: Fundamentalists in the Modern World.* New Brunswick, NJ: Rutgers University Press.

Anderson, Sherry Ruth and Patricia Hopkins. 1991. *The Feminist Face of God: The Unfolding of the Sacred in Women.* New York: Bantam Books.

Bellah, Robert N., Richard Madsen, William M. Sullivan, Ann Swindler, and Steven M. Tipton. 1985. *Habits of the Heart: Individualism and Commitment in American Life.* New York: Harper and Row.

Bendroth, Margaret L. 1993. *Fundamentalism and Gender, 1875 to the Present.* New Haven: Yale University Press.

Christ, Carol P. and Judith Plaskow, eds. 1979. *Womanspirit Rising: A Feminist Reader in Religion.* San Francisco: Harper San Francisco.

Daly, Mary. 1973. *Beyond God the Father: Toward a Philosophy of Women's Liberation.* Boston: Beacon Press.

———. 1985. *The Church and the Second Sex.* Boston: Beacon Press.

Davidman, Lynn. 1991. *Tradition in a Rootless World: Women Turn to Orthodox Judaism.* Berkeley and Los Angeles: University of California Press.

DeBerg, Betty A. 1990. *Ungodly Women: Gender and the First Wave of American Fundamentalism.* Minneapolis: Fortress Press.

Evans, Mary J. 1983. *Woman in the Bible.* Downers Grove, IL: InterVarsity Press.

Fiorenza, Elisabeth S. 1985. *Claiming the Center: A Feminist Critical Theory of Liberation.* New York: Harper and Row.

————. 1986. *Bread Not Stone: The Challenge of Feminist Biblical Interpretation*. Boston: Beacon Press.

————. 1992. *But She Said: Feminist Practices of Biblical Interpretation*. Boston: Beacon Press.

————. 1993. *Discipleship of Equals: A Critical Feminist Ekklesia-logy of Liberation*. New York: Crossroads.

Hirschman, Albert O. 1970. *Exit, Voice, and Loyalty: Responses to Decline in Firms, Organizations, and States*. Cambridge, MA and London: Harvard University Press.

Kaufman, Debra Renee. 1991. *Rachel's Daughters: Newly Orthodox Jewish Women*. New Brunswick, NJ: Rutgers University Press.

Klatch, Rebecca. 1987. *Women of the New Right*. Philadelphia: Temple University Press.

Kolbenschlag, Madonna. 1987. *Women in the Church*. Laurel, MD: Pastoral Press.

Martin, Faith. 1988. *Call Me Blessed: The Emerging Christian Woman*. Grand Rapids, MI: William B. Eerdmans Publishing Co.

Mollencott, Virginia R. 1987. *Women of Faith in Dialogue*. New York: Crossroads.

Neitz, Mary Jo. 1987. *Charisma and Community: A Study of Religious Commitment within the Charismatic Renewal*. New Brunswick, NJ: Transaction Books.

Plaskow, Judith and Carol P. Christ, eds. 1989. *Weaving the Visions: New Patterns in Feminist Spirituality*. San Francisco: Harper San Francisco.

Riesebrodt, Martin. 1993. "Fundamentalism and the Political Mobilization of Women." Pp. 243–71 in *The Political Dimensions of Religion*, edited by Said Arjomand. Albany, NY: SUNY Press.

Ruether, Rosemary R. 1974. *Religion and Sexism*. Old Tappan, NJ: Simon and Schuster.

————. 1984. *Sexism and God-Talk: Toward a Feminist Theology*. Boston: Beacon Press.

————. 1986. *Womanguides: Readings toward a Feminist Theology*. Boston: Beacon Press.

Stacey, Judith. 1990. *Brave New Families: Stories of Domestic Upheaval in Late Twentieth Century America*. New York: Basic Books.

Thistlethwaite, Susan Brooks and Mary Potter Engel, eds. 1990. *Lift Every Voice: Constructing Christian Theologies from the Underside*. San Francisco: Harper San Francisco.

Van Leeuwen, Mary Stewart. 1990. *Gender and Grace: Love, Work, and Parenting in a Changing World*. Downers Grove, IL: InterVarsity Press.

Warner, R. Stephen. 1988. *New Wine in Old Wineskins: Evangelicals and Liberals in a Small-Town Church*. Berkeley and Los Angeles: University of California Press.

Wuthnow, Robert. 1988. *The Restructuring of American Religion: Society and Faith Since World War II*. Princeton: Princeton University Press.

Chapter 5

What Is Right? What Is Caring?

Moral Logics in Local Religious Life[1]

PENNY EDGELL BECKER

What does it mean to be Jewish in a largely Gentile community? The members of a Conservative synagogue in Oak Park, a suburb of Chicago, found themselves discussing this very question when their leaders helped to organize a homeless shelter in which they hoped the synagogue would participate. Opposition to the shelter among the synagogue's neighbors and village officials was vocal, and included, by some reports, openly anti-Semitic remarks directed at synagogue members supporting the shelter. Concerns about anti-Semitism moved some congregants to question the wisdom of participating in a project that was running up against community objections. Several members feared becoming the target of discriminatory comments and hard feelings. Some felt that their welcome in the community was tenuous, and that "making trouble" was not a good idea.

Raising these concerns in public meetings, those who opposed getting involved in the shelter found that many members, particularly younger ones, rejected the idea that the congregation should back down just because the shelter was unpopular. These members also contended that one reason some opposed the homeless shelter was because they feared that their beautiful, well-kept building would be damaged by the overnight guests. Shelter supporters rejected fear—of anti-Semitism, of the homeless—as a legitimate basis for withdrawing. More generally, they insisted that this decision had to be made on moral grounds, not out of apprehension or inconvenience. As the rabbi told me, shelter supporters finally forced the rest of the membership to confront the issue on their terms. As he put it, they successfully forced people not to ask, "Is this the easy thing to do?" but rather to inquire, "Is this the right thing to do?" The latter is a moral question (cf. Tipton 1982).

After heated public meetings and private conversations, the congregation voted to participate in the shelter project. Through this debate, members rejected an interpretation of Jewish identity as marginal and the accompanying expectation that the congregation would remain apart from community affairs. Instead they advanced a self-image that stressed their history of marginality as grounds for ministering to another marginal group, the homeless. The conflict was never about whether being Jewish was a marginal identity in this particular suburban Chicago community. Rather, it centered on the implications of this identity for practice, programs, resource allocation, and a more general stance toward community involvement.

This Conservative synagogue's conflict over the homeless shelter did more than reveal a shared understanding of the marginal nature of Judaism in mainstream suburban America and divergent interpretations about what this recognition implies for participation in local community life. The conflict became the locus for constructing a new public consensus among the congregants. It provided an occasion for interpreting their identity as a rationale for engaging in compassionate outreach, for changing the overall direction of the congregation's involvement with the community. The final resolution stressed compassion, inclusion, and connection.

During conversations with me, congregants noted that questions of meaning and identity had long received considerable public attention and conscious reflection. This synagogue is not afraid of heated debate. As Rachel, a clinical psychologist and a board member, reported

"This is a culture here which is not shy about conflict. It is part of Jewish culture in general, not just this synagogue. You confront, you question, you ask, you look for a better way." So sometimes people yell, and feelings are hurt, and apologies are forthcoming, and it's patched up and you move on.[2]

Thus conflicts in this congregation often become public arenas for negotiating boundaries and identity. In this case, the boundary between the temple and the "outside" was well demarcated and consensual. What was being contested was what action to take given the congregants' shared understanding of this boundary.

In contrast, conflicts over the role of the non-Jewish spouse in inter-married couples within congregational life raised precisely the question of the location and meaning of the congregation's boundaries. These conflicts were not about how to relate to the outside but about how much—or which parts—of the outside to incorporate into full member-ship. This Conservative congregation and a Reform congregation up the street both confronted the issue of intermarriage and the role of the spouse in temple life. The Conservative temple decided that the non-Jewish spouse was welcome to participate in any congregational activ-ity but could not sit on the board. The Reform temple initially allowed the non-Jewish spouse a seat on the board, but the decision proved to be an unstable solution because some members continually worried that non-Jews might make the synagogue's important decisions. These dis-senters repeatedly raised the issue for further discussion. At the time of my fieldwork, the Reform synagogue was working out a policy to grand-father in the non-Jewish spouses already on the board, but to prohibit any more from being elected. Satisfied with the solution, the syna-gogue later sent congregants to conferences to share their model for handling this issue and distributed copies of their written policy upon request.

The conflicts about the implications of Jewish identity in these con-gregations evolved from an awareness of anti-Semitism in society at large and in this community in particular. Anti-Semitism is one among a constellation of issues that are particularly troublesome for mainstream American religion. Charles Glock (1993) has argued that issues of race and ethnicity, gender roles, sexuality, and sexual morality have become the primary arenas of conflict for churches in the United States through-out this century.[3] Subject to rapid social change in the larger society, these issues have posed particular problems of adaptation for religious organizations. Perceived from the start as moral issues, Glock argues, these topics have been difficult for religious leaders to ignore. Accord-ing to him, tensions over gender, sexuality, race, and ethnicity reflect the reactions of national religious organizations to ongoing moderniza-tion, and, in particular, to the increasing universalism and liberalism of public life. He concludes that liberal, accommodating churches have fared badly, losing members and resources, while conservative churches, which have resisted accommodation on these issues, have thrived and grown.

Critiques of the accommodation thesis of denominational growth and decline abound, and my purpose here is not to engage that debate. Whether

Glock's analysis of the relations between these social issues and changes in national religious organizations is correct in its particulars, his observation that gender, sexuality, race, and ethnicity are central issues in American religion was substantiated in my study of local religious life. In the 23 congregations I studied, nearly one out of three conflicts (21 out of 65) reflects one of these hot button issues. Even when these social issues are not the subject of overt conflict, they often figure prominently in people's discussions of "potential conflict" or "troubling issues," or as factors that influenced how people felt about conflicts over other issues, like music or liturgy.

However useful for understanding denominational dynamics, Glock's concepts—accommodation and resistance—and the accompanying culture wars thesis do not sufficiently explain the impact of these issues on congregational life (see Hunter 1991, 1994, cf. Ammerman 1994). At the local level, these issues are not, primarily, arenas for ideological battles between those who are more liberal/progressive and those who are more conservative/orthodox. At the local level, these represent issues of inclusion and exclusion, of boundaries and identity, of who is and who is not part of the moral community. Certainly, some differences emerge in which particular issues trouble liberals and conservatives. Yet marked similarities characterize how liberals and conservatives negotiate the meaning of social issues that arise in congregational life. Liberal and conservative congregations alike tended to frame these issues as "moral" conflicts, or conflicts over "What is the right thing to do here?" They tended to resolve these conflicts by open and participatory processes, to favor compromise, and to stress that solutions needed to be "compassionate" or "caring."

A more useful analytical approach for understanding how the issues that Glock highlights affect local religious communities considers their role in provoking conflicts over how to reconcile different moral logics that crosscut, rather than reinforce, a liberal/conservative divide. Specifically, most conflicts over issues of social inclusion are struggles over when to apply a moral logic of caring and when to apply a moral logic of authoritative religious judgment or truth seeking.[4] These conflicts are triggered when a member transgresses an agreed upon boundary or calls for the renegotiation of the boundary itself.[5] The particular issues that trigger conflict are influenced by the content of a church's belief and so differ between liberal and conservative congregations and between Jewish and non-Jewish congregations in this community. But the similarities in the processes by which conflict plays itself out once it has begun indicate a crosscutting correspondence in moral logic within these congregations. This moral logic determines which issues of social inclusion are interpreted as moral and affirms that the right decision balances the moral imperatives of truth seeking and compassion.

Conflict, then, can provide a good window on the ongoing construction and negotiation of moral order, the shared and divergent expectations about the community's boundaries, and the moral obligations of membership.[6] Elaine Tyler May's (1980) study of divorce in late Victorian and post-Victorian America supports this view of conflict. May discusses what conflict reveals about moral expectations of family life. According to May, the claims and arguments that divorcing parties made during the late Victorian era reveal a basic consensus on the goals of marriage and the expected behaviors and temperaments of husbands and wives. Couples divorced when these shared expectations were violated. In a later period of rapidly changing economic arrangements and diversification of gender roles, May finds that the rhetoric of divorce reveals divergent expectations of what marriage should be like and what husbands' and wives' roles ought to be within it in post-Victorian society.

In small face-to-face groups like congregations, rhetorics of conflict reveal more than established moral expectations; they also participate in the ongoing production of moral order among people who have decided, in essence, not to "divorce" or exit when they are dissatisfied, but to stay and work things out (cf. Becker et al. 1993). In conflict, divergent expectations are revealed, shared expectations are discovered and articulated, and the implications for specific decisions are negotiated.

Conflict in Context

Understanding the links between the public discourse surrounding conflict and the moral expectations of participants in local congregations became the goal of my ethnographic study of congregations in Oak Park, Illinois. For 18 months from 1991 to 1993, I collected information on 23 congregations in and around Oak Park, a collar suburb nine miles from the center of Chicago. I interviewed more than 230 people, reviewed congregational histories and other documents, and observed worship services and other meetings.[7] Focusing on conflict and its role in making and remaking moral order in local religious communities, I asked people to tell me about all of the conflicts their congregation had experienced in approximately the past five years.

My research resulted in information on 65 conflicts that had become public and that were serious enough to be remembered by at least two people. It also yielded a list of issues that were privately labeled as conflicts or potential conflicts but which never made it into the arena of public discourse or overt conflict. This latter group of potential conflicts will also be included in my discussion, because they reveal gaps or inconsistencies between private discourse and the moral logic of public argumentation. No doubt my inventory is somewhat incomplete. Although people proved far more willing to talk about even serious conflicts than I had anticipated, some more sensitive issues or details were likely omitted, either from the congregation's own public discourse or from private talk with me. And the details of earlier and less serious conflicts may also have slipped from memory.

The time, place, and particulars of Oak Park shape this account of conflict. This village and the two to the west of it, River Forest and Forest Park, are dominated by middle- to upper middle-class professional couples with children, who make up the largest demographic group and provide leadership in many community institutions, including churches and synagogues. Oak Park and Forest Park are racially mixed and have progressive, tolerant reputations, while River Forest, more white and affluent, has a reputation as comparatively conservative.

In Oak Park and River Forest, nearly half the voters went Democratic in the 1992 presidential election, and half, Republican. The area's Pentecostal and fundamentalist churches are filled on Sunday morning, as are the United Methodist and Unitarian congregations. If the culture wars thesis worked anywhere, one might expect it would be applicable here. In fact, some evidence of culture wars exists. For example, Oak Park has an active gay and lesbian community, and, recently, a village ordinance to grant benefits to partners in same-sex unions passed but not without open opposition from more conservative churches and individuals. However, village leaders in all three suburbs identified problems that cut across the liberal-conservative divide. Communities that have avoided the white flight experienced by other Chicago collar suburbs, they nevertheless have some racial tensions. Communities that have remained economically viable, they still worry about their ability to compete with far-flung suburban malls for retailers and to maintain an adequate tax base.

Oak Park and its surrounding communities provide a good place to study the use of moral rhetoric and the public negotiation of religious identity and boundaries. These congregations, when confronted with issues of social inclusion, begin public conversations about "What are the obligations of moral community?" and "What are the boundaries of moral community?" (cf. Nippert-Eng 1996). I do not claim that Oak Park, or the three-village area of Oak Park, River Forest, and Forest Park, is somehow typical or a microcosm of American religion. In fact, quite the opposite is true. Oak Park is unusual in that it is a community where issues of race, ethnicity, sexuality, and gender have received public attention and debate and where there are well-defined groups of liberals and conservatives. Plenty of professionals and activists reside here, the ones who, according to Hunter, create and spread the culture war. If conflicts over issues of social inclusion are not well explained by the culture wars thesis in this community, then this thesis needs rethinking. This study suggests that the rethinking involves keeping the categories of liberal and conservative, while also taking into account those moral divisions that cut across, rather than reinforcing, a liberal/conservative divide.

Locating and Interpreting Moral Conflicts

To say that roughly a third of the conflicts involve issues of race, gender, or sexuality implies a broad and even distribution of concern over these issues. But conflicts about social inclusion were not evenly distributed among these congregations. Rather, they only emerged in those congregations that embraced, as part of their mission, providing members a public forum for debating deeply felt social, political, and religious issues. Out of 23 congregations, 12 contain all of the conflicts addressed in this chapter. These 12 congregations, to some extent, foster the kind of atmosphere that Rachel described in her Conservative temple, an atmosphere that embraced conflict, seeing it not only as inevitable, but as a constructive and important element of religious seriousness. Some congregations, which view their primary mission as worship or providing a close and familylike fellowship for members, did not engage in public conflict over these social issues at all. In fact, they actively avoided it.[8]

Figure 1 identifies the conflicts. Figure 2 describes the potential conflicts—tensions that were mentioned to me privately as narrow escapes, controversial issues, or problems waiting to happen. Figure 2 includes conflicts in which issues of social inclusion became a complicating factor but were not considered its primary focus. The latter are included in the table as potential conflicts.

Figure 1—Conflicts

Conflict Issue	Where Located	Number of Conflicts
Adultery or premarital affair—congregational members	Plymouth Brethren, Assemblies of God, Missouri Synod Lutheran	4
Ordination/Woman preaching	Independent Baptist, Episcopal, Catholic	3
Inclusive language	United (Presbyterian/UCC), Congregational	2
Survival of Sisterhood (women's organization)	Conservative Jewish	1
Adopt an official statement of openness towards lesbians/gay men	United (Presbyterian/UCC), Congregational	2
Minister to AIDS patients	Episcopal	1
Intermarriage—Jewish/non-Jewish	Reform Jewish	1
	Total:	14

As these figures demonstrate, the most common conflicts centered on women's roles, the participation of homosexual persons, and violations of traditional heterosexual morality in conservative Protestant churches. In the two synagogues, the only conflict generated internally was intermarriage. Anti-Semitism complicated at least one synagogue's relationship with the larger community, a complication that also caused internal strife. Race also influenced several of the conflicts that respondents were willing to discuss.

The figures also highlight differences among conflicts. Liberal Protestant congregations had all the conflicts over inclusive language and about policies regarding lesbians and gay men, while conservative Protestant congregations had all the conflicts over violations of traditional

Figure 2—Potential Conflicts or Conflicts where Issues of Social Inclusion were Contributing or Complicating Factors

Potential Conflict Issues or Complicating Factors	Where Located	Total Number
Form a "small group" for lesbians/gay males	Lutheran (USA), UCC	2
Woman preaching	Episcopal	1
Anti-Semitism (in conflict over homeless shelter)	Conservative Jewish	1
Intermarriage—Jewish/non-Jewish	Conservative Jewish	1
Race in conflicts over:		
parish school and admitting poor black community children	Missouri Synod Lutheran	1
music/worship style	Independent Baptist	1
woman preaching	Catholic	1*
	Total:	7

* Note that this conflict is also counted in Figure 1, so is not added to the total here.

heterosexual morality. Conflicts over women's roles occurred in both liberal and conservative congregations, as did conflicts over race and intermarriage. This pattern shows that the categories liberal and conservative are useful in understanding some shared moral expectations in local congregations. Conservative Protestant churches are the only ones in which the discovery of adultery or premarital sexual relations by members is cause for public comment, concern, or debate. This locus of conflict underscores expectations that heterosexual marriage is not only the norm but is also a public institution with public moral implications. Though conflicts over gender and race reveal that liberal and conservative churches are ambivalent about these issues, inclusive language is primarily a liberal Protestant strategy for incorporating feminist critiques of dominant religious practices, and tensions over this issue do not appear in other congregations.

Competing Moral Imperatives and Conflicts over Inclusion

Competing moral imperatives naturally arise in systems of religious ideas and symbols that are abstract, multivalent, and polysemous. More specifically, local congregations that decide to engage in public religion in some form combine within their mission potentially contradictory moral logics. They incorporate the communal logic of caring for members and preserving important particular relationships as well as the potentially exclusionary logic of designating some positions as true (or right, or authoritative) and others as false (or wrong, or illegitimate). Below I examine how these moral imperatives play out in different groups of conflicts.

Violating Sexual Norms

Conflicts over heterosexual morality include strife over premarital and extramarital sex in the conservative Protestant churches. Since these issues are similar and the responses to them have several common characteristics, I consider the various conflicts as a group. No disagreement existed over whether the behavior in question—premarital sex, extramarital sex—was right. No one in the conservative Protestant churches argued that this behavior was acceptable. In fact, in some ways, these incidents, reported by respondents as conflicts, are unlike most other conflicts reported, because no sides advocated different solutions. Everyone agreed that this behavior was wrong.

Nonetheless, these incidents were conflicts simply because congregants characterized them as such. First, the congregants perceived these incidents as problems that required solutions. Viewed as disruptions in the normal, day-to-day decision making of the congregation, for which there existed no convenient, routine solutions, these incidents were characterized negatively. People described them as "problems," not "opportunities" or "challenges." Second, congregants, especially church leaders, were called upon to respond to these situations. Ignoring the situation was not acceptable when a teenager became pregnant (by the son of a deacon) at the Assemblies of God church; when the elders at the Plymouth Brethren congregation discovered two different affairs among members (one involving a married woman, one between single members); or when the pastor of the Missouri Synod Lutheran Church was asked to perform a marriage ceremony for a member's son who had been living with his fiancée for more than a year.

Congregants framed these predicaments as conflict because when they sought the correct solution, they realized that two potentially contradictory moral imperatives applied to the situation. The first imperative required an authoritative interpretation of religious values that govern sexual behavior. This mandate was revealed in the proof-texting[9] and the congregational rhetoric of "following what the Bible says." In each of these conflicts, the congregations agreed that traditional, biblical ideas about heterosexual morality had to be upheld, and some public statement had to be made to that effect.

The second moral imperative addresses the congregation's need to be loving and compassionate. This obligation grows from the rhetoric of "loving the sinner, but condemning the sin." It also stems from the idea that judgment involves responsibility for helping the sinner to repent and remain part of the community. Providing support and encouragement that would allow the person to stay in fellowship while changing the immoral behavior was central in respondents' discussions of these conflicts. For example, the pastor at the Missouri Synod Lutheran church told me that he tried to do the right thing and be understanding too when he offered to marry the young couple who had been living together. If the man would just move out and stay out for six months before the wedding and if the couple would undergo premarital counseling, then he would conduct the ceremony. These strategies attempted to change the offending behavior while maintaining close ties to the couple and encouraging their continued commitment to the church.

Most members rejected judgmental, rigid rhetorics and sanctioned those who used them. For example, the pastor of the Assemblies of God church told me about the need to "lovingly rebuke" one of the deacons, who kept bringing up the subject of the teen pregnancy long after the young woman and her boyfriend had publicly apologized to the congregation and announced their forthcoming marriage. Several church members privately characterized this deacon, who thought that both individuals should have left the congregation, as a troublemaker precisely because he was judgmental, would not forgive, and seemed bent on driving the young couple away rather than encouraging them to stay.

The pastor's reaction illustrates the difficult position of official leaders in conflicts over sexual norms. Pastors and elders were judged by how well they balanced the competing moral imperatives. In this Assemblies of God church, the apology before the congregation and the agreement to marry satisfied the requirement of upholding the authoritative view of appropriate sexual activity; an insistence that the congregation be forgiving and treat the young couple well satisfied the requirement to be compassionate.

This dynamic operated in the other congregations, as a quote by a member of the Plymouth Brethren church suggests. She judged the leadership by their treatment of two members of the congregation, one of them married, who were discovered in an adulterous affair. My fieldnotes from this conversation read:

> Before the elders handled it, people were a little concerned. Would they do a good job, would they handle it well? They were close to the couple . . . but they held a congregational meeting and were loving and compassionate [pause]. Afterward, there was no qualm or question, people felt they had done a good job, were "pleased with their discretion and their compassion."

In these conservative Protestant churches, respondents claim that both moral logics—follow the authoritative teaching, do what is caring—emanate from their religious beliefs. Specifically, these approaches reflect the rhetorics of judgment and forgiveness, both of which are seen as requirements of religious community. Moreover, these conflicts articulate and institutionalize an agreement that the right thing to do involves both living the congregation's religious values and forgiving violators of moral expectations when they have demonstrated their willingness to change.

Redrawing the Boundaries

The second group of conflicts involves controversies over how to include previously excluded groups or persons into full participation and membership in congregational life. This group includes two conflicts over inclusive language; two over becoming "open and affirming" of lesbians and gay men; one over how to minister to two men diagnosed with AIDS; one over the role of intermarried couples in the life of a Reform synagogue; one over the continuing role of the Sisterhood in a Conservative synagogue; and three conflicts over women speaking from the pulpit (in an Episcopalian, a Catholic, and an independent Baptist congregation).

These conflicts differ from the first group in several ways. First of all, they are all conflicts in the sense of having at least two competing groups with two different preferred solutions. In this sense, they are more than just problems to solve; they are disagreements. In fact, in one case, the conflict resembles more a fight with great emotion, an inability to compromise, and a conclusion prompted by the exit of one group of members.

Like the first group of conflicts over sexual norms, these conflicts represent moral dilemmas for members and leaders. Early in the debates, congregants rejected nonmoral ways of framing the issues. For example, at the Conservative synagogue one group suggested disbanding the Sisterhood. It was inefficient, they said, taking time and resources away from other organizations. The Sisterhood had lost most of its members and it no longer fit with most women's lives and work schedules; it should just be dropped. Many members of the synagogue roundly rejected this assessment as a crass and inappropriate argument regarding an organization that still gave meaning to some members and provided an important outlet for older women to socialize and engage in service to the temple.

Unlike the previous group of conflicts, in these there is no underlying agreement about what is the right thing to do. "What is right" is hotly debated. In most of these conflicts, both sides couch the dispute about what is right in religious terms. In an Episcopal church, for example, members invoked a religious framework to debate how to respond to two members with HIV-AIDS. One man was well loved, but the other was identified by several people as a difficult personality. Additionally, the difficult man led a flamboyant life style that disturbed many members, especially older ones. When each man became debilitated by AIDS-related complications, he was placed on the church's home communion list along with other ill or older house-bound members of the church.

A conflict ensued when an older member wrote a letter to the vestry condemning homosexuality and sexual irresponsibility, based on certain biblical passages. This letter sought to define the central issue at stake as homosexuality. According to the letter writer, these men should not be on the home communion list; it was tantamount to a congregational endorsement of their life style, which this man viewed as sinful. Congregants informed me that the letter writer was also upset because he felt that his own wife, who had died from cancer, had not received as much attention from the congregation as were the men dying of AIDS. This neglect, they told me with some display of guilt, had led to hurt feelings that surfaced in the present conflict.

The man's letter prompted public discussions in several venues, including the vestry, Sunday sermons, small group classes, and private, informal discussions among members. In these discussions, the letter and its arguments were rejected in favor of a frame that made AIDS the central issue. This way of framing the issue focused on Christ's compassion for the sick. Those who spoke about this told stories of Jesus healing the sick from the Gospels. In the end, the illness frame prevailed. The congregation rallied around these two men as they had previously for other terminally ill members.

The pastor and a majority of lay leaders successfully employed the frame of ministering to the ill as Christ had done, of embodying Christ's ministry in contemporary times. This approach had several consequences. First, it channeled the activity of the congregation into existing organizational routines. Being placed on the home communion list along with other house-bound congregants is normal when the issue at hand is illness, not sin. When one man was hospitalized, church people cleaned his house before his mother arrived from out of town. When they discovered that she could not drive, church members drove her to the hospital to visit her son. These were common congregational activities in caring for ill members and their families.

Framing the issue in this manner also allowed the congregation to depoliticize and contain the conflict. The letter to the vestry did not lead to a sustained discussion of whether or not AIDS is related to sin—whether the sin was homosexuality or a specific irresponsible life style. Attempts to use the deaths of these two men to institute an AIDS education program in the parish succeeded, but the effort to include detailed discussion of homosexual life styles in the program was entirely unsuccessful. Rather, AIDS was treated as an "illness like any other," as it had been constructed in the initial congregational negotiation prompted by the letter. The pastor and lay leaders labored to make the question of sin irrelevant from the start, and they succeeded in quickly foreclosing any debate about it.

This conflict occurred in a congregation with an open gay and lesbian presence, a group of members who are self-conscious and are perceived by others as a gay subgroup. The congregation has tried to avoid the internal politicization of homosexuality. Thus the illness framing of this issue kept a potentially divisive conflict from escalating. In the end, most every one felt good about the congregation's response, although the man who initially wrote the letter to the vestry stopped attending church for a long time.

In this conflict, both frames—condemning sin and ministering to the ill—were based in religious language and imagery. Like the first group, this second group of conflicts focused on how to apply multiple or contradictory religious and moral imperatives to actual situations. The two churches in conflict over whether to ratify an official statement affirming openness to lesbian and gay members experienced this tension. One side argued that "doing what is right" involves rejecting homophobia, while another faction contended that "doing what is caring" involves not making the local congregation into a political forum, excluding those from fellowship who do not agree on an essentially political issue.

In another church, the inclusion of gay men and lesbians never became a public conflict, but might have if one member had pushed for a public discussion. This man, a member of a Lutheran church (ELCA) reported that he approached the pastor about forming a small fellowship group explicitly for lesbians and gay men. The pastor responded that their mission statement welcomed members regardless of sexual orientation, thus, addressing the justice issue. But, the pastor also pointed out that politicizing the issue by forming a small group might damage fellowship and was thus uncaring. Justice and fellowship need not logically be contradictory, but this pastor interpreted them as so in this case. This gay man told me that he had concluded that the pastor's response was, perhaps, right for this church. He also noted his regret that the congregation could not be a forum for activism on gay issues. However, he did not see any reasonable likelihood of that happening; he had not pursued the issue, and instead channeled his activism through denominational and community organizations other than this congregation.

The conflicts over inclusive language were also rooted in competing religious arguments. One religious argument highlighted what is right doctrinally, which in these liberal churches is understood as condemning injustices such as sexism. Another sought to preserve the beauty and tradition of some worship practices and rituals (the Lord's Prayer). Yet another consideration is the desire not to exclude those congregational members who value traditional practices, thereby potentially damaging fellowship. The conflict in the Catholic parish over a sister's practice of speaking from the pulpit raised these arguments on the same terms. One side wanted to preserve the tradition and follow the official church rules. The other side told me that their religious beliefs told them that sexism was a moral wrong and should be eradicated. The arguments about intermarriage in the two synagogues, discussed earlier, raised the same issues. Some argued that the spouse in the interfaith marriage should be included because that is the caring thing to do, while others insisted that another religious and communal imperative required the Jewish basis of the leadership.

Though most moral arguments that arise in these conflicts have their roots in a religious rhetoric (justice and fellowship), a few do not. A conflict in an independent Baptist congregation over women's roles is one example. A woman was elected to the church council. The church then moved toward a two-board system: a board of elders, composed of men only, and an administrative board of deacons, which could contain women. This action prompted some younger professional women (and a few men) to argue against the church's teaching that restricts women's roles. The pastor wrote a position paper and led several adult Bible study classes on the topic. In the end, the church adopted the two-board system, and more women stepped into approved positions, such as serving on the board of deacons and leading prayers in the Sunday services.

Those who challenged the church's stance on women in leadership roles used rhetoric from their business and professional environment. As one woman explained to me, in that world, "the criterion is, 'Can you do the job?' If the answer is 'yes,' then restrictions are discriminatory." This group made the moral argument that restrictions on women's roles are sexist, and sexism is wrong. But in this case, she and others made no attempt to link a "sexism is wrong" argument to a larger biblical or religious frame. The pastor explicitly rejected this argument and claimed that the church must maintain the right to make its own judgments about appropriate gender roles, which are quite different from the secular world's. It may be sexist to deny women promotions in the secular world, but a gender-based division of labor in the church is not sexist, the pastor argued, it is biblical, and there is a difference.

This conflict over women's roles in the church underscores the pastor's rejection of a nonreligious framing as a legitimate part of the moral debate. Further, the pastor successfully used a religious framing to depoliticize and contain the conflict. At the end of the conflict, the minister made a public statement from the pulpit that this issue was one about which Christians could disagree in good conscience. He then recruited more women into approved positions, hiring a woman director of Christian education and inviting more women to pray and do readings on Sunday mornings. Even some women who had been most vocal in questioning the new policy told me that, although they disagreed with him on this issue, they liked and respected the pastor, and did not feel that he was trying to exclude them.

What We Speak of In Private

In general, these congregations reject the moral arguments that take a political or ideological stand rather than those that advocate the issue in religious terms. This rejection can prevent congregants from talking publicly about political factors that inform conflict. At one church, two or three people privately told me that the conflict over inclusive language started when a group of "radical lesbian feminists" wanted to change the God-images. These respondents privately resented that a few radical people could change the liturgy. When I asked them if they had talked about their concern in the open meetings, they were aghast. They told me quite definitely that they could not say that kind of thing in public. More generally, in the conflicts over the role or representation of women and homosexuals, respondents noted that the conflict began with the concerted action of a congregational subgroup, usually a group of professional women or gay men. But all reported that it was illegitimate to say in public, "Oh, it's just a small group making trouble." Even less legitimate to say, "Oh, it's just a group of gays (or radical feminists) making trouble."

Likewise, when an individual or a small group argued that sexism is wrong or homophobia is wrong, congregants might agree or they might not, but they often did not perceive a congregational issue if these assertions could not be tied to broader religious themes. In the case of liberal churches, this necessary connection usually was made through a call to live up to their social justice doctrine. But arguments like "We're gay, and we want equal representation," or "We're women, and we feel excluded by references to a male God" were not legitimate in and of themselves and needed further justification to avoid dismissal as merely political claims.

Local religious conflicts, therefore, are influenced in some degree by the religious repertoire developed by members of the larger religious community in other times and places. The women at the independent Baptist church had a difficult case to make in part because nothing like an inclusive language movement exists among fundamentalist congregations. Evangelical feminists are present, and some of the women in this congregation were familiar with evangelical feminist writings. But women in this congregation chose not to use the arguments of the evangelical feminists in the public discussions in their local church. Instead, they made their argument in secular terms. When questioned about this, one woman responded that they had thought this approach would relate to a common experience (work outside the home) among congregants, whereas most rank-and-file Baptists were not familiar with evangelical feminism. Lacking a common religious rationale for gender equality, they chose a secular one but were unable to make a compelling case for its relevance in this arena. Ironically, the pastor, who wanted to restrict women's participation in leadership roles, referred explicitly and at length to the work of evangelical feminists, portraying this work accurately and fairly, although rejecting its claims.

In these congregations, linking matters of social inclusion to a religious framework makes them relevant to congregational life and makes it possible for members to translate private experience into legitimate claims for public attention and action. Correlating private experiences to political frameworks also enables congregants to claim public attention in many arenas; however, most members of the churches and synagogues in my study view political frames as irrelevant—or even dangerous—to the congregation. Hence in religious traditions whose leaders have not historically connected theology and social justice explicitly, public debate in local congregations almost always favors the status quo politically.

In more liberal congregations with histories of linking political and private concerns in a legitimate religious discourse, congregants have more latitude to raise issues. But, here, too, challenging such linkages on the bases of personal or political discomforts that cannot themselves be cast in religious terms is unacceptable. Congregants in a liberal congregation cannot publicly oppose a claim by a homosexual person just because of the person's homosexuality. On the other hand, members can always claim that the person's actions are creating an uncaring environment that excludes more traditional members and, by so doing, temper the radical political potential of experiential claims by insisting on compromise on all politically divisive issues.

The issues of gender, sexuality, and sexual behavior operate in this manner because these issues generate disagreement within the largely professional, middle-class group that comprises the majority of leaders and members in these congregations. Race and ethnicity are fundamentally different types of issues in the Oak Park community with its progressive reputation and community pride in its racial tolerance. Virtually no publicly legitimate way of talking about racial differences exists here; there are no rules for civil disagreement about racial matters.

In these congregations, no conflicts were understood as being about race, but, in private conversation, race entered into several of the conflicts. One example illustrates themes common to these conflicts. One Catholic congregation clashed over the role of a popular African American sister, who had been encouraged by the priest to take on leadership roles, including leading some liturgies. Some parishioners always found this troubling but said nothing until the arrival of a new pastor, who was far more conservative on women's roles in the church and who instructed the sister to curtail her public speaking and leadership in religious services. This exchange led to a highly charged and very emotional conflict that, at one point, featured a group of members picketing the church in support of the sister and in protest of the new pastor's policies.

This particular parish, a racially mixed group on the eastern edge of Oak Park, had merged several years previously with an all-black congregation on Chicago's West Side that closed down. The former pastor was white, and most of the sister's supporters were white Oak Park liberals. The new pastor is black. Nobody in this congregation mentioned race until I asked if it was an issue. The new pastor was the first to tell me that most of the black parishioners supported his decision. When I returned to talk with some of the white lay leaders, asking explicitly about race, I was informed that some black parishioners saw the protest of the pastor's decision as a racial matter and assumed that a white priest would have received more respect. However, they asserted race did not enter into the public discussion of this issue. Black lay leaders agreed that they heard a lot of private discussion among black parishioners about the issue of race. Many black congregants contended that a white pastor would have been more highly regarded, but, among black lay leaders, opinions varied. Regardless, these private understandings of the role that race played in the conflict received no public airing during this long conflict.

Though parishioners were publicly silent on how race entered and complicated conflicts, they voiced their affirmation of racial differences within congregational life. Two mixed-race congregations, the Catholic one just discussed and an independent Baptist one just up the street, embraced multiculturalism that included encouraging traditional black music forms such as gospel and jazz along with maintaining other musicial and liturgical traditions. Like the community as a whole, these congregations upheld tolerance and diversity as central to their self-images as progressive bodies. Additionally, congregations drew on their religious traditions to support their commitments. In the case of the Baptist church, tolerance and diversity were linked to the Baptist tradition of missionary work. The pastor told me, and several members echoed, that it would be racist to minister to blacks in the context of

African missionary work but not to welcome the blacks who live up the street. They also used the image of New Testament church as racially, ethnically, and economically diverse to justify a multicultural ministry here and now. Drawing on religious symbols and rationales that are not commonly associated with a comprehensive theology of social justice, to say the least, the congregation linked multiculturalism to a religious, not a political, rationale and made it morally acceptable within the congregational arena.

Implications

If some congregations become arenas for open debate about the boundaries of the moral community and the implications of membership, then the question arises: What kind of arenas are provided? What kinds of discussions can take place? With what consequences? First and foremost, these churches provide arenas where these social issues are understood primarily as moral matters, not political ones. That is, they are not about organized groups seeking their special interests in instrumental ways. They are about interpreting the requirements for living a faith in ongoing community.

As such, these congregations, liberal and conservative, Protestant, Catholic, Jewish, are places where certain kinds of moral logics are institutionalized. The first is the logic of compassion or caring, a relational logic that keeps conflict, in most cases, from escalating into "winner take all" contests. This logic emphasizes dialogue and compromise. The second is the logic of religious authority, implementing the guidelines agreed upon in advance as originating from an authoritative text or person.

Overall, these approaches lead to an expressive moral style (cf. Tipton 1982, Becker et al. 1993). These communities engage in the process of interpreting together the implications of deeply held values. The source of these values varies, including personal experience, pastoral sermons, authoritative religious texts, and symbols sufficiently ambiguous so as to need reinterpreting in any given moment. The congregations agree that their church should uphold, interpret, and express moral views on social issues that members care about.

When possible, leaders sought compromise in these conflicts. When the pastor at the independent Baptist church resisted ordaining women or allowing them to preach, he included more women in administrative positions and featured women more prominently in Sunday services. In one conflict over inclusive language, congregants compromised by changing part of the service to inclusive forms, while other parts, such as the doxology and the Lord's Prayer, kept their traditional language.

Even when compromise was not possible, the same rhetoric of balancing value judgments with caring appeared prominently. This approach can lead to what I call "exhaustive process"—exhaustive because it explores all possibilities, but also because it takes a real toll on members' time and energy. The inclusive language conflicts, and the conflicts over becoming open and affirming of lesbians and gay men, all took between one and two years, with open meetings, draft resolutions, and other time-consuming processes geared to generate maximum participation. The opportunity for expression is not only given lip service in these congregations, it is also structured into the decision-making process. The conflict over women's roles at the Baptist church took a similarly long time, although in the end the pastor was more willing to declare a resolution and move the congregation forward.

This view suggests that we should reject the idea that religious conflict is inherently absolutist or escalatory (Simmel 1971, Kurtz 1986). This very common view of the uniqueness of religious conflict conflates a truth seeking or authoritative moral logic with a religious logic more generally. This common fallacy informs Friedland and Alford's (1991) discussion, in which they say that truth seeking is the paradigmatic cultural logic of both science and religion. In its present institutional arrangement, American congregational religion is an institutional arena that simultaneously privileges a moral logic of religious authority and a moral logic of religious community, at least in congregations (cf. Warner 1994).

The culture wars thesis also subscribes to this absolutist and escalatory view of religious conflict, particularly in later versions (Hunter 1994). But this study suggests that this thesis needs to be modified, precisely because it misunderstands local conflict processes and does not recognize the multiplicity of religious moral logics in local congregations. Conflict in these congregations, even over the most divisive issues, has similarities to Ginsburg's (1989) discussion of abortion activists in Fargo, North Dakota. She found that local activists on both sides of the abortion debate were willing to engage in dialogue, refrain from demonizing one another, use a language of compassion as well as judgment, and seek compromise whenever possible. Local conflict over abortion only escalated and became intractable when national activists entered the arena and began to play off of one another for a national media audience.

Findings like Ginsburg's and those presented here lead to an important qualification of the culture wars thesis for the local level of religious, and perhaps political, life. In local arenas, liberals and conservatives certainly do have different moral expectations regarding which issues should make it to the table, but, once there, both groups favor compromise and dialogue, recognizing complex and competing moral imperatives. In order to understand moral conflict at the local level, we need categories of analysis that cut across liberal and conservative.

Conversely, it is possible that Hunter finds liberal/conservative ideology to be so important because of the level of analysis on which he concentrates. The warring tendencies that Hunter identifies may have nothing to do with the nature of the issues involved or a societywide, unbridgeable split between liberals and conservatives. Culture wars may not be inherent in the religious grounding of liberal and conservative world views. Hunter may have found an accelerating cycle of liberal/ conservative conflict because of the particular features of the place that he examined, a national policy arena oriented to the mass media in which religious professionals and ideological experts battle for soundbites on CNN by emphasizing the outrageous and in which activists have no commitment to one another as part of ongoing, face-to-face moral communities. In local communities and community institutions, conflict generally means a complicated balancing of the equally compelling imperatives to do what is right and what is caring.

It is important to note that this expressive moral style that combines justice and caring has its own logic. It minimizes politics, and while that keeps the culture wars out, it also makes it difficult for some congregations to confront their most painful divisions honestly. Race, by far the most salient issue in private conversations with the people I interviewed, cannot be spoken of in any sustained way in most public discussions of congregational life, especially in the context of an ongoing conflict.

More generally, using conflict as a window into the moral order allows an understanding of what may be publicly and legitimately said, into public and shared moral expectations, but not into the private hearts of participants. Yet it is precisely in this construction of expectation, of what may legitimately and publicly be said and done, that culture exerts one of its more important shaping influences on social life (Caplow 1984). Ethnography is a method particularly suited to developing a better map of the cultural cleavages—the systems of shared and divergent moral expectations—that shape the public discourse and practices of local religious life.

NOTES

1. An earlier version of this paper was presented at the 1994 Association for the Sociology of Religion Annual Meeting in Los Angeles. Members of the Culture and Society Workshop at the University of Chicago gave helpful feedback on an early draft of this work, as did Nancy Eiesland. The Louisville Institute for the Study of Protestantism in American Culture provided funding. I thank the members of the churches and synagogues in and around Oak Park, Illinois, who shared their stories with me, an outsider.

2. All personal names are pseudonyms. This is an excerpt of my fieldnotes on my conversation with Rachel and is a combination of paraphase and direct quotation. The directly quoted portion is in quotation marks.

3. He follows the lead of Herberg (1960) and treats Protestant, Catholic, and Jewish traditions in the United States as the three major "churches."

4. See Friedland and Alford (1991) for a discussion of these institutional logics. Scholars of religious groups have noted these differing moral logics before; see Tipton 1982. Elfriede Wedam's chapter in this volume also explores a similar kind of tension between a moral ethic of caring and a moral ethic of justice. Nancy Ammerman (forthcoming) suggests that taken together, this concern with doing what is right, but also caring, is characteristic of what she calls Gold Rule Christianity, an ethic and set of practices that informs both congregational culture and decision making and individual religiosity in American religion. She further shows that this ethic is found among both liberals and conservatives.

5. The literature on boundary work is huge and growing, an interest in this formal process having been recently revived in the sociology of culture by influential work such as Michele Lamont's (1992) study, *Money, Morals, and Manners*. One of the best examples of an analysis of boundary work is Christena Nippert-Eng's (1996) *Home and Work*; this book also contains an up-to-date literature review on the study of boundary creation and maintenance.

6. If "the coherence of social life rests on the convictions we share about its moral meanings," (Tipton 1982:xiv), then conflict provides a good window into the shared or divergent expectations that constitute this coherence—the moral order. I use "moral order" here to indicate both a broad sense of identity and mission and a more specific sense of what the group's boundaries are and what are the requirements of membership (cf. Wuthnow 1987).

7. A longer introduction to the study's methods and overall findings is available elsewhere (Becker, 1995, 1997, forthcoming). This sample includes 19 Protestant congregations from a wide range of denominations, as well as two Catholic churches and two synagogues (one Reform, one Conservative). The

congregations were chosen to span polity types and cultural orientation (liberal/consevative).

8. See Becker (1995, forthcoming) for a discussion of the differences between more privately oriented congregations, which I label "house of worship" and "family," and those more publicly oriented ones, which I call "community" and "leader" congregations.

9. Citing of particular scriptural passages to prove a point or provide a rationale for a specific action.

References

Ammerman, Nancy Tatom. 1994. "Telling Congregational Stories." *Review of Religious Research* 35:289–301.
———. Forthcoming. "Golden Rule Christianity." In *Lived Religion in America*, edited by David Hall. Princeton: Princeton University Press.
Becker, Penny Edgell. 1995. "'How We Do Things Here': Culture and Conflict in Local Congregations." Ph.D. dissertation, Department of Sociology, University of Chicago.
———. 1997. "Congregational Models and Conflict: A Study of How Institutions Shape Organizational Process." Pp. 231–55 in *Sacred Companies: Organized Aspects of Religion and Religious Aspects of Organization*, edited by Jay Demerath, Peter Dobkin Hall, Terry Schmitt, and Rhys H. Williams. New York: Oxford University Press.
———. Forthcoming. *Culture and Conflict: The Moral Order of Local Religious Life* (Working Title). New York: Cambridge University Press.
Becker, Penny Edgell, Stephen J. Ellingson, Richard W. Flory, Wendy Griswold, Fred Kniss, Timothy Nelson. 1993. "Straining at the Tie that Binds: Congregational Conflict in the 1980s." *Review of Religious Research* 34:193–209.
Caplow, Theodore. 1984. "Rule Enforcement without Visible Means: Christmas Gift-Giving in Middletown." *American Journal of Sociology* 89(6):1306–23.
Friedland, Roger and Robert Alford. 1991. "Bringing Society Back In: Symbols, Practices, and Institutional Contradictions." Pp. 232–66 in *The New Institutionalism in Organizational Analysis*, edited by Walter W. Powell and Paul J. DiMaggio. Chicago: University of Chicago Press.
Ginsburg, Faye. 1989. *Contested Lives*. Berkeley and Los Angeles: University of California Press.

Glock, Charles. 1993. "The Churches and Social Change in Twentieth-Century America." *The Annals of the American Academy of Political and Social Science* 527:67–83.

Herberg, Will. 1960. *Protestant-Catholic-Jew*. Garden City, NY: Doubleday Anchor.

Hunter, James Davison. 1991. *Culture Wars*. New York: Basic Books.

———. 1994. *Before the Shooting Begins*. New York: Free Press.

Kurtz, Lester. 1986. *The Politics of Heresy*. Berkeley and Los Angeles: University of California Press.

Lamont, Michele. 1992. *Money, Morals, and Manners*. Chicago: University of Chicago Press.

May, Elaine Tyler. 1980. *Great Expectations*. Chicago: University of Chicago Press.

Nippert-Eng, Christena. 1996. *Home and Work: Negotiating Boundaries through Everyday Life*. Chicago: University of Chicago Press.

Simmel, Georg. 1971. "Conflict." Pp. 70–95 in *On Individuality and Social Forms*, edited by Donald N. Levine. From the "Heritage of Sociology," series, edited by Morris Janowitz. Chicago: University of Chicago Press.

Tipton, Steven M. 1982. *Getting Saved from the Sixties*. Berkeley and Los Angeles: University of California Press.

Warner, R. Stephen. 1994. "The Place of the Congregation in the American Religious Configuration." Pp. 54–99 in *American Congregations*, Vol. 2., edited by James P. Wind and James W. Lewis. Chicago: University of Chicago Press.

Wuthnow, Robert. 1987. *Meaning and Moral Order*. Berkeley and Los Angeles: University of California Press.

Chapter 6

SPLITTING INTERESTS OR COMMON CAUSES

*Styles of Moral Reasoning in
Opposing Abortion* [1]

ELFRIEDE WEDAM

An Encounter with Families for Life

Before you became involved in pro-life you may have thought abortion
was wrong, but I myself didn't realize what it really was. When I was
faced with that reality—oh my gosh, this is what an abortion is at eight
weeks, at four weeks. I see arms and legs here. That was it. I got involved.

Diane,[2] an active volunteer and stay-at-home mother of three, cofounded
Families for Life (FL) in 1976 after being startled by the human features of
an aborted fetus pictured in a library book. She and three other members of
Families for Life explained to me how they had become interested in the
abortion issue while they stapled and stuffed envelopes around a kitchen
table, a site where many women-run projects begin. Sharon, then president,
had responded to my request for a one-on-one interview by urging me instead to meet and talk to other members while they prepared the mailing of
their newsletter. I suspected she was not willing to express her pro-life views
alone to a stranger who might not be trusted to portray them in a favorable
light. Sharon's response was my first exposure to the wariness with which
people in the pro-life movement regarded academics; it was small comfort that I came to know that they held members of the media with even
greater suspicion.

Members of Families for Life live in a cluster of suburbs about an hour southwest of downtown Chicago. These suburbs, like many around Chicago, were carved from farmland about 20 years ago and today consist of primarily bedroom communities with increasing numbers of shopping malls on the main thoroughfares. The group meets in the dining hall of a retirement center located near a major suburban intersection. This meeting place was a deliberately chosen neutral location void of association with a religious group or an individual's home that might imply identification with a particular leader or wing of the anti-abortion movement. While their mailing list contained more than 600 names, approximately 20 were core members. This core group consisted of mostly married couples and a mixture of professional and blue-collar workers. Both Catholic and Protestant families belong to the group. The Catholics attended any of several local parishes, and the Protestants belonged to a variety of local, independent evangelical churches. FL members maintained connections to local congregations, but no one church dominated. The members' ages ranged from mid-20s to late 50s, but the majority was between 30 and 40 years of age. All the married couples had children; family size ranged from one child to six. All the core members were white.

An active mother of three Cub Scouts, Sharon developed her pro-life commitment as part of an emerging consciousness. A neighbor approached her over a cup of tea six or seven years after the 1973 *Roe* v. *Wade* Supreme Court decision legalizing abortion in the United States. She had been "ignorant" about the issue, despite having three children. Her neighbor "slowly and carefully began to educate [her] as to what the issue was."

Claire, a younger mother with one child, spoke about the transformation in her anti-abortion convictions that began at the birth of her child. Prior to childbirth, the abortion issue was not a "big deal." She had felt the decision was up to women's "own judgments about what they wanted to do." Lydia, a lively woman who raised six children after graduating from college, recalled how her public high school classmates all "kept their babies when they got pregnant. I think it was our biology class. I always knew [the fetus] was a baby. I knew what it looked like."

None of the women invoked religious reasoning to justify their moral position. Diane responded to Sharon's story by emphasizing, "I think that's why when a girl's in a situation [of being pregnant] you have to make her understand the humanity of that baby. . . . You couldn't decide abortion was wrong unless you realized that that was a human being in the womb." Diane and the others expressed their commitment to pro-life issues as a learned conviction founded, in part, in their status as mothers but more generally in a humanistic, moral stance.

These core members of Families for Life expressed that opposition to abortion had evolved from their conception of justice. Lydia, who had been the group's long-time president, related her life-long commitment to justice. "I was speaking up for the blacks when nobody else [around me] was." She noted that the pursuit of justice has always required people to put their personal beliefs on the line, even if it meant infringing on someone else's beliefs. Sharon, too, pointed out that the civil rights movement could not have happened without individuals' personal beliefs propelling them into "some kind of action." Lydia recounted an episode in American history often cited by pro-life advocates. "Where would we be if Abraham Lincoln didn't say what he said about slavery?" Through such comments, Lydia and other pro-lifers reconstructed Lincoln as a principled opponent to slavery, whose commitments prompted action. Likewise, these women believe abortion is an act against a human being, and justice demands an intervention on behalf of his or her life.

In my first encounter with Families for Life, these activists articulated secular rather than religious motivations for their moral evaluations of abortion. Initially, I believed this emphasis reflected an effort to mute religious reasoning for the benefit of an academic listener. On closer inspection, however, I discovered an intragroup variation that persisted in several dimensions of members' beliefs and practices. This variability gave me a lens into the layered reasoning that existed within a movement known more for its convergent moral stance.

Finding Peaceful Solutions

I first encountered Peaceful Solutions (PS) at a conference on Chicago's north side. Throughout the conference, speakers connected their pro-life position with a world peace platform and identified anti-abortion advocates who objected to the peace issue as "short-run pro-lifers." Participants discussed the exploration of these social issues by placing them in a larger context of life issues and examining their moral connections.

As a result of attending this conference, I received a call from a Peaceful Solutions member inviting me to a picnic. I attended with my daughter and found about a dozen families and plenty of food. When I introduced myself to several women and stated my research interest, I was quickly directed to two of the officers whom they considered the most articulate. Both officers were fathers in their early 30s; one was the president, the other was the cofounder (together with his wife) of the organization.

The president described the group's interest in opposing both war and abortion and explained the moral imperative against both forms of violence. He clarified that Peaceful Solutions takes a multi-issue view of the abortion debate, espousing a "consistent ethic of life" philosophy that opposes not only abortion but also nuclear war, capital punishment, and euthanasia. This ethic also calls for social and economic justice. The cofounder described how the members of the group, who hold predominantly leftist social positions while maintaining a rightist position in opposition to abortion, felt politically isolated. The PS members found reasoned discussion of abortion practically impossible among most of their friends and relatives who held socially and politically liberal views. At the same time, when the members went to pro-life meetings and conferences, they found their liberal perspectives on capital punishment and social and economic welfare were not welcomed. John, the cofounder, described their views as "politically miscegenated," and the members felt themselves socially marginalized.

The Peaceful Solutions meetings rotated among the homes of the core members of about six to seven couples, most in their 30s, not all with children, who lived in an urban neighborhood on the far north side of Chicago. The Catholics in the group attended the same parish. Two of the active Protestant couples were members of an independent evangelical church, and two of the other couples divided their time between the Catholic church and a Mennonite community. Members displayed a range of religious attachments as evidenced by a few members, for example, who expressed ambivalence about their faith commitments in general. But such ambivalence tended to be the minority view and created some tension when members discussed Peaceful Solutions' place in the religious landscape. Members openly wondered about their connection with religious bodies. When archbishop of Chicago, Joseph Cardinal Bernardin, publicly articulated the consistent ethic of life in a series of speeches (U.S. Catholic Conference 1983; Bernardin 1987), Catholic and Protestant members of the group felt an easing of their sense of marginality within the American church. Having to fight the Catholic right and both the secular and religious left had pushed PS members inward. But having institutional support from the cardinal's own words helped them "come out of the closet," as they sometimes expressed it. Despite this boost, the tensions within the group over peace and pro-life agendas were never fully resolved.

Variation within the Pro-life Movement

In contrast to researchers who emphasize the consistency in the pro-life world view (Luker 1984; Ginsburg 1989), my study of Families for Life and Peaceful Solutions revealed considerable variability—both between the groups and within each organization.[3] These differences resulted in two distinct moral cultures. The moral discourse of these groups and their practices underscored a multiplicity of ideological, political, and religious views in their construction of the abortion debate. Three sets of social and cultural dimensions differentiated the moral cultures of these two organizations: first, styles of moral reasoning with different legal implications; second, ideological critiques of American society and culture including an analysis of gender roles and sexuality; and third, organizational structures that have implications for the strengths and weaknesses of moral reform movements. In this chapter, I confine myself to a discussion of the different styles of moral reasoning these two pro-life organizations invoked through the selected, but representational, voices of its members.

Carol Gilligan (1977, 1982) suggests two orientations to the construction of a moral problem. While maintaining an empirically open stance about whether contrasting styles of moral reasoning can be substantially identified with gender differences, Gilligan compares women and men's different approaches to the resolution of an abortion dilemma. She concludes that women construct the moral problem in terms of an ethic of care while men espouse an ethic of justice. Women tend to use a psychological logic of responsibility and relationships to solve a moral problem, while men tend to use a formal logic of equality and reciprocity. The ethic of care is set within a "contextual particularity," a real and specific situation that allows women to visualize consequences (1982:100). This ethic of care leads women to solve moral problems so that no one is hurt. A male orientation to moral reasoning focuses on respect for the rights of others and on protection from interference of an individual's rights to life and self-fulfillment. According to Gilligan, the ethic of justice is based on a hierarchical ordering of choices rooted in universal and abstract principles of rights and autonomy. Using this ethic, people adjudicate moral problems by seeking what is fair among competing rights. But the ethic of care requires that a person seek to avoid harm to all parties in an effort to resolve competing responsibilities.

In examining the two anti-abortion groups, the care versus justice orientation did not appear to be distributed by gender in regard to their moral reasoning styles. That is, both the women and men of Peaceful Solutions employed an ethic of care to explain their opposition to abortion, while the mostly female membership of Families for Life opposed abortion based on an ethic of justice. The single-issue pro-life organization emphasized an absolutist orientation regarding the nature of abortion, and the application of their belief was absolutist in style. The consistent ethic organization is also absolutist regarding the moral nature of abortion, but the ethic of care revealed how contextualist reasoning was applied to people's specific situations. Attention to both care and justice emerged from the words of many of the participants with whom I spoke. Compassion and concern for dialogue among all parties characterized the consistent ethic group, Peaceful Solutions, while Families for Life, the single-issue group, emphasized commitment to principle and conforming behavior.

The Moral Nature of Abortion: A Shared Belief with Different Applications

Both groups believed that abortion is a moral matter and that, in principle, abortion is always wrong. Although some Peaceful Solutions members admitted an uncertainty about the exact beginning of human life, they argued that due to the gravity of the issue—a matter of life and death—the benefit of the doubt must be given to the fetus. Families for Life and PS shared an absolute principle regarding the immorality of abortion, despite variations in their styles of expression.

Peaceful Solutions member Jody, who at the time of the interview was a homemaker with three sons in elementary school, stated, "Life is a mystery and [since] we can't create it, then I don't think we should end it either." Another PS member, Elizabeth, a registered nurse who worked part-time to accommodate her three young children's schedules, claimed that the irrevocability of an abortion raises questions that cannot be satisfactorily answered on the level of human feelings and needs. Elizabeth judged human beings as simply too fallible; she could not trust fully the choices humans make.

While initially secular justifications predominated in my conversations among Families for Life members, I later learned that some members base their opposition on religious beliefs. For example, Doris, in her early 60s and whose careers ranged from technical work in an engineering firm to exotic dance, invoked the biblical prohibition, "Thou shalt not kill" and asserted, "killing a baby is wrong." Another member, Constance, a former teacher, single, and now a full-time pro-life activist, cited the frequently used Jeremiah 1:4 passage as the basis of her religious justification: "Before I formed you in the womb I knew you, and before you were born I consecrated you."

Constance invoked traditional Catholic theology when she explained that conception is not simply a naturally occurring phenomenon but rather an expression of the will of God. As a speaker at a FL meeting member put it, "The Bible says children are a gift from God. If those children are a gift from the Lord, you don't throw it back in God's face— 'I don't want this!'" But Constance also invoked an incarnational theology in which humans participated in divine creation: "When you don't hold life to be sacred but just hold it to be human, then you've lost the divine beginnings of all of our lives."

Families for Life and Peaceful Solutions members also shared the conviction that abortion represents insensitivity to life. PS member, Katherine, a young married woman who worked full-time as an editor until her children were born, remarked, "I don't think we've ever had an incredibly healthy attitude towards human life. The way we've treated black people in this country, the way they [were] treated in South Africa. The way we treat anybody who doesn't look or talk or act the way we do." She also pointed to the vulnerability of "the elderly and children who are born retarded or handicapped. I just hate to think the value of a life is how productive it is or how much it fits the norm. That scares me. . . . I think of Hitler and his perfect race."

Emma, who worked full-time as a dental assistant before her children were born, and her husband, who operated a Christian bookstore, were members of Peaceful Solutions. Emma contended that while "abortion is evil," it is only one among many evils that exist in the world today, including oppression, torture, and genocide. She believed these evils are created by "a very casual attitude toward the sacredness of life."[4]

Despite the use of religious rationale by both groups, a countervailing tendency exists in both. Families for Life members often framed their opposition in humanistic terms. To avoid being dismissed as sectarian, some Catholic members of FL hesitated to identify their beliefs with those of the Catholic teaching. FL member Sharon stated, "I don't think it has anything to do with my religious beliefs, it was my biological beliefs." Peaceful Solutions members also questioned the biological logic of distinguishing middle- and late-term abortions from first trimester ones in justifying their opposition to abortion on grounds other than religious reasoning. Toni, a full-time mother of three from Peaceful Solutions, suggested, "To me there isn't any kind of logical cut off— [that] it's life after this but it's not life before this. There is no logically consistent way that you could do that."

Divergence between the two groups appeared in their distinctions between "innocent" life and the consistent ethic principle that claims culpability makes no difference. As in the pro-life movement generally, much of the rhetoric of Families for Life focused on the innocence of the fetus and the deliberate harm women do to protect their own interests. They discussed the "innocent victim," these "littlest ones." FL members see the aborting mother and those aiding her as enemies of those "least able to defend themselves." If defenseless human beings are threatened, then those who are threatening them must be stopped. Implied in the argument is the belief that if a creature is defenseless, it must be innocent. Furthermore, if persons are doing harm to an innocent, they are not deserving of our sympathy.

Families for Life member, Doris, who had hosted several pregnant teenagers in her home, explained that abortion differs from a deadly assault because the latter incidence lacks the element of innocence. If you have a fight with someone, Doris observed, and "you kill in heat" while it is wrong, it "doesn't cut you to the quick." In the case of an unborn child, where there is such an innocence, she asked, "What is the reasoning? An innocent child who can't fight back. What kind of humanity is that? What kind of compassion is that?" Here, the emotionally demonstrative comes to be intellectually persuasive. Constance described an unborn child in an abortion. "You're talking about innocent, defenseless human lives that cannot speak for themselves, cannot do anything on their own, and need to be protected."

In contrast, Judith explained the universalistic stance toward life in the consistent ethic of Peaceful Solutions:

> It's a philosophy or moral attitude that starts from the point that all life is sacred and that we can't—we as human beings—can't distinguish or start selecting parts of life or types of life that should not be held sacred. . . . Human life is a gift and no body of people or no single person ever has the right to take that away from any other human being. . . . Either because

they're only a zygote, because their I.Q. is less than 50, because they've murdered 45 people, or because they support a foreign government that is our declared enemy.

When Lori, a homemaker with four children and FL president for one term, explained her disagreement with the consistent ethic of life, she expressed her view that only abortion, and, by extension, euthanasia, represented a threat to innocent life. Criminals, for example, made conscious choices that removed them from the sanctity of life protection. Warring governments are also not innocent and therefore not deserving of our protection.

Common belief that abortion is always wrong based on the sacred nature of life diverges, in the case of Families for Life and Peaceful Solutions, when group members discussed the moral status of the unborn. On the one hand, most members of Families for Life distinguished between innocence and culpability in their reasoning about abortion, capital punishment, war, and euthanasia. Peaceful Solutions, on the other hand, emphasized the sacredness of all life and, therefore, the immorality of all deliberate actions to end it. These different views affected directly the application of the life principle to individuals' moral decision making.

Applications of Two Principles: Splitting Interests or Common Causes

The groups differed in their approaches to adjudicating the conflicting interests between mothers and their fetuses. The members of Families for Life identified their cause as saving babies' lives. Concern for the life of the fetus was placed above concern for the mother's situation, except when pregnacy threatens the mother's life. Nevertheless, while their concern for the woman is diminished, it is not absent. Diane took pains to point this out:

> I know a lot of people think, those pro-lifers, those crazy maniacs, they don't care what happens to these women. What do they know about what happens? I don't want to sound like that, I really do care. I think a lot of us really do care about what happens. We know it's traumatic. Pregnancies aren't always convenient. And, um, I'd really like to get these girls into counseling, somehow . . . make sure that that decision they make is what they're not going to be sorry for later.

Other members of Families for Life stated their priority more vigorously, clearly ranking the interests of the fetus above the mother. "The importance for the unborn child has to be the interest, because that's where the exact definite killing is going on everyday in this country. You cannot ignore that, you cannot diffuse the emphasis," stated Constance.

While Peaceful Solutions held that the fetus has moral standing, their beliefs about life and morality included a wider range of concern. Thus, they found it impossible to speak about the life of the mother or the life of the potential child separately or independently from one another. The PS members refused to split the interests of the mother from the interests of the fetus. They sought a resolution that would not privilege either one. I call this style of moral reasoning "contextualist." The contextualist approach considers the consequences of a decision on the lives of both individuals. In addition, this reasoning recognizes that the harm done to both lives merits moral sympathy and requires acts of compassion. Jody said, "I think of myself as being pro-choice for life. The difficult choices [are] when it comes to unwanted pregnancy—that the life of the mother and the life of the child are both considerations."

Jody repeated her moral position on abortion without implying that rightness or wrongness of action follow inevitably from the posing of the position. In other words, more than one correct choice may exist. "But I really believe that a fetus is a baby and that, when a woman has a baby growing within her, that is a real life that is taking place. And that abortion is always taking that life," Jody stated. "Now I'm not making a judgment whether that is justified or not."

Peaceful Solutions member Judith tried to make a moral claim by drawing an analogy between the moral independence of the fetus and the moral independence of women. Judith, one of several PS members who identified themselves as feminists, argued that fetuses, like women, should not be dependent on the control or decision of others, including their mother-hosts for their lives or right to life. She tried to show the inconsistency in the feminist claim that women do not need men to establish their legitimacy, identity, or right to exist when that same claim is applied to fetuses:

> [I]f we say that a fetus' life can be judged to be valuable simply on the . . .
> individual decision of the mother, then we're undercutting the argument that
> a woman shouldn't be just considered valuable if her husband or her father

grants [it]. . . . You can't have it both ways, either you have that principle or you don't.

Katherine, also from PS, offered a justification based loosely on a civil rights principle of equality and noninterference. "[P]eople don't have that sort of authority over each other. . . . I just don't feel like we have that sort of right, who should live and who shouldn't live."

Another contextual factor that PS members took into account is how an absolute prohibition against abortion may, if strictly applied, create hardships that cannot be ignored. Pete, the president, enunciated some of them:

> I am sympathetic to those women who do have an abortion, because I can understand the pressure that they are under, and I can understand that pressure [to abort] is seemingly greater pressure than they might experience if they did carry [the child] to term. [If they] ended up being a single mom, perhaps, and facing all kinds of discrimination, in a workplace, housing, within their own families, within their churches, and so forth. At that moment of crisis, . . . deciding whether or not to abort, it would seem very painful but perhaps less difficult to have an abortion, faced with all the obstacles [to] continuing the pregnancy.

Pete's statement illustrates how real human needs are central to the abortion dilemma. The choice between the fetus' life and the mother's needs can be a choice between two evils. Jody admitted, "I think in general that abortion is really a moral wrong, but I think, sometimes, a person is in a situation where all of the choices are deadly choices."

Because Peaceful Solutions framed the issue such that the interests of the woman are joined to the interests of the fetus, they worked to obtain a "win-win" outcome for unplanned pregnancies. Ideally, a woman would freely choose to forego an abortion and receive all the support and resources her choice required. PS member Claudia declared it would take a revolution in the structure of society to allow such a win-win solution. "I think that it would be a situation where people really have the possibility of fulfilling themselves to the maximum without having to fit into the patriarchal structures."

Claudia, born in Cuba, spent her high school years developing her radical Catholicism and worked for Cesar Chavez's Farm Workers' Union and several VISTA projects. She argues that while *Roe* v. *Wade* uses the right to privacy to protect the right of women to choose abortion, it secretly perpetuates men's interests by barring women from engaging in the full range of complications that childbearing and childrearing requires. If abortion frees women to work, according to the feminist argument, it also prevents women from choosing motherhood on their own terms. Affecting the structures of society has always been a goal of PS, but the group clearly understood it was a long-term effort. PS members realize they must supply practical, short-term answers or they will be dismissed as idealists. As Toni said, "It's true that it is no easy answer to just say to [women] 'Don't have an abortion, you have a life living within now.' What do you do with the woman who's unmarried? What do you do with the woman who already has more children than [she and her husband] want? There are not easy answers."

In the short term, PS expressed an unwillingness to outlaw abortion, thereby identifying with the feminist rights claim, while opening lines of dialogue with both the left and the right. Because PS applied contextualist reasoning, they were unwilling to draw moral boundaries distinguishing women from their fetuses. Families for Life sought the moral clarity of a hierarchical ranking among evils. An ethic of justice demarcates moral boundaries in which women's interests are separated from those of their fetuses, and, applying absolutist reasoning, the life of the fetus will always take precedence.

Ethical Practices: Certainties versus Ambiguities

The members of Families for Life and Peaceful Solutions saw abortion as evidence that people were careless about their lives and their sexuality. Both groups recognized abortions have existed and will continue to occur, regardless of the law. Keeping abortion legal permits the morally "easy way out," in which people will never have to face the consequences of their actions. As Constance said, "She should carry [the pregnancy] to term. You don't take the product of your love and destroy it because you're not talking about a blob of tissue."

Both Peaceful Solutions and Families for Life members believed a moral ideal should not be changed simply because people had difficulty conforming to it. However, the two groups differed in enacting these ideals. Families for Life members believed the legal and cultural warrants should conform directly to their moral ideals. In contrast, Peaceful Solutions permitted a heterodoxy or pluralism of approaches to the legal and cultural warrants of society regarding the moral ideal. As a nurse, Elizabeth has been consulted regarding abortion choices: "I think my basic approach is for a person to look at what they're doing and knowing what they're doing and then making a decision." She asserted, "I can't force my beliefs on somebody else. I can try to counsel somebody, I could try to give them what I consider an accurate picture of their choices and then have them make the choice."

PS member Claudia, a pediatrician with the Chicago Board of Health, was similarly sought out by clinic patients. "I have to be very clear before I give any kind of advice what sort of advice they're asking for. Because I would feel bad if I just instilled guilt on someone who had kind of already made up their mind or who had already done it." When she felt they were "genuinely struggling with making a decision" and asking her advice, she participated. "And I feel that people need to make informed decisions, but they also need to have that in a real supportive environment." She added, "Not like—'Here, this is what [the fetus] looks like'—I don't think that's a supportive environment. That's a very unsupportive environment."

The members of Peaceful Solutions are sympathic to women who have been forced into decisions about which they were ambivalent because they felt no other options were available. To counteract this situation, suggested John, we "create a lot of alternatives. Let's provide a situation where women are not going to feel so hopeless that they're forced into an abortion." Besides aiding organizations like Bridgings, a support group for older pregnant women, he and Jody also hosted several pregnant, unwed teens in their home in recent years and supported them emotionally and financially, in some cases, after the birth of their babies. Members of Families for Life participated in similar support services although, in contrast to PS, their rhetoric emphasized "ways to save babies' lives."

To correct one wrong—the current narrowing alternatives to abortion—Peaceful Solutions worked hard to avoid another. If changes in the law made abortion illegal again so that a pregnant woman's only choice was to carry her child to term, society would have only shifted sides of the same coin. Both legal resolutions impose unacceptable consequences according to PS. Some members of PS were feminists committed to women's freedom. They asserted true freedom comes only from having choices; it cannot come from being forced to make a choice, however morally upstanding.

In the end, Families for Life argued for a legal injunction as the prominent solution; Peaceful Solutions members were agnostic regarding the law, struggling with the meaning of tolerance and often trailing off with the admission ". . . there is no *the* answer."

Strategies for Change: The Legislative Option

Families for Life members believed reducing the incidence of abortion must begin with a change in the law, either a constitutional amendment prohibiting abortion or the reversal of *Roe* v. *Wade*. Peaceful Solutions members believed that while legislation would prevent some abortions, many would continue. Furthermore, PS recognized that strictures against abortion would create hardship and possibly result in a societal backlash with long-term consequences.

The effect on individual lives was a secondary concern among Families for Life members. Their moral ideals need to be institutionalized to promote social change. Constance asserted that "[f]or some [people] it will be very difficult, but . . . if a free nation is going to speak a message to the rest of the world, we have to reverse [*Roe* v. *Wade* Supreme Court decision]. How things affect our own personal life is not the question. The question is what will the nation be speaking to the world."

Many people who oppose abortion compared slavery in this country to the development of the abortion debate. Just as the black slave was once considered a nonperson without a right to life, so the fetus is given the same status by *Roe* v. *Wade*. As FL member, Doris reminded me, "We had a right to kill a slave at one time. That was no punishable offense. 'Hey, that's my slave, if I want to kill him, I'll kill him.' Today, the woman says, 'Hey, it's my body, if I want to kill that baby, I'll kill it.' Same difference." Why did the laws about slavery change, she asked rhetorically. "Simply because they found out they were wrong. . . . The court ruled wrong at one point [slavery]. The court ruled wrong at another point [abortion]. So there simply has to be a correction."[6]

The members of Families for Life did not accept public opinion as a legitimate reflection of the American moral ethos. Judie Brown, president of the American Life Lobby, one of the organizations with which Families for Life identified closely, told me that the correct moral stance on important issues does not emerge from opinion polls. "You have to take an NBC–*Time* Magazine poll to find out what's right and wrong, and that's determined by what people tell you they want. [Polls] have nothing to do with right and wrong."

In contrast, the pragmatism of Peaceful Solutions respected the need for social consensus; negative consequences had to be considered. "Because people vote anti-abortion legislation does not mean that abortion stops. It just doesn't mean that, and it could have the opposite effect," claimed John.

Not surprisingly, the members of both organizations agreed that legalizing an action leads toward its general acceptance, regardless of the moral ambiguity involved. FL member Lori asked, "What makes people not steal if there's not a moral and a legal [prohibition] against it? How many people won't steal just on morals alone?"

While the evaluation of legislative strategies by Peaceful Solutions differed dramatically from that of Families for Life, the concern for the relationship of morality and legality is nonetheless similar. Pete noted that in most people's thinking legality and morality are conflated. "Most people think, 'Well . . . so it is written, so it is true. If it's the law, it must be right. . . .' It then lends some validity to one's own action." However, even though Pete credited the law with carrying some "vague kind of moral authority," he was less persuaded by the meaningfulness of law than were members of Families for Life. "'If it's the law, it must be right,'" Pete noted. "I personally don't believe that, because there have been a lot of unjust laws written."

PS member John explained that although he favors legal restrictions on abortion in the abstract, he opposes them in fact, because they would have the opposite effect of what is intended. "Pro-life people, like a lot of liberals, ironically think that because they introduce a legislative solution, it is going to have the effect they intend. A lot of interventions in society don't have the intended effect, and I don't think this one would at this point in time." In linking principle and application, John's reasoning was pragmatic. The value of an action lies in its success. If a moral position does not reflect beliefs and sentiments of a society, then the position had to be reconsidered. John reasoned that anywhere but in a totalitarian society, determined women would obtain abortions. "There are all kinds of things that are illegal but continue to happen." Unless public opinion changed, John felt abortions would continue. He determined that affecting public opinion was an appropriate way for him to engage the issue. "In terms of stopping abortion, my efforts ought to be in trying to convince people not to want to abort, not to prevent them once they've decided to abort."

At the same time, John found it "disingenuous" of liberals to oppose anti-abortion legislation on the grounds that it is a moral issue and, thus, not the perview of politicians. He contended that almost all remedies for social ills in this country precipitated some legislative action. John referred to the 1960s civil rights legislation to illustrate his view:

We [liberals] did not hesitate to prescribe school integration because it would have negatively affected the rights of whites who didn't want to go to school with blacks. We didn't buy the whole states' rights thing. . . . Our formula for righting wrongs has always, or generally certainly, has included a dimension that was political, that involved a change in legislation. . . . I mean why would you legislate anything at all if it wasn't morally objectionable? I mean obviously there are some things that should be and some things that shouldn't, but just as a catch phrase, it's sort of silly.

Nevertheless, John conceded that legislation against abortion "at this time would be inappropriate and futile: inappropriate because there is no societal consensus and futile because abortion in cases of extreme need would be denied, thereby creating a societal backlash against any form of legal protection for the unborn."

Other members of Peaceful Solutions voiced different views on the role of law. Judith declared her support for a constitutional amendment (the Human Life Amendment, which subsequently failed) to ban abortions, while at the same time recognized that, in light of current judicial interpretations, such an amendment would likely be judged unconstitutional. In addition, she supported the Equal Rights Amendment. To her, these proposed amendments symbolized "that we are a just society, that we want all of our citizens protected and more than protected, to live out their fullest potential." On the other hand, Judith expressed some ambivalence about her legal position. She wondered if she could accept a law that would ban abortions in the second and third trimesters only. "In order to save some lives, do we still allow some abortions to take place? . . . I don't know where I stand on that."

Jody also expressed ambivalence on the legal question. Although she thinks it is wrong for the law to condone abortion, she does not condemn a person for seeking one. "You know that I feel abortion is wrong. I think that it's wrong that it's legally sanctioned. I don't necessarily think it's wrong if an individual seeks an abortion. . . ." Likewise, Claudia conceded some situations are so desperate that abortion is probably the only solution. Katherine focused on the second victim of abortion, the woman herself. "Legal or illegal [abortion] is going to happen. What matters is the effect it's going to have on those that are involved." Peaceful Solutions' goal is to create a climate in which people find it "unconscionable" to choose abortion, Jody asserted. Such change requires other changes as well. "I only see that day coming when there are other really viable alternatives for women. [That is,] when a woman choosing to keep her baby and being a single parent is not ostracized, not economically just doomed, and those sorts of things."

PS member Emma objected to people who think their duty rests in what laws stipulate. "I wish that our society was more mature than it is in terms of taking laws so seriously as to let the law tell us how we should live." For Emma, "real life is beyond laws." Jody elaborated, "I wish that [abortion] could be neither right nor wrong in the eyes of the law, but I don't think that's going to be possible."

Families for Life and Peaceful Solutions basically disagree over the appropriate means to enact social change: PS favored persuasion, while FL preferred legal restraint. Multidimensional reasoning led PS members to adopt the conviction that "changing hearts and minds," while impractical in the short term, was morally compelling. FL expressed a unidimensional reasoning in which the overriding integrity of the moral principle led directly to the establishment of legal prohibitions against abortion.

Strategies for Change: The Call for Dialogue

Pete suggested that the purpose of the dialogue Peaceful Solutions encourages is to "help people along in their thinking, to free them up from entrapped positions or from political positions, to help them rethink things." The group deliberately chose dialogue, in contrast to the political activism supported by Families for Life members. Pete recalled, "When we were first trying to piece together what our vision was, we didn't have coercion in mind, or pinning people down, because then you get into a litmus test, and you're immediately in opposition to someone or to someone's position." Toni, a PS member, illustrated, "If you're going to take the feminists on, you have to show how far you can agree with them."

To demonstrate their approach, Peaceful Solutions devoted the second of two major conferences to Moving toward Dialogue: Understanding Different Viewpoints on Abortion and Nuclear Defense. The workshops offered techniques of conflict management and how to promote dialogue among people holding different views on abortion and nuclear arms. The keynote speaker was psychologist Sidney Callahan, coauthor with her husband, ethicist Daniel Callahan, of the book *Abortion: Understanding Differences* (1984). The Callahans hold opposing views on the abortion issue yet were able to bring both pro-life and pro-choice supporters into a forum in which they explored their common ground as well as their differences.

In the two years following this conference, many PS members lamented the group's inability to attract new members. Because of its unique combination of principles, Peaceful Solutions had difficulty building membership. Nevertheless, many members found their efforts "personally transforming." Many appreciated finding people with whom they could share politically and socially marginal views. But John concluded with some disappointment: "I had some illusions that we could really have some major impact. I don't think we really did. I think we touched a few people. But what is coming to me is that maybe that's how real change takes place—that you touch a couple of people and they touch a couple of people."

Families for Life objected to conjoining issues under the consistent ethic approach and drew on recent history for support. Constance pointed out that no people have been killed in a nuclear explosion since World War II, but there are "innocent, defenseless human lives" being killed every day in abortion. Lori, an amateur historian, related that "the [cardinal's] criteria [are] to sit there and try to talk things out, try and work things out. As Hitler was, you couldn't talk to him. You couldn't reason with him, and he was ready and willing and possibly able to take over the world, you know. . . ."

While PS raised pragmatic objections to the effectiveness of legal constraints on abortion, FL advanced pragmatic objections to the political effectiveness of the ideology of the Catholic bishops' consistent ethic platform. "[The bishops] want the whole ball of wax. That's going to take who knows how long. In the meantime, millions of babies are being slaughtered," argued Joseph, Claire's husband. FL members expressed two kinds of objections to the consistent ethic: substantive or doctrinal (the bishops are wrong on just war) and pragmatic (abortion is a more urgent crisis; the consistent ethic won't work). All of these objections can be traced through historical theological debates within Catholicism.

In 1988, the organizers of Peaceful Solutions disbanded the group because they were unable to sustain their membership. They judged their failure on pragmatic grounds—the political climate could not support moral reasoning based on principles of nonviolence and care, because the particular outcomes of these principles were too ambiguous to predict. Families for Life continues; their principles of justice and fairness have provided sustainable moral clarity.

Conclusion

Both Families for Life and Peaceful Solutions viewed abortion as a moral wrong, but FL members applied an ethic of justice to the abortion issue—adjudication based on the principle of the right to life. PS applied an ethic of care in which the principle of nonviolence determined adjudication.

These distinct styles of moral reasoning can be related to the debates within philosophical ethics and moral development theory. Flanagan and Adler (1983) contrast Kohlberg's theory of right with Gilligan's theory of good using John Rawls' terms: "The theory of right is that part of moral theory which deals with the basic structure of society, with the ground rules for adjudicating conflicting claims about rights and property" (1983:588). The theory of good involves considerations about the quality of relationships, the obligations of friendship, the requirements of being a responsible parent or citizen, and how to improve the quality of one's own as well as others' lives. Kohlberg's ethic of justice is hierarchical, procedural, and abstract, that is, lacking specific content. The resolution of competing rights is adjudicated by formal rules. Gilligan's ethic of care is embedded in responsibility to relationships, is content specific and not generalizable. Her ethic seeks to avoid harm in making moral choices and understands rights within the context of humans living out their lives. Rawls claims that neither theory follows from the other but, rather, that both are essential. Flanagan and Adler point out that Gilligan's and Kohlberg's theories require a synthesis in which truth and goodness are, finally, not conflicting claims, but interdependent ones.

In Tolstoy's two questions cited by Weber (1946), the issues are: "What shall we do?" which is a question about justice. "How shall we live?" is a question about the nature of the good. Sociologists have attempted to answer questions about how to seek justice, equity, or fairness in studies on race and ethnic relations, stratification and social class, work and economic structures, deviance and social control. Sociology can pursue less easily investigations into issues of the good, or how to determine whether something is better or worse. Yet studies that investigate socially appropriate behavior versus deviant behavior and the justifications that support them begin to ask questions about better and worse. In one example, sociologist Samuel Oliner and his wife, educator Pearl Oliner, investigated the nature of altruistic behavior. They asked the question, "Why did some ordinary people risk their lives to rescue Jews from Nazi-occupied Europe during World War II while others who had an equal opportunity refuse to do so?" The researchers found a major part of the answer in the rescuers' personal conceptions of moral behavior that had been nurtured by family, community, and religion. I cite this example only to highlight its relevance to moral analysis and not to draw comparisons between the Holocaust and abortion.

The narratives of Peaceful Solutions and Families for Life construct communities of moral discourse in which the participants engaged their various past histories yet came together to seek a different way forward. Robert Wuthnow suggests the need for a sociology of culture to "find underlying rules of dialogue and expression that will help us address the major challenges facing our society and our world" (1992:7). Groups like Peaceful Solution and Families for Life struggle with the values and beliefs that constitute one of the important public issues today. This struggle is often poorly understood by academics and the public. Indeed, my initial discovery about these two groups was that moral movement organizations are neither inherently monolithic nor preordained to hold polarized positions. This account provides little support for a culture wars thesis; it also suggests that both liberal and conservative groups have more nuanced views than generally recognized. Peaceful Solutions is one such group that suggests an opening for discussion among activists on all sides and between activists and sociological practitioners; Families for Life suggests a critique of the contemporary moral codes that are taken for granted in wider American culture.

NOTES

1. I am very grateful to the following people whose helpful suggestions substantially improved this work: Robert E. Lammers, David Rubenstein, Rhys H. Williams. I am especially grateful to Issac D. Balbus, Lois Gehr Livezey, and Lowell W. Livezey whose discussions on moral reasoning helped me clarify my position. Many thanks to the editors of this volume for their insightful directions. Most of all, thanks to the members of the organizations I studied for their willingness to talk to me and teach me.

2. All personal names are pseudonyms. The names of the organizations have been slightly altered.

3. This account is based on dissertation research (Wedam 1993) I conducted between 1984 and 1990. I collected four types of data: extensive fieldnotes on meetings and other types of group activities such as conferences, prayer breakfasts, social gatherings, marches, and pickets; tape-recorded and transcribed

in-depth interviews with informants; archival materials produced by the organizations themselves and by organizations within their networks; and, a self-reflexive account of the research process. I became a dues-paying member of both organizations and participated in many activities. Nevertheless, I remained something of an outsider, occupying a not always comfortable status between being an official member yet not really belonging.

4. Many feminist writers share these concerns, although they express their ideas in secular terms. Gordon writes, "The abortion opponents . . . are afraid of a loss of mothering, in the symbolic sense. They fear a completely individualized society with all services based on cash nexus relationships, without the influence of nurturing women counteracting the completely egoistic principles of the economy, and without any forms in which children can learn about lasting human commitments to other people . . . their fear of unchecked individualism is not without substance" (Gordon 1982:151).

5. Some Peaceful Solutions members acknowledge the resemblance between their thinking and the positions of Catholics for a Free Choice. This ethic argues that morality must be determined by the context in which an act occurs, particularly, the human relationships among the participants. In this sense, morality is emergent. Moral status is determined as the participants work through their understandings of the situation with particular reference to certain virtues, principally compassion, nonviolence, justice, human dignity, and love. These last criteria thus function as emergent boundaries through which the starting point principles must be routed. Nevertheless, the members disagreed with this position when it is left completely open ended.

6. Doris was likely referring to the U.S. Supreme Court's 1857 decision in the case of *Dred Scott* v. *Sandford*, a ruling that upheld the instititution of slavery. After the American Civil War, slavery was made illegal in the United States and its jurisdictions by the ratification of the 13th Amendment to the U.S. Constitution.

References

Bernardin, Joseph Cardinal. 1987. "A Consistent Ethic of Life: An American-Catholic Dialogue," Gannon Lecture, Fordham University, December 6, 1983, collected in *Consistent Ethic of Life Symposium Papers*.

Callahan, Sidney and Daniel Callahan, eds. 1984. *Abortion: Understanding Differences*. New York and London: Plenum Press.

Flanagan, Jr., Owen J. and Jonathan E. Adler. 1983. "Impartiality and Particularity." *Social Research* 50:576–95.

Gilligan, Carol. 1977. "In a Different Voice: Women's Conception of the Self and of Morality." *Harvard Educational Review* 47:481–517.

———. 1982. *In a Different Voice: Psychological Theory and Women's Development*. Cambridge: Harvard University Press.

Ginsburg, Faye D. 1989. *Contested Lives: The Abortion Debate in an American Community*. Berkeley and Los Angeles: University of California Press.

Gordon, Linda. 1982. "Why Nineteenth-Century Feminists Did Not Support 'Birth Control' and Twentieth-Century Feminists Do: Feminism, Reproduction, and the Family." Pp.140–54 in *Rethinking the Family: Some Feminist Questions*, edited by Barrie Thorne and Marilyn Yalom. New York and London: Longman.

Luker, Kristen. 1984. *Abortion and the Politics of Motherhood*. Berkeley and Los Angeles: University of California Press.

Noddings, Nel. 1984. *Caring: A Feminine Approach to Ethics and Moral Education*. Berkeley and Los Angeles: University of California Press.

Oliner, Samuel P. and Pearl M. Oliner. 1988. *The Altruistic Personality: Rescuers of Jews in Nazi Europe*. New York: The Free Press.

United States Catholic Conference of Bishops. 1983. "The Challenge of Peace: God's Promise and Our Response." Compiled and edited by Catherine M. Pilley. Haverford, PA: Catholic Library Association.

Weber, Max. 1946. "Science as a Vocation." Pp. 129–56 in *From Max Weber: Essays in Sociology*. Translated, edited, and with an introduction by H. H. Gerth and C. Wright Mills. New York: Oxford University Press.

Wedam, Elfriede. 1993. "Moral Cultures and the Movement Against Abortion." Ph. D. Dissertation, Department of Sociology, University of Illinois at Chicago.

Wuthnow, Robert. 1992. "Introduction: New Directions in the Empirical Study of Cultural Codes." Pp. 1–16 in *Vocabularies of Public Life: Empirical Essays in Symbolic Structure*, edited by Robert Wuthnow. London and New York: Routledge.

Chapter 7

THE CHURCH AND THE STREET

Race, Class, and Congregation

TIMOTHY J. NELSON

Charleston, South Carolina, is a historic city of graceful buildings and charming, quiet streets. Horse-drawn carriages filled with tourists plod slowly past the city's famous "single houses" with their grand piazzas and well-tended gardens. Many of these homes were built before the Revolutionary War and have been carefully maintained inside Charleston's historic district—the first architectural preservation district in the nation. It is a town where church spires still dominate the skyline and where visitors stroll by the azaleas and bougainvillea that cling to the high stone walls and wrought-iron fences.

Yet within this quaint panorama of colonial and antebellum Charleston lies the landscape of another city. In this Charleston, pedestrians move quickly past corners where emaciated men and women furtively exchange money for small plastic bags. Abandoned buildings, many of them blackened by long-forgotten fires, lean over curbs littered with used hypodermic needles. Laughter erupts from a group of young men in front of a run-down corner store, idly talking and sharing a 40-ounce bottle of malt liquor. These are the impoverished African American neighborhoods of Charleston. In geographic terms, they lie just several blocks from the streets plied by the tourist carriages, but, by social reckoning, they occupy a different hemisphere.

One of these neighborhoods is known as the Eastside, a historic but impoverished community bound by two major streets on the south and west, the Cooper River on the east, and the Silas Pearlman bridge on the north. For 12 months in 1991 and 1992, I attended an African Methodist

Episcopal (AME) congregation that sits in the heart of the Eastside and draws most of its members from the neighborhood. My research at Eastside Chapel[1] focused primarily on religious experience and ritual, both of which were greatly influenced by the social composition of the congregation and the environment surrounding the church (Nelson 1997, 1996). These factors, however, had an even greater effect on the relations among church members and on the structure of participation at Eastside Chapel. These social dynamics provide the focus of this chapter. First, I show that the distrust and isolation that characterizes relationships among residents of high poverty areas is reproduced to a certain extent within the congregation. Second, I discuss the congregants' high normative levels of participation at and financial contributions to Eastside Chapel, arguing that it was the church's immediate social environment among the urban poor that necessitated these high demands on members' commitment.

Studying Eastside Chapel

During my year of participant observation at Eastside Chapel, I attended Sunday services, revivals, Bible studies, prayer meetings, and many fund-raising services. I informally interviewed approximately 40 church members, conducted formal interviews with 20 congregants, and had lengthy discussions with the pastor on many occasions. I also taped and transcribed over a dozen sermons and made video recordings of five entire worship services.

I chose Eastside Chapel in part because of its location within a poor and almost entirely African American neighborhood. Because my research was primarily a congregational study, information regarding the surrounding neighborhood comes from several sources.[2] First, I used census data to give some sense of the demographic composition of the community. I also relied on previously published studies of the social composition of neighborhoods like the Eastside. My participant observation and interviewing permitted an understanding of the congregation itself as a social and cultural entity. The census figures located the economic and social status of the church and its immediate community, while the published ethnographic material lent insight into some of the dynamics operating within impoverished African American neighborhoods. The combination of these sources allowed an examination of how the internal world of a church like Eastside Chapel is influenced by its social environment. It also allowed me to move beyond previous research on social status and religion—much of which takes the individual as the unit of analysis—to consider the institutional and social environments structuring members' participation.

Eastside: The Setting

Charleston's Eastside is an old community developed in the early 19th century and annexed to the city in 1849. Unlike the patterns of racial invasion and succession typical of northern cities, Eastside has always been home to a significant African American population. These residents gravitated to the area because of lower rents and the attraction of cheaper, wooden houses prohibited within the more densely built (and thus fire prone) areas of the city (Rosengarten 1987). However, like many inner-city neighborhoods in all parts of the country, the residents of the Eastside are largely impoverished African Americans, struggling to survive in an environment plagued by drugs, crime, unemployment, a rapidly decaying housing stock, and many other problems.

A brief look at the federal census data offers a statistical portrait of Eastside's social reality. The Eastside has suffered impoverishment for several generations. The 1970 census (the first after the official poverty standard was established)[3] reported that 65.1 percent of the African American residents in Eastside had annual incomes below the poverty line. This figure well exceeds the 40-percent threshold used by many scholars to define a ghetto area (Danziger and Gottschalk 1987; Jargowsky and Bane 1991; Kasarda 1993). As poor as they were, however, Eastside residents were not much worse off than other African Americans in the Charleston metropolitan area, 51.6 percent of whom lived in poverty in 1970. Twenty years later, poverty levels among black Eastside residents had dropped only slightly—the 1990 census shows that 54.2 percent of black persons in Eastside were living below the poverty threshold. However, during these intervening decades, the poverty level of all African Americans within the Charleston metropolitan area dropped over 20 points (to 31.9 percent). Both the housing stock and the population of the Eastside declined substantially during this same period. The 1970 census reported 6,719 individuals living in 2,069 units on the Eastside. Only 2 percent (152) were white, and over half of them lived on two blocks at the southern tip of the neighborhood. By 1990, there were only 3,397 persons living in 1,574 housing units, a 49.4 percent decline in population and a 23.9 percent drop in housing units from the 1970 figures.

Table 1 compares the African American residents of the Eastside (who made up 97 percent of the neighborhood in 1990) to both the white and black population of the Charleston Metropolitan Statistical Area (MSA) in 1990. The substantial inequities between whites and African Americans in the Charleston metropolitan area are quite apparent from these figures. Yet those who lived in the Eastside were anywhere from 30 to almost 100 percent worse off on each of these indicators than the average black resident in the metropolitan area.

Table 1: Selected Economic and Social Characteristics, 1990

	Charleston SMSA		Eastside
	White	*Black*	(Tracts 8 and 9)
Median household income in 1989	$32,125	17,037	7,433 (8) 9,640 (9)
Percent of persons with income below poverty line	7.6	31.9	54.8
Percent of households with public assistance income	3.2	16.3	27.9
Percent of persons 25 years old and over with less than a high school diploma	17.4	42.1	63.8
Percent of unemployed males 16 years old and over	1.9	6.7	11.7
Percent of employed persons in service occupations	7.9	20.9	37.8
Percent of families with female head, no husband present, with own children under 18 years of age	6.1	22.1	32.2

Source: United States Bureau of Census, 1990 Census of Population and Housing, CPH-107.

Eastside Chapel AME

Within this troubled neighborhood lies the congregation I call Eastside Chapel African Methodist Episcopal Church. Eastside Chapel grew out of a small mission organization planted in the early decades of this century, and the present church building was completed in 1942. At the time of my research in 1991 to 1992, Eastside Chapel drew most of its membership from present or former neighborhood residents. Although some congregants had never lived in the Eastside, most of these members resided in areas of Charleston and North Charleston that resembled the Eastside in their socioeconomic and racial makeup.

The social composition of Eastside Chapel did not exactly reflect its surroundings. Almost all of the men and women had low-wage jobs, and only a few collected public assistance.[4] In this respect, they resembled the "mainstreamers" rather than the more disorganized "street families" identified by Ulf Hannerz (1969) 25 years ago in a similar neighborhood in Washington, D.C. Most of the men held jobs as unskilled and semiskilled laborers in the construction trades or in service occupations like catering and janitorial service. Many of the older women had been domestic servants, and several had been cooks for local schools. As Reverend Wright, Eastside's senior pastor, told me

> This is a low-income crowd. . . . We don't have high-dollar workers. I think we've got some people that work for the phone company, and one of the ladies works at job services and does counseling. Those are the more lucrative jobs you'd find in this congregation. Everybody else is basically running a cash register for somebody, working in somebody's kitchen, or cleaning motel rooms.

The poverty of the community and the church members, and the severity and intractability of the problems they faced on a daily basis, has two significant consequences for this congregation. They lead to isolation and distrust in congregational relationships and high normative demands on members' time and money.

The Street in the Church: Distrust and Isolation

Relationships among residents of extremely poor neighborhoods often breed suspicion, distrust, and isolation. Several factors account for this wariness. First, poor urban neighborhoods have much higher crime rates than other communities, and the Eastside follows this pattern. Lieutenant Ronald Hamilton, head of Team One of the Charleston Police Department whose assigned boundaries included the Eastside, told the *Charleston Post-Courier* in November 1990 that "crime on the Eastside is out of control." In the same article, a local merchant reported that his store had been broken into on 20 different occasions in 1989 and 36 times in 1988. Five days later, the paper ran an article with the headline "Eastside Heavy on Homicides," indicating that the majority of homicides in Charleston (60 total) from 1983 to 1990 had occurred in the Eastside. Much of the crime related to the sale of narcotics, and several intersections in the neighborhood were notorious centers of drug activity. The many abandoned houses in the area also attracted addicts who used them as "shooting galleries"—a problem so severe that the city began to seize these properties and board them up (*Post-Courier* April 9, 1992).

The second reason ghetto residents tend to distrust one another has to do with the images that outsiders have of African Americans who live in inner city neighborhoods. While community members generally reject these negative stereotypes for themselves, they often apply them to their neighbors. As Gerald Suttles has written of such a neighborhood in Chicago: "[The] Addams area resembles a prison community or any other population that is not credited with a capacity to behave in an approved social manner. Insofar as the residents depend upon the public definition of each other, there is very little basis for trust. . . . " (1968:27). More recently, Elijah Anderson has described how young black men in the inner city are generally regarded as dangerous and looked upon with suspicion—even by other young black men (1990:163–89).

Finally, conditions of oppression and marginality often produce an exploitative individualism as people try to get as much as they can from others without themselves appearing vulnerable to manipulation. In his ethnography of a mostly African American housing project in St. Louis, Lee Rainwater observed that: "Techniques of relating to other people are markedly defensive; individuals manipulate and exploit others where possible and at the same time try to ward off manipulation and exploitation by others. This contributes a pervasive tone of guardedness and mistrustfulness to interpersonal relations within the community" (1970:372).

This attitude of competition and exploitation contributes to the formation of street gangs in these neighborhoods (Jankowski 1991) and can be found not only among lower-class African Americans, but also among other ethnic groups and in other industrialized nations. Paul

Harrison, writing of slum conditions in Britain in the early 1980s, observed that, "Low incomes and poor services, private squalor compounded by public squalor, are not the only tribulations of deprived areas. For poverty can also weaken the bonds between human beings and generate conflict within the family, between neighbors, and between races" (1985:301).

This guardedness and mistrust that is endemic to the Eastside and neighborhoods like it appeared, to some extent, within Eastside Chapel, although it took a somewhat different form. For example, members had little fear of criminal victimization at the hands of another parishioner. Rather, distrust in the congregation centered on issues of psychic and emotional vulnerability that might damage one's reputation and leave one open to exploitation by others. This type of vulnerability was a clear threat in the St. Louis housing project studied by Lee Rainwater:

> Perhaps the most commonly perceived danger is the less specific fear of losing one's identity resources. Pruit-Igoeans fear that losing control over information about oneself and one's life will interfere with or even destroy one's chances of being what he wants. . . . The detrimental effect of openness can come about directly through a change in one's image in the eyes of a friend or relative, or indirectly as a result of gossip about you that is spread to others (1970:71–72).

Ronald Huger, a construction worker in his early 30s and a relative newcomer to Eastside Chapel, told me, "I'm the type of person that I normally hang with myself. I don't hang too much with [other] individuals." I asked him why that was and he replied, "What it is—basically, what it is is a lack of trust." Pressing further, I asked him why he and other members did not trust each other. He answered

> I think a lot of people are afraid of one another. Now me, I find myself, when I begin to open up, I always find myself weeping. See, I constantly still do that. See you got people look at you and think—a lot of people in the church, when they see you going to the front, they thinking you got a problem. Even when like you go up for prayer, you find a lot of people are afraid—a lot of people got problems in that church, and they are afraid to go up to that altar on Sunday for prayer.

In Ronald's estimation, "Even though they are in the church, a lot of people in the church say they are saved, but [they are really not]." In other words, instead of encouraging and praying for those who have shared their weaknesses, some members will use the information to judge and criticize them. In my conversations and interviews with church members, I was often surprised and dismayed by the harsh and critical attitudes that congregants displayed toward one another. For example, Sherman Davis told me that the church was divided up into many small groups and that these cliques "might do for each other if you're in that group, but not for anyone else." However, just after complaining about these divisions in the church, he criticized several of the lay ministers and his mother-in-law, condemned one of the older men for drinking and cursing, and denounced the man's son for "putting the flesh before the spirit." Ironically, Sherman himself was notorious for his inconstancy, periodically leaving his job, family, and the church for months at a time while he returned to his drug and alcohol habits.

As the most visible member of the congregation, Reverend Wright was often a target of harsh criticism, and he frequently condemned this type of backbiting from the pulpit. In the following sermon excerpt, he compares the violence of the ghetto streets to the "spiritual violence" of gossip and discord within the church:

> They talking about the violence in the street. But there's another kind of violence—it's a spiritual violence, and it's in the churches. And it's goin' to and fro [to] tear the churches apart. The Devil is out to tear you apart. And it's not a drive-by shooting with a gun, with a Saturday Night Special. It's a drive-by shooting with this Monday through Sunday Special right up here with this tongue on the inside. It's a trigger and it's always shooting off garbage.

However, Reverend Wright was perhaps the most openly critical person at Eastside Chapel. He would often publicly chastise people for their lack of commitment and other failings, a trait that exacerbated some of the divisions in the congregation and earned him several enemies in the church.

Deborah Watson expressed dismay that the harsh and critical attitudes that characterize street life also ruled within the church:

> There's just as much [criticism and gossip] out in the world as there is in the church. But you know, it shouldn't be in the church. . . . [You] hear that out there, so why hear it when you come inside the church? The church is supposed to be helping and encouraging [people] to get closer

with God, not to come in and hear what you done come out from! That throws you back out in the wilderness.

Sherman Davis seemed to think that things were actually worse in the church than on the street. After talking with him about the divisions at Eastside Chapel, I asked if it was the same way with the men he periodically hung out with on the corner. "No, man," he replied, "if they have one bottle or one cigarette, they share it. But in church, if you ask somebody for a quarter, 'No man, I ain't got it.' There is more unity on the street than there is in the church."[5]

One result of the harsh criticism and the distrust it engendered was that, like Ronald Huger, people tried not to appear vulnerable in front of other congregants. On more than one occasion Reverend Wright declared from the pulpit, "Don't ever let anybody know your weaknesses." Deborah Watson acknowledged that all Christians were subject to human frailty and a propensity to sin; but she upheld the idea that these shortcomings should be a private matter between God and the individual believer. She noted, "You know we all fall sometimes, but we don't need to share with our sisters and brothers how we have fallen."

The distrust Eastside members had of fellow congregants and the resulting fear of vulnerability had several consequences for the structure of church events. First, worship services, Bible studies, prayer meetings, and revivals left no room either for "fellowship," or for the informal sharing of personal failures and struggles. In fact, Eastside Chapel members often used very individualistic and antagonistic language to characterize their struggles. Not only did they not conceptualize themselves as sharing their spiritual journeys with fellow congregants, but often testified that they were "pressing on" in spite of being "talked about" and otherwise scorned by other members of the church. The recitation of testimonies, a traditional part of the ritual structure, relied upon heavily formulaic declarations that revealed little personal information. For example, when testifiers referred to their life style before salvation, they generally used deliberately vague phrases such as, "when I was out in the world. . . ."

One important consequence of distrust within the larger ghetto community is that residents tend to keep to themselves. Although the term "social isolation" has come to mean the disconnection of ghetto inhabitants from social networks outside of their communities (Wilson 1987), many residents of ghetto neighborhoods remain isolated even from one another (Hannerz 1969; Rainwater 1970). This isolation characterized relations among Eastside Chapel's congregants. I asked some members if most of their friends were also members of the church. Like Ronald Huger, many people informed me that they didn't have any friends— either inside or outside of the congregation. For example, Mother Pinckney, who had gone to Eastside for over 40 years, reflected on my question for a few moments before replying, "Well, I don't know . . . you know I ain't never been a person to have a lot of friends. . . . I just thought of that." Deborah Watson, Mother Pinckney's daughter-in-law said, "I don't really have a friend. . . . I have family through marriage [that attend the church]." When I pressed further and asked if there were any persons at all in her life whom she would consider a friend, she replied firmly, "None."

Like Deborah Watson, many Eastside Chapel members attended services as members of nuclear and extended families, not because, as individuals, they were drawn to the church. For example, four of Mother Pinckney's adult children as well as their spouses and teenaged children attended the church. In addition, the children and grandchildren of Eastside Chapel's founding pastor dominated congregational leadership. While the presence of these families mitigated the distrust and isolation described above, the social context of the neighborhood also acted to weaken familial bonds within the congregation. A high percentage of these nuclear and extended families consisted of only adult women, their grown daughters, and grandchildren of both sexes. Females headed many of the families, which reflects the high rates of female headship within the Eastside community reported in Table 1.

However, even when the husband was present in the household, often he either did not attend church or attended the congregation in which he was reared. Several highly visible and active leaders at Eastside Chapel, including the worship leader and daughter of the founding pastor, had spouses who were members of other congregations, a fact which is consistent with other research on marital role segregation among the working and lower classes.

In sum, the distrust and isolation that characterizes social relations in poor urban communities affected relationships within Eastside Chapel. This effect was somewhat mitigated by the presence of extended family ties within the congregation, although these relationships often showed strains as well. The fragile nature of social ties among church members might have contributed to an even greater emphasis than usual on the traditional evangelical conception of a personal relationship with Jesus— for this type of spiritual relationship was often portrayed as a substitute for friendship, kin, and even marital relations.

The Church versus the Street:
Involvement, Participation, and Contribution

When I first began this ethnographic study of Eastside Chapel, I had little idea of the scope of participation such a project would require. I quickly learned, however, that the weekly menu of church activities presented an exhaustive list of events, none of which lasted for less than two hours. Sunday school and the Sunday morning worship service (which began at 11:00 and often lasted until 2:30 or 3:00 in the afternoon) inaugurated each week's regularly scheduled events. The schedule also included Thursday night prayer service and Bible study; "midnight" prayer service on Saturday nights (which actually started at 10:00 and lasted until well after midnight); and the occasional Sunday evening service.

In addition to this fixed calendar of services, Reverend Wright and several assistant ministers frequently preached at other congregations for revivals and Sunday evening services. A dozen or so Eastside Chapel members always accompanied the ministers to these engagements, some of which were 90 miles outside of Charleston. Eastside Chapel had two adult choirs with weekly rehearsals—the Senior Choir and the Evangelistic Choir—in addition to a Youth Choir and the Rainbow Choir for small children, each of which had rehearsals twice a month.

Eight administrative boards for the church, as well as two "prayer bands," and the men's and women's auxiliary met at least monthly. Each group also sponsored one-night, three-night or even week-long revivals, as well as yearly anniversaries and many special fund-raising services. These services depended upon the participation of other invited congregations and often had a numerical theme (such as, 100 Men in Black, 100 Women in White, 12 Tribes of Israel, Seven Speakers Program) which determined the number of other congregations invited and the structure of the service itself. In return, other congregations often invited Eastside Chapel to participate in their own fund-raising services.

Like most congregations, Eastside Chapel had an easier time drawing members to church on Sunday mornings than at other times during the week. The turnout for prayer services and special meetings, however, was considerably higher than that for the other two neighborhood AME congregations I observed, even though these higher-status churches had much larger memberships. The Sunday morning service at Eastside usually drew a capacity crowd, particularly on the first Sunday of the month when Reverend Wright was sure to preach, communion service was held, and class dues were collected. Sometimes, overflow crowds set up folding chairs in the center aisle. The Thursday night Bible study and prayer service drew an average of 20 to 25 members who filed in over the course of the evening, and even the Saturday night prayer service consistently brought out between ten and 15 of the faithful. The many special services and revival meetings tacked on to this full calendar were also well attended.

Attendance at church functions and participation in its organizations was costly, not only in the amount of time members spent at these activities, but in financial terms as well. Each worship service and revival meeting included at least one offering, every choir member needed several robes, and all church boards and auxiliaries charged monthly dues over and above the "class dues" of ten dollars a month assessed each adult parishioner in the congregation. For Eastside Chapel's 50th anniversary, every member was supposed to contribute $500 (although it was understood that many would not be able to reach that goal). Because most parishioners held low-wage jobs and were sometimes between work for extended periods of time, their contributions represented a substantial portion of their incomes.

High rates of participation and financial contribution were customary and normal. Members were expected not only to attend the Sunday morning service but also revivals, fund raisers, and weekly Bible study. They were also expected to join at least one of the church's organizations and to tithe their earnings. (I was asked to be on the Usher Board and to teach the men's Sunday school class on the same day my wife and I joined the church.)

Eastside Chapel had several structures in place for maintaining these commitments of time and money. Reverend Wright repeated the strict standards of participation and contribution in his sermons, during Bible study services, and at every other opportunity. The members themselves also upheld these norms and would often informally sanction one another for any perceived deviations. According to standard Methodist practice, Eastside was divided into "classes," and class leaders were responsible for contacting their members when they did not appear in church. In order to maintain standards of giving, church leaders published the members' contributions. Every Sunday, the bulletin contained an insert showing each person's offering from the previous Sunday (both children and adults), and the names were arranged according to class membership. Even the revivals and special meetings placed maximum pressure on participants. Members filed to the front, one row at a time, to put their money in the plate, and the church organized competitions among participating congregations.

Social Class and Sectarian Commitment

The pattern of involvement, participation, and contribution at Eastside is characteristic of sectarian religious organizations and has long been identified as a particularly lower-class phenomenon (cf. Drake and Cayton 1962). Sociologists offer several explanations for the link between class and this type of sectarian commitment. Some make the assumption that the lower classes simply have less access to alternative arenas of participation and thus concentrate their activities within the church. For example, Rodney Stark points to structural factors which " . . . deprive [the poor] of secular opportunities for organizational life and for forming friendships" (1972:493). Others, like Laurence Iannaccone, argue that individuals with high socioeconomic status do not join such sectarian organizations because: "The opportunity costs are simply too great. But the costs are substantially less, hence the odds of joining substantially higher, for people with limited secular opportunities, such as those with low wage rates, limited education, or minimal job experience" (1994:1201).

These approaches are called "supply side" explanations. In Stark's formulation, individuals' demand for organizational participation is assumed to be stable; it is the supply of opportunities for participation within a range of organizations that varies by socioeconomic status. According to Iannaccone, the demand for strictness is stable because it is a rational mechanism for maintaining church strength; it is the supply of potential converts that varies by social status, thus producing the preponderance of highly committed church members among the lower class. Both of these explanations center on individuals' choice within already existing arenas of participation. For Stark, the poor simply have no choice—religious institutions are their only alternative.

But this monopolistic situation cannot explain why the poor would allow the church to make such extraordinary demands upon them. For Iannaccone, individuals weigh the costs and benefits of joining established churches or sects. But, as he himself notes in an earlier article, "one wishes to explain not only why certain people are more attracted to existing sects but also why such sects emerge in the first place" (Iannaccone 1988:S263). Also, the very monopolistic characteristic that is supposed to increase participation among the poor appears in other rational-choice accounts as reducing attendance and commitment (Finke and Stark 1992). Why a monopoly increases participation for the poor and decreases it for everyone else remains unclear.

One problem that Stark, Iannaccone, and others have in accounting for religious commitment among the poor is their use of Benton Johnson's formulation of a sect as a "religious group that rejects the social environment in which it exists" (1963:542) without adhering to his "guidelines for the definition's proper use." In Johnson's words, "It is necessary to specify the group which is to be classified *and the environment to which it is to be related*" (1963:543, emphasis added). Most analyses simply assume a generic white, middle-class American society as the relevant sociocultural environment for all religious organizations. For example, Hans A. Baer and Merrill Singer characterize all African American religious groups as "sectarian" because,

> [T]hey all exist unavoidably in a state of some tension with the larger society. This is so because the racial status of their adherents automatically insures both the experience of oppression, individually and/or collectively, and the use of the religious group to respond in some fashion to this experience (1992:58).

While congregations like Eastside Chapel do respond in religious, social, and political ways to the experiences of racial injustice, they direct their activities not toward their white oppressors but toward the conditions of the ghetto that this racial oppression has spawned. These conditions include segregation, poverty, unemployment, and their effects: crime, drug abuse, alcoholism, and unstable family formations.

During my initial meeting with Reverend Wright, I asked him about the neighborhood surrounding the church. He described it as a "negative zone," full of "drug addicts and alcoholics" and people with "no jobs and no future." The following excerpt from one of Reverend Wright's sermons captures the perception that church members had of the world around them and of their difficult place in it:

> I am so broken up inside when I see the conditions of our people. [Someone] was talkin' with my brother last night and told him, said, "A little girl ten years old came to sell me her body for ten dollars." And what is the world come to when a little ten-year-old child, who hasn't even lived yet, is already destroying her life? And the sad part about it is, the mothers sometime send their children out to sell themselves. 'Cause the moth-

ers are hooked on that nasty dope. That filthy, nasty, low-down drug. It's awful. And Jesus told me to go and preach the gospel. Lord, what can I do in a world where people would rather kill themselves with drugs than to turn to You? When the drug dealers are takin' all of their money? And Lord, You tell me to preach the gospel. He said, "Preach the gospel anyhow. Preach it if they hear it, preach it if they don't hear it. But you preach to them that there's a better way."

While the Eastside neighborhood represents a "negative zone" of despair and destruction, it is also a powerfully seductive force that pulls members, particularly men, from the congregation. Many of the younger men and women at Eastside Chapel had come out of drug and alcohol addictions, and several of the men had sold crack cocaine for years before "getting saved" and moving into the legitimate labor force (often at much lower wages). The availability of drugs presented a constant temptation to the young (and sometimes not so young) members of the church. In my year of attendance, three new and promising members slipped back into their drug habits after coming to the church for several months. One of the older members, a former trustee, went back out on the streets and was arrested for possession of narcotics. He is currently in prison.

Contrary to supply side explanations of religious participation, lower-class individuals do have alternative arenas of participation and friendship. These alternatives, however, center on the activities associated with "the street": drug use, criminal activity, fighting, drinking, and running with members of the opposite sex. This set of alternatives has long been noted by scholars writing of intensive church attendance, particularly in "emotional" worship services, as a functional equivalent to " . . . patterned indulgence in whisky, sex and tavern behavior" (Lewis 1964:153; see also Clark 1965 and Anderson 1979). While the secular opportunities of Eastsiders are certainly limited within the legitimate economy, they are, at least for the men, plentiful within the underground economy—particularly in the sale and distribution of drugs.

It is not a lack of alternatives to church participation or secular opportunities, but the nature and abundance of available activities that is the driving force behind strict norms of commitment. In short, the abundant supply of negative alternatives to religion, and the power of these alternatives to pull members from the church, creates the demand for these norms among poor urban believers. I once remarked to Darryl Lawson, a teacher's aid in his early 20s, that the church seemed to demand a lot in terms of time and money. He said that he didn't mind these demands because they kept him from doing things that might get him into trouble: "The Devil sort of plays tricks on you if you're not doing something constructive. [He] puts things in your mind where you know you can be doing this or you could be doing that. So I enjoy the services, and any of them that I can get to, I go."

Because of its ghetto environment with its many dangers and temptations, services at Eastside Chapel often had the emotionally charged atmosphere of a besieged military outpost struggling to survive behind enemy lines while preventing defection from within the ranks. Indeed, members used this metaphor of the church as an army encamped in hostile territory to characterize their relationship to the world just beyond their doors. The image of the congregation as a tiny piece of God's Kingdom, isolated in the midst of hostile territory, was given even greater currency by several incidents in one month. One night, several members' cars were stolen out of the church parking lot while they were attending a revival service. On several different occasions, the Saturday night prayer service was almost drowned out by an unruly crowd of young men congregating in front of a corner store just down the block from the church.

The Christian as God's soldier is the dominant theme in many sermons and several popular spirituals, such as "I'm on the Battlefield for My Lord," and "I'm a Soldier (In the Army of the Lord)." The anthropologist James Fernandez (1986) has pointed out that such metaphors often serve as templates for collective and individual action, and this was certainly true at Eastside Chapel. For seven consecutive weeks (a conscious allusion to the biblical account of Gideon's attack on Jericho), Reverend Wright led the members of the Saturday night prayer group through the most notorious housing project in the Charleston area. As they marched, they prayed for the residents and cast out the demons of drug addiction, alcoholism, incest, and other social ills.

Constantly confronted with the destructive effects of drugs, alcohol, and crime—which members of Eastside Chapel attributed to oppression in both the social and the spiritual realms—Reverend Wright and other church leaders spoke often about the need for spiritual power (Nelson 1997). This emphasis on the Holy Spirit and spiritual empowerment was directly tied to the social conditions of the community. Reverend Wright once exclaimed in a sermon

But don't you understand? The dope dealers needs a heavy fire! These children that are messed up on crack cocaine, you can't walk them down the aisle and say, "Repeat after me." That ain't gettin' rid of no addiction!

In other words, simply standing new converts before the congregation to repeat a set of formal religious vows will not break the incredible psychic and spiritual bondage of cocaine addiction; only a "heavy fire"—a powerful encounter with the Holy Spirit—can accomplish that difficult task. Perhaps the perception of destructive social forces surrounding the church and a consequent need for spiritual power to confront them is one reason that Pentecostalism and other religious movements which emphasize the Holy Spirit have historically appealed to members of the lower class.

Although the line between "the street" and "the church" was sharply drawn at Eastside Chapel, it is important to note that this line was primarily one of behavior rather than belief.[6] Norms of church going among African Americans remain much higher in the South than other geographic regions (Stump 1987; Welch 1978); and most children are still raised attending church. For this reason, most adults both in the church and on the street hold very similar religious precepts and moral principles.[7] Lenard Singleton, a former crack dealer and addict, told me

When I was out in the world, you know, doing the things of the world—drugs and womanizing—I really never lost contact with God, even though I knew I was sinning. I always had growed up to have that seed planted in me. A Catholic all my life, and always being taught about God, I believed in God and I knew that He was my creator and savior. When I was out in the drug world, I knew I was doing wrong and eventually, if I lived long enough, I wanted to stop all that. But I was just having fun serving the Devil and trying to serve God part-time too.

On several occasions that I observed, men came into the monthly men's prayer group right off of the street corner. These men, who in some cases were clearly still high on alcohol or drugs, would pray fervently and sometimes almost preach to the regular members of the group. When I discussed one of these incidents with Lenard Singleton he remarked, "Basically, the average wino and drug addict out there came up in the church, and some of them know the Bible better than me and you." Wondering about the attitude that street corner men had toward the church, I asked Lenard if his friends had given him a hard time when he made his decision to leave the streets and devote himself to religion. He replied, "I never had a problem with that. All of the people that I ran into told me they respected [my decision]. That made me feel good, but when they were saying that, I was wishing they could do the same too and follow [my example]."

This dynamic is very different from the two-way tension described by Bainbridge and Stark (1980), in which sectarian groups and their social environment reject each other and disagree over beliefs, norms, and behavior. While those "out on the street" may condemn the church and its members as hypocritical (which they often do), they accept as legitimate the beliefs and values the church represents and even apply these moral judgments to themselves. Several men outside of the church told me that they were "going to hell" because they knew that they were not "living right." One alcoholic confided to me that he kept a Bible on the top shelf of his closet, but that he did not consider himself worthy even to touch it until he could manage to stop drinking.

Conclusion

This ethnographic study describes how an African Methodist Episcopal congregation was influenced by its physical and social location within a poor and segregated urban neighborhood. I examined two such effects: the high level of distrust that permeated the internal relations of congregants and the creation of a "strict" church with high normative levels of commitment that protected members from the destructive pull of the ghetto environment. In effect, two contradictory forces operated on Eastside Chapel. One force, reflective of the sociocultural environment surrounding the church, tended to keep members isolated and distrustful of each other. The other force pulled the members tightly together and unified them in opposition to the lure and danger of "the street." The interplay of these forces had several consequences for the congregation.

First, the high commitment that Eastside Chapel members displayed was not oriented toward the congregation as a community of fellow believers. That is, their loyalties were not tied to one another in any personal way but to the church as an institutional representation of God's authority—and even that only provisionally. Reverend Wright was replaced in 1993 with a pastor who relaxed the demands of the congregation somewhat. As a result, Eastside Chapel began to lose members to stricter churches in the surrounding area. By and large, these members did not leave as a group but drifted off individually or with their kin groups to several different AME and nondenominational congregations.

The second and more pragmatic consequence concerns the amount of social capital available to Eastside's members, an important concern within the ghetto community. In the words of Ulf Hannerz: "[I]n a society where life on a small income is a continuously unfolding series of instant crises, the small informal loans and services granted between neighbors may ease the burden by channeling resources each moment to the point where there is a current need" (1969:52). By distinguishing between "insiders" and "outsiders" and enforcing high levels of commitment and participation, sectarian religious organizations can create strong relationships among their members and thus represent a potentially powerful source of social capital. Yet as James Coleman (1990) notes, trust is crucial for the creation and maintenance of social capital. Thus the potentially high level of social capital in a congregation like Eastside Chapel can often go unrealized. While several Eastside families borrowed small amounts of money from the church itself, systems of mutual exchange like those described by Carol Stack (1974) did not exist outside of certain extended kin networks.

In sum, both the high levels of commitment at Eastside Chapel and the fragile relationships of its members can be traced to its location within a high-poverty area plagued by drugs, crime, and fear. These findings are admittedly provocative. Yet they highlight the ability of ethnographic research to interrogate and extend accepted theories and sensibilities within sociological research. The distrust and discord I documented at Eastside Chapel challenges many traditional assessments of the African American church as an institution unified by racial oppression and segregation. Instead, in the case of Eastside Chapel, these very forces fractured the bases of trust and solidarity in the larger ghetto community, and this distrust and isolation permeated the boundaries of the church. Second, the finding that certain social environments tend to produce high-demand churches challenges the individualistic approach currently dominating the literature. The link between social class and strictness must be seen not merely as an aggregate of individual choices conditioned by status-defined "opportunity costs," but as an expression of life within physical and cultural environments profoundly shaped by patterns of stratification in modern society.

NOTES

1. The names of the congregation and all persons have been changed to ensure confidentiality.

2. I interviewed some local community activists and pastors of several other AME churches in the neighborhood. I also attended about a dozen services at congregations other than Eastside Chapel. Although these experiences did influence my approach to these issues, the data were not collected systematically enough to include here.

3. Though deficient in several important respects (Ruggles 1990), the federal poverty standard is the only widely available measure of impoverishment. In 1990, the poverty threshold for a family of three was $10,419 (Census 1991: Table A-2).

4. However, this might be somewhat unique to the time and place of research. In the early 1990s, Charleston had a relatively low unemployment rate for African Americans, probably because of the expanding tourist industry, the presence of a navy yard and air force base (both of which have since closed), and the continuing reconstruction of the city after Hurricane Hugo in 1989. Also, benefits from Aid to Families with Dependent Children (AFDC) for South Carolina were among the lowest in the nation, which discouraged participation in the welfare system.

5. However, as Hannerz (1965:56) notes, these claims of street corner solidarity among the men are often exaggerated.

6. Martin E. Marty (1976) offers a more general discussion of the reletionship between religious belief and behavior, particulary as it relates to historical studies, than is possible here.

7. This somewhat surprising fact was also noted by Drake and Cayton in pre–World War II Chicago (1962:616), and by Hannerz several decades later in Washington, D.C. (1969:147).

References

Anderson, Elijah. 1990. *Streetwise: Race, Class, and Change in an Urban Community*. Chicago: University of Chicago Press.

Anderson, Robert Mapes. 1979. *Vision of the Disinherited*. New York: Oxford University Press.

Baer, Hans A. and Merrill Singer. 1992. *African American Religion in the Twentieth Century*. Knoxville: University of Tennessee Press.

Bainbridge, William Sims and Rodney Stark. 1980. "Sectarian Tension." *Review of Religious Research* 22:105–24.

Clark, Kenneth B. 1965. *Dark Ghetto.* New York: Harper & Row.

Coleman, James S. 1990. *Foundations of Social Theory.* Cambridge: Belknap Press.

Danziger, Sheldon H. and Peter Gottschalk. 1987. "Earnings Inequality, the Spatial Concentration of Poverty, and the Underclass." *American Economic Review* 77:211–15.

Drake, St. Clair, and Horace R. Cayton. 1962. *Black Metropolis: A Study of Negro Life in a Northern Community.* New York: Harper & Row.

Fernandez, James. 1986. *Persuasions and Performances: The Play of Tropes in Culture.* Bloomington: Indiana University Press.

Finke, Roger and Rodney Stark. 1992. *The Churching of America, 1776–1990.* New Brunswick, NJ: Rutgers University Press.

Gans, Herbert J. 1962. *The Urban Villagers.* Glencoe, IL: The Free Press.

Hannerz, Ulf. 1969. *Soulside: Inquiries into Ghetto Culture and Community.* New York: Columbia University Press.

Harrison, Paul. 1985. *Inside the Inner City: Life under the Cutting Edge.* Revised Edition. New York: Viking Penguin.

Iannaccone, Laurence R. 1988. "A Formal Model of Church and Sect." *American Journal of Sociology* 94:S241–S268.

————. 1994. "Why Strict Churches are Strong." *American Journal of Sociology* 99:1180–211.

Jankowski, Martin Sanchez. 1991. *Islands in the Street: Gangs and Urban American Society.* Berkeley and Los Angeles: University of California Press.

Jargowsky, Paul A. and Mary Jo Bane. 1991. "Ghetto Poverty in the United States: 1970 to 1980." Pp. 235–73 in *The Urban Underclass*, edited by Christopher Jencks and Paul E. Peterson. Washington, DC: Brookings Institution.

Johnson, Benton. 1963. "On Church and Sect." *American Sociological Review* 28: 539–49.

Kasarda, John D. 1993. "Inner-City Concentrated Poverty and Neighborhood Distress, 1970 to 1990." *Housing Policy Debate* 4:253–302.

Lewis, Hylan. 1964. *Blackways of Kent.* New Haven: College & University Press.

Marty, Martin E. 1976. *A Nation of Behavers.* Chicago: University of Chicago Press.

Nelson, Timothy J. 1996. Sacrifice of Praise: Emotion and Collective Participation in an African American Worship Service." *Sociology of Religion* 57: 379–96.

————. 1997 "He Made a Way Out of No-Way: Religious Experience in an African American Congregation." *Review of Religious Research* 39:5–26.

Rainwater, Lee. 1970. *Behind Ghetto Walls*. New York: Aldine.

Rosengarten, Dale, Martha Zierden, Kimberly Grimes, Ziyadah Owusu, Elizabeth Alston, and Will Williams. 1987. "Between the Tracks: Charleston's East Side in the Nineteenth Century." *Archeological Contributions* 17, Charleston: Charleston Museum.

Ruggles, Patricia. 1990. *Drawing the Line: Alternative Poverty Measures and Their Implications for Public Policy*. Washington, DC: Urban Institute Press.

Stack, Carol B. 1974. *All Our Kin: Strategies for Survival in a Black Community*. New York: Harper and Row.

Stark, Rodney. 1972. "The Economics of Piety: Religious Commitment and Social Class." Pp. 483–503 in *Issues in Social Inequality*, edited by Gerald W. Thielbar and Saul D. Feldman. Boston: Little, Brown.

Stump, Roger W. 1987. "Regional Contrasts within Black Protestantism: A Research Note." *Social Forces* 66:143–51.

Suttles, Gerald D. 1968. *The Social Order of the Slum*. Chicago: University of Chicago Press.

Welch, Michael R. 1978. "The Unchurched: Black Religious Non-Affiliates." *Journal for the Scientific Study of Religion* 17:289–93.

Wilson, William Julius. 1987. *The Truly Disadvantaged*. Chicago: University of Chicago Press.

Chapter 8

CONTENDING WITH A GIANT

The Impact of a Megachurch on Exurban Religious Institutions[1]

NANCY L. EIESLAND

At the corner of Fence and Hebron Church Roads outside of Dacula, Georgia, stands a weather-worn wooden sign announcing the location of Hebron Baptist Church.[2] The primitive marker belies what seekers will find around the bend. There sprawled on a plaza of pavement is Hebron Baptist Church, composed of several mobile classrooms, a small brick chapel that formerly served as the sanctuary, a Quonset-like gymnasium, a multistoried Christian Living building, and a modern brick auditorium that seats approximately 1,300 worshipers. Across the street sits a crowded old cemetery; its entrance doubles as overflow parking space. This architectural pastiche of old and new structures reflects the congregation's history and practice. In 15 years, this country Baptist congregation has been transformed into a trendy, exurban megachurch. With this transformation has come not only significant changes in the internal life of Hebron, but also vast alterations in Dacula's religious environment.

This chapter highlights the internal dynamics of a trend-setting institution—a megachurch—and the interorganizational response to this innovator among the other churches in its field. New institutional theory provides insights into the processes of organizational change within

Dacula's religious milieu. However, it fails fully to account for the diverse responses of congregations in this organizational field.[3] John Meyer and Richard Scott (1983) note that success of an early organizational innovator disrupts the taken-for-granted relational framework operating in the locale and initiates a process of restructuring. This restructuring may take the form of increased isomorphism within an organizational field (DiMaggio and Powell 1991), or it may result in increased mimesis initially when no centralized authority exists, moving toward greater diversity as more centralized authority emerges (Scott and Meyer 1991). My findings suggest, however, that within religious organizational fields, early, successful innovation results in a diversity of religious organizational responses that are sustained over time, because at the local level, no centralized legitimating authority exists.

My study also highlights how restructuring within American religion generally (Wuthnow 1988) has increased the salience of local relations among congregations (Warner 1994). According to R. Stephen Warner, denominational affiliation is also becoming a less useful predictor of the practices of congregations as these local groups "vary widely in theology, liturgy, and social values" (1994:74). He argues that a de facto congregationalism has emerged as congregations within denominations increasingly become ideologically homogeneous collectivities conforming to the focal populations in their local environment rather than to a common denominational identity. With the declining significance of denominationalism, congregations have defined their identity and mission somewhat less in relation to their denomination and somewhat more in relation to other religious organizations nearby.

Researching the effects of exurbanization on the religious institutions of a small town, I spent more than two years doing participant observation in the religious institutions in the Dacula area. Dacula was once a bustling cotton-ginning town before it fell on hard times when the boll weevil hit the South. In the 1950s, as the community's farming base became saturated, rural residents often commuted more than 30 miles to work in the General Motors plant in Atlanta. By the early 1970s, deindustrialization also made this employment option unstable and limited. During the early 1980s, however, Georgia Highway 316 tied Dacula's blue-collar community into Atlanta's freeway system and provided easy access for pioneering exurban families to settle in the community. The relatively cheap land prices during the 1980s and 1990s, the community's reputation for quality public schools, and the picturesquely rural environment attracted middle-class newcomers. Since that time Dacula has become a full-fledged exurb.

Between April 1992 and January 1994, I attended the worship, fellowship services, and planning meetings of several congregations in Dacula. I conducted more than 60 interviews with members of local congregations, denominational officials, and community leaders. The bulk of my interviewing and field research has been conducted at Hinton Memorial UMC, Trinity Christian Fellowship, and Hebron Baptist, although I have also attended several services and interviewed lay persons and the minister of First Baptist Church–Dacula.

In this chapter, I focus on the impact of Hebron Baptist, a megachurch, on several surrounding congregations. In recent years, researchers have chronicled the emergence of megachurches as part of this restructuring of American religion (Eiesland 1995; Vaughan 1993; Thumma 1993; Miller 1993; Schaller 1992; Richardson 1991). These very large congregations harmonize with the suburban institutional scene's mega-malls, warehouse supermarkets, and the multiplex cinemas and, according to one media observer, have an "increasing edge in the competitive marketplace of U.S. religion and an inexorable attraction to choosy members" (Ostling 1991:62).[4] No scholarly or even popular consensus yet exists regarding an operational definition of a megachurch. Vaughan (1993) and Thumma (1993) confer megachurch status at 2,000 members; Schaller (1992) places the numerical cutoff at 1,000. Still others (Olson 1988) place the limit as low as 800. In part, because of these different definitions, counts of the total number of such congregations vary. Thumma (1993) places the figure of churches at more than 350 nationwide, whereas Schaller (1992) estimates the number at approximately 1,000.[5] The vast majority of these congregations are conservative evangelical or fundamentalist. By most accounts megachurches are overwhelmingly located in the Sun Belt.[6]

Some case studies of megachurches highlight their ability to provide high-intensity experiences of communality with relatively weak systems for insuring individual religious accountability—the assurance of right without the punishment of wrong (Thumma 1993; Eiesland 1995). Their individualized and small-group programs provide emotional and spiritual support, whereas the large worship services evidence an intensity made possible in a throng of like-minded believers (cf. Wuthnow 1994). Typical of most megachurches, Hebron Baptist has developed a symbiotic relationship of specialized support groups, age-graded programming, and big-theater liturgy.

Making A Megachurch: Hebron Baptist Church

Founded in 1842, Hebron Baptist is a historical congregation in the community. Fifteen years ago, it was the smallest of the dozen or so small Baptist churches in and around Dacula. In 1995, drawing congregants from seven surrounding counties, Hebron was a congregation of nearly 3,400 regular worshipers, surpassing the total number of Dacula residents. The congregation's story is a classic tale of church growth on a metropolitan frontier. In the 1980s, when Gwinnett was the fastest growing county in the United States, Hebron kept pace with the steady population inflow, becoming the primary beneficiary of exurban growth in the area. Its optimal location on the periphery of Dacula near the community's newly constructed elementary school and abutting several high-density subdivisions has given it high visibility among exurban newcomers.

The church's pastor, Reverend Larry Wynn, whose 17-year tenure has provided leadership stability and consistent outward vision, has been very deliberate in addressing the needs of exurbanites by implementing relevant programs and updating the congregation's worship services. In 1977, when the South Georgia native came to the church as a 24-year-old Mercer University graduate, he began accompanying the Dacula Fire Department on its emergency calls. As he sat with victims of tragedy, he realized that many had no local support during difficult times. Observing these newcomers' lack of community, Wynn led the Hebron congregation in aggressive evangelism in the area's burgeoning subdivisions. Members canvassed each neighborhood once or twice a month, inviting families to attend special programs at the church. The evangelistic blitz spawned a new verb in the community: locals inquired if new subdivisions had been "hebroned" lately.

Though some newcomers responded negatively to the persistent outreach, many were swayed by age-graded evangelism, as youth visited other youth; singles, other singles; and young families, other young families. A relatively recent convert, Dick Lee reported on his visit from Hebron members upon moving into a subdivision nearly ten miles from the church

One thing that happened immediately, just immediately, was a visitation. They were just so good about it. Tuesday night they came. We had about ten or 11 people in our age groups in this [living] room. I was out shooting baskets in the backyard, and my son and twin daughter came and said, "Dad, there are some people here to see you." And they were from Hebron. Then the doorbell rang and another group came in. And then the doorbell rang a little while later, and another group came in. They didn't know that the other groups were going to be here. Just a lot of laughing and things. You could tell that they just really worked at [witnessing].

A police officer, Lee was immediately invited to attend the public safety support group, in which he soon became active, helping to make arrangements for several high-profile Gwinnett County police funerals held at Hebron in 1994.

In exurbia, populated by commuters with demanding work schedules, getting in and staying in touch with people is vital to organizational survival and vitality. Hebron's leadership has adopted the resources of most contemporary businesses, seeking to increase their market share. Desktop publishing and computer labels are real "God-sends." Hebron uses these relatively low-tech and inexpensive means to produce a newsletter for individuals who are not regular attendants but who consider the congregation their home church.[7] The regular weekly newsletter, *The Vision*, is distributed to three times the number of weekly worshipers, about 7,000 recipients.[8]

One individual who receives the newsletter but attends services at the church only occasionally, told me, "I love the newsletter because it always has a good word, I can read it when I have time, and it keeps me in touch with *my* [speaker's emphasis] church." Many Hebron congregants spoke of the encouragement they received from Wynn's short spiritual commentaries in the newsletters. These messages include encouragement to find a place of service in the congregation, a testimony of spiritual support received, or a celebration of the church's impact on the community. The church newsletter has become an important way for Hebron to keep marginal members tied to the church and to encourage committed and peripheral participants alike.

On-line communication may be the next means the congregation adopts for this purpose. In 1994, Wynn commented that he hoped to be on-line via the Internet with members in the near future. Wynn notes that he does not want to get "hung up" in the medium for the message, but that he wants to use whatever technology people are using to get the congregation's theological vision out to area residents. This megachurch pastor does not, however, see the newsletter or computer-driven communication as a substitute for physically gathering for worship and mutual support.

The church's success in retaining exurban newcomers has been due, in part, to its innovative and extensive programming and its celebrative and spiritually challenging worship experiences. Balancing conservative Baptist theology with a therapeutic personalism, Hebron has sought to address the specific familial and life style stresses of exurban baby boomers. The occupational and special-needs support groups have been particularly successful in incorporating new members. Initiated by a police department chaplain and associate pastor at Hebron, the support group for public safety personnel and their families provides peer and professional counseling, seminars in stress management, and topical discussions. The support group also reaches out to other families concerned with public safety, especially those who have experienced loss. The church provides many services for people in the throes of personal crisis. According to an announcement in the church's weekly newsletter, Grief Relief, a group designed to assist individuals who have lost loved ones, whose businesses have failed, who are in poor health, or who have lost self-esteem, encourages "unhurried healing to help bring life back into focus after the blur of pain, confusion, and bewilderment caused by loss." Creating Awareness spearheads the congregation's efforts to address the needs of people with disabilities, especially children, through special Sunday school programs and headphones and signing during services for the hearing impaired. Other support groups include Divorce Recovery, Christian Alcohol Recovery, Christian Al-Anon, and Adult Children of Confusion. The church also operates the AlphaCare Therapy Services, an on-premises professional counseling group that provides free or low cost "Christ-centered" individual, marital, and family therapy. In addition to ongoing support and service groups, Hebron offers one-night LifeSkill seminars designed to develop practical skills for real-life issues such as parenting, finances, dating, and Christian sexuality.

With individual staff members for children, singles, students, senior adults, high school, middle school, and preschool ministries, the church offers a sophisticated array of age and life-stage specific programs, choirs, Sunday school classes, and support groups. In 1995, Hebron supported a youth program with 500 members. Led by a pastor of high school ministries who had been an acclaimed football hero and valedictorian in Dacula's only high school, the youth program incorporates films, special guests, fellowship and discussion groups, summer and winter retreats, Discipleship Now weekends, and numerous impromptu and planned parties. Youth from Hebron have also begun prayer groups at several local schools, including the Second Chance prayer group at nearby Duluth High School. The annual Vacation Bible School, serviced by an extensive bus ministry, draws more than 500 children with daily visits from Captain Hook and Arte the Aquaman, drawings for bicycles and other prizes, Bible stories and songs, and a Hippo-party-mus. The Young at Heart, for individuals 50 years and older, offers separate weekly Bible studies and fellowship gatherings for men and women, as well as coed meetings.

Additionally, the congregation's single largest event, the Starlight Crusade, which typically falls the week before Memorial Day and runs Sunday through Friday nights at the Dacula Football Stadium, features dinners of special emphasis. The college/career and singles groups cook out; public safety officials from northeast Georgia sit down banquet-style; middle and high school students have a pizza blast; and hamburgers are served to children of the fifth grade and younger. The revival under the stars often draws more than 6,000 people to enjoy the 180-voice Hebron choir and nationally known contemporary Christian musicians, such as NewSong and Michael English, who perform each evening. Wynn, who attended the Billy Graham School of Evangelism where services in an open-air setting were encouraged, said, "Starlight is an opportunity for people to come and hear really great Christian music and positive preaching in a neutral environment. We rent the stadium. Second, it's a lot of fun. Our people want folks to be able to come and be totally relaxed without any requests for money" (Sibley 1993). The more than $45,000 annual bill for Starlight is paid by the congregation which takes up a special "love offering for the community" during Easter. The congregation's 1993 budget of $1.9 million permitted a great deal of programming innovation. The church is not, however, spendthrift. Wynn refuses to go into debt for any projects, including building construction—explaining the congregation's architectural pastiche.

Despite good planning and execution, the congregation's innovative programming sometimes fails. In April 1993, Hebron began a Saturday evening worship service and Bible study designed in particular to serve public safety employees who were thought to find Saturday services more convenient within the confines of their work schedules. Wynn promoted the Saturday services as one more way that the church's role in the 1990s was changing to respond to the life styles of its busy exurban members. "In doing this, we are showing that Hebron is willing to break with tradition," said Wynn. "Like I have said: We have to understand that the message of Christ is the same, but the methods of delivering that message are not sacred" (Matlock 1993). Despite more than 350 pledge cards from people saying they would be attending the Saturday services, the participation was well below that total. By midsummer 1993, Hebron stopped holding Saturday services for lack of participants.

The failure of the Saturday evening service may be due, in part, to many congregants' preference for services with a big group. An integral element of this congregation's ethos and identity is the worship atmosphere made possible by its large size. At the 9:00 and 11:00 o'clock Sunday morning worship services, the auditorium, decorated with simple brass chandeliers, powder blue carpet, and department-store drapes, is crowded with predominately white, middle-class young families, middle-age couples, and teenagers. (A children's worship is held elsewhere on the campus.) A typical Sunday service at the church begins with a water baptism, performed by one of the church's eight pastors dressed in a black clerical robe.[9] Accompanied by the 15-member orchestra and 75-person robeless choir murmuring a chorus, such as "Let's Just Praise the Lord," the believer is immersed as the pastor recites a traditional baptismal formula. The individual rises from the water to the 1,300 congregants' vigorous applause and loud "amening." Such a welcome to the company of Baptists is both enervating and energizing.

Afterwards, the pastor of music ministries quickly rises from his blue-padded platform chair to lead the congregation in several fast-paced choruses. Often between the first and second chorus, the minister instructs congregants to "turn to your neighbor and tell them how good they look—even if they don't." Mostly, neighbors deftly shake hands and return to singing, ignoring the proposed conversation starter. But when Wynn approaches the microphone to encourage members to greet newcomers, worshipers make the rounds. Leonard Boswell, a new member and a former Episcopalian, related his experience me this way

> When they introduced the visitors, everybody shook our hand—they'd come from other pews. It was a real friendly place. But the thing that was really good was the preaching. And the singing, too. It is conservative fire and brimstone, but with everything all together it isn't scary. It is just the Truth.

Leaning nonchalantly against the oak cross-shaped pulpit, Wynn generally begins his sermon with jocular, Christian small-talk with the congregation. After a downpour during Youth Night at the recent Starlight Crusade, Wynn commented that it had rained on Youth Night for three years. He teased that if it rains again next year, "we'll look for sin in the youth ministry camp." Often as he makes self-deprecating jokes, Wynn calls on individuals in the congregation by name to "back me up now." But when Wynn instructs congregants to "turn with me in your Bibles to . . . ," the mood turns serious. With the rustle of turning pages sounding like rain inside the sanctuary, Wynn offers a pastoral prayer for all those who will hear this message: "Father, just let it convict them of their need for You."

Minimizing the congregation's denominational affiliation (despite his role as one-time president of the Georgia Baptist Convention), Wynn's sermons often reinforce Hebron's unique character both in the Southern Baptist Convention (SBC) and in the northeast Georgia region. Mentioning the number of water baptisms in the church during the past month, Wynn commented one Sunday that there were more people saved at Hebron in a month than many SBC churches can claim in a decade. Local churches also come in for unflattering comparison, although as a general category, not by name. Wynn sermonizes, "We can't afford to wait until [the area's newcomers] come and beat down our doors, we've been called by God to go out and get them. We're a church that's willing to take risks to do that." His messages do not, however, simply reinforce the congregation's sense of uniqueness. They also press worshipers to be more conscientious employees and merciful employers, to win souls to Christ, to be more devoted parents, to grow in the faith, and to be a more playful spouse.

Similar in content to his biweekly "Spiritual Life" columns in the *Gwinnett Post-Tribune*, whose titles included "Only with God's Help Can We Learn to Love for a Lifetime," "No Matter What Your Status, God Can Use Your Talents," and "My Encounter with Personal Pain Taught Me We Don't Suffer Alone," Wynn's sermons also go beyond these more public messages to detail for congregants the dire present-day and otherworldly consequences of failing to heed his and the Bible's call to right living. Wynn intends this conservative fire and brimstone theme, as Boswell termed it, to press through the superficiality of contemporary suburban life, convincing Hebron congregants that Christian commitment really matters now and hereafter. The sense of gravity that his tone and topic convey is welcomed by many congregants. Charlene Lemond, a teenager involved in the high school ministry and a member of a Soul Winning Accountability Team, commented, "He's not just another person telling you, 'stop and listen to me.' What he's saying really matters."

Wynn concludes each service with an all-eyes-closed, all-heads-bowed altar call. Sometimes as many as 20 people file forward to pray with pastors arrayed across the front of the auditorium. After a brief time of prayer, Wynn announces who responded and their reasons for coming forward. Applauding, the congregants stand, and a receiving line assembles at the front of the sanctuary, as converts, new members, and the troubled claim their hugs and greetings.

The Contenders

Hebron's success in attracting and holding the area's newcomers has not gone without notice. Among the other congregations in the area, comment on Hebron's rise to prominence was ubiquitous. I heard laments about members lost to Hebron, tirades over Hebron's dominance in the school system or parks department, and questions about the internal workings of the megachurch, since many interested parties had never attended services at Hebron. Interviews, participant observation, and archival exploration in three congregations—Hinton Memorial United Methodist Church, Trinity Christian Fellowship, and First Baptist Church—revealed the particular salience of Hebron's presence in the community for their self-identity and mission.

In size, polity, and theology, these congregations are representative of the 21 congregations in the Dacula environs. Besides Hebron Baptist, no congregation in Dacula had more than 300 members or regular attendants; most had fewer than 150. All congregations in the Dacula area evidenced a high degree of de facto congregationalism (Warner 1994), regardless of their formal denominational ties. Likewise, no congregations within the Dacula sample would be categorized as theological liberals. Although all were theologically conservative, there were dimensions of variation. The variations related to Pentecostal or charismatic identity and/or self-identification as fundamentalist. Leaders of seven congregations identified themselves as charismatic or Pentecostal, while 14 said this category, though sometimes accurate for a subgroup in the congregation, did not characterize the congregation's primary theological orientation. Five congregations were identified by their leaders as fundamentalist while 16 were not. Trinity Fellowship advertises itself as Pentecostal or charismatic; First Baptist calls itself fundamentalist; while Hinton Memorial UMC is characterized

as conservative, though neither Pentecostal/charismatic nor fundamentalist.

Trinity Fellowship, First Baptist, and Hinton Memorial UMC are also
less than fully representative of the 21 congregations in the Dacula area,
in that each of these congregations has a historical connection to Hebron
or its leaders. Thus, they are particularly attentive to the changes at the
megachurch. Yet in the 21 congregations, 16 pastors or primary leaders
identified Hebron Baptist first when asked which other congregations
were particularly influential in the environment. While Trinity Fellowship, First Baptist, and Hinton Memorial UMC have particularly strong
connections to Hebron, the majority of congregational leaders have
Hebron firmly on their minds. Analysis of these three congregations,
therefore, is particularly useful for determining how a megachurch affects the missions and identities of congregations within a common organizational field.

Hinton Memorial United Methodist Church

Until the 1960s, Hinton Memorial UMC and Hebron Baptist each held
services only every other Sunday, and congregants regularly worshiped
together. Alfred and Lula DeVries, former Dacula shopkeepers and re-
tired farmers, vividly recall holding joint meetings with Hebron. Alfred's
father led singing at the combined services. Yet the recent histories of
the congregations have varied dramatically. Founded in 1837, Hinton
Memorial, long known as Dacula's establishment church, evolved from
a small church dominated by a single extended family during the 1960s
to become a steadily growing congregation in the late 1980s. But in
1990, the congregation split when Reverend Gerald Gerhard, their pastor of six years, and more than half of the members left the Methodist
church to found an independent charismatic congregation, Trinity Christian Fellowship. Prior to the split, the congregation had tripled in size in
five years, growing from a weekly attendance of 40 to 120.

Several long-time Hinton members contend that Hebron contributed
to the schism by feeding Hinton's young minister with visions of the
congregation's rapid growth. Nowell Altoona, head of the Trustees'
Committee during the schism, reported

> [Gerhard] was seeing that Hebron Baptist Church up the road from us,
> which is growing by leaps and bounds, and talking with some of the
> people there. I know he was having regular dialogue with Larry Wynn

and several others. He got depressed that things weren't going like that down here. He was not accomplishing what he thought he needed to do as fast as he wanted to do it. He felt as though the music needed to be different. Then things really started changing drastically.

Wounded by the schism, Hinton Memorial members also report that their church has been raided by Hebron. Lula DeVries expressed bewilderment that her children have left Hinton, their family's church, for the competitor up the road:

My daughter is a member there [at Hebron]. And our young son, he left our church and goes to Hebron Baptist. I guess they like it. There's a lot of activity there. Of course, when you have maybe 2,000 members or something like that, or more, there's a lot of activity going on, and that's what young people like. Of course, with our limited membership, you can't have a whole lot of activity. You know the teenage kids, they like to be where all the other teens are. My daughter doesn't have children. But I mean, I think that's one of the reasons why Hebron has grown so fast. They have a lot of programs and all the teenagers want to go there.

Alfred DeVries responded to Hebron's phenomenal growth and Hinton's loss of young families with a somewhat stunned admiration:

We have probably the stiffest competition in the world just up the road there—Hebron. Boy, they have tremendous services. And I mean they have a tremendous preacher. It is hard to compete with that fellow. And they've got a good program. We don't really have a good program for the children. We're trying to get one, but it's hard. I think we're doing real well with the senior citizens. We've got them participating and doing well. I think we need to try and appeal to the retirees moving into the area.

In addition to losing young members whose material and spiritual resources would have provided much needed support after the schism, Hinton has also lost considerable status. Long-time Hinton Memorial members have felt their standing in the community slip as Hebron has grown in size, gradually becoming the area's congregation of note. Some Dacula old-timers perceive that the community has been the subject of a hostile takeover by high-powered mega-developers. They see evidence of this in the 11,500-acre, 1,400-home development in their backyard, with a golf course and homes costing from $110,000 to $325,000. They also see the evidence in Hebron, the upstart megachurch snatching up their few remaining hometown kin along with the new development folks.

From 1990 to 1993, as Hebron added more than 1,000 worshipers, Hinton Memorial stayed in a holding pattern under the pastorship of Reverend Luther Dawson, a traditional Methodist minister of retirement age. The congregation, hampered by the financial strain of a heavily mortgaged parsonage and sapped of programmatic incentive, allowed youth and children's programs to die slowly. Although Hinton made some efforts to attract the area's retirees, this population represented only a handful compared to the rapid inflow of young families. The congregation mostly waited for new members from families who actively sought religious fellowship, who retained denominational brand loyalty (an increasingly uncommon circumstance among unchurched suburbanites), or who were contacted personally and informally by long-time Hinton members.[10]

In early 1993, however, as Hinton Memorial sought new pastoral leadership, the district superintendent urged the church to become a "redevelopment congregation." This program of the North Georgia Conference of the UMC enables congregations in the midst of changing communities to gain the financial resources, programming, and training for active outreach. Denominational officials and consultants pressured the congregation to participate. One official noted that if Hinton did not want to grow "there will soon be another United Methodist congregation on your doorstep." Although the Hinton members decided to join the redevelopment program, some members perceived it as the only option available to them if they did not want the denomination further to undermine their status in the community.

Hinton congregants, newcomers and old-timers alike, do not relish the prospect of denominationally induced growth. They assert that they joined Hinton exactly because they did not want to get lost in a large church. Many of the exurban newcomers joined Hinton after rejecting Hebron. Hearsay and personal interactions have left them with bad feelings about the megachurch. Linda and Bill Lyle decided to attend Hinton, despite the superior programming that Hebron could offer their daughter with learning disabilities and their preteen son:

When Bill came here, he was like "Why don't we try the Baptist church?" because it's the biggest. He's worried about a youth program. Hinton doesn't really have one. It's growing though. But I've heard some really, really strange stuff about that Baptist church. It's too big. And they're not very nice. The Cub Scouts wanted to use one of their facilities, and they told them they couldn't do it because none of them were members. I mean, that's too big for your britches. Dacula isn't that big that they can't help. I mean if they're not going to help these kids, who are they going to help?

A Georgia native and full-time mother, Liza Mayeux, was particularly offended by Hebron's visitation programs:

They've visited us. Three times. Knowing—I point blank told him I was going to Hinton Methodist Church. I was teaching Sunday school. They had visitation. "We were just in the area and thought we'd come by." Well, you don't really "drop by" down our driveway. You can't do that. They came down in here for a purpose. Why were they pushing? Lord, they've got more than they can handle, obviously, with three services— although I think it was just two at that time. We call them "Hebronites." I mean, that's a pretty good word for them. Some of the people in this subdivision who are unchurched lock their doors and turn out their lights when they see [the Hebron visitation group] coming. Or they've got a watch out in the subdivision. They'll start calling each other. "It's Tuesday night. They're hoofing it on the street again."

Despite denominational officials' inducement (or what some at Hinton perceived as coercion) to grow, Hinton Memorial grew slowly and only slightly. The church did not attempt to match the programming and styles of Hebron Baptist, but it increased programs that capitalized on what they perceived as their unique character. Bob Tracy, a coach at Dacula High School, believed that United Methodist denominational officials are naive to think that Hinton can compete with Hebron to become a mainline megachurch. He stated, "We can't fight that. So really the only people that we're gonna get are the ones who want to come to a small church where we are friendly." Billy Sue Hammond, a long-time resident and real-estate agent, maintained that Hinton should give up any notion of trying to "out Hebron Hebron" and instead invest their energies in finding something that is impossible for a megachurch to do.

As part of this strategy, Hinton members have been active in preserving the unique history of Dacula and in promoting a community boosterism. Congregants contrast their local focus with Hebron's appeal to the Atlanta metro area. Hinton trustees began selling plates and Christmas ornaments with etchings of the area's historical buildings. A Hinton member, an Ohio native and exurban newcomer, spearheaded the town's first Dacula Days and Memorial Day parade. And several Hinton members, including Linda Lyle, planned community storytelling events at the church, in which congregational old-timers tell mostly exurban youngsters what the area was like before it became an exurb of Atlanta. Under the leadership of a new energetic young pastor, a slightly growing number of committed white, middle-class young couples with children, and a preponderance of elderly old-timers, Hinton is slowly reckoning with the nearby megachurch. But instead of aggressively pursuing growth as denominational officials had hoped, the congregation, hampered by continued financial instability, developed a niche by exploiting their historical identity and began programs that did not have to compete directly with Hebron for participants.

Trinity Christian Fellowship

As evidenced by the bulletin board notice that announced "Souls saved in 1994—134; Goal—500," Trinity Christian Fellowship, established in 1990 after the schism at Hinton Memorial UMC, is vigorously pursuing growth. By attracting the area's incoming white, middle-class exurbanites, the congregation has expanded rapidly, swelling from approximately 50 adherents following the split to more than 280 in mid-1994. TCF (as the congregation is known to insiders) is an independent, interdenominational church affiliated and in mission with the Trinity International Fellowship of Churches, a consortium of some 15 charismatic (mostly former Methodist) congregations in the Southeast. After nearly three years of itineracy, often holding meetings in the Dacula High School auditorium, the congregation built and occupied in late 1993 a new brick and Quonset-like facility, located in a rapidly suburbanizing area approximately six miles west of Dacula. Similar to Hebron Baptist, which defines its mission as "reaching northeast Georgia for Christ," Trinity Christian Fellowship identifies its area of influence as the "northeast metro [Atlanta] community." Despite this wide net, the congregation continues to draw primarily from Dacula and Lawrenceville, a larger, primarily exurban, community south of Dacula.

With Gerald Gerhard continuing as pastor, Trinity Christian Fellow-ship has developed programming apace or slightly ahead of the demand created by the church's newcomers. The congregation currently sup-ports 12 age-graded Sunday school classes and 14 small care groups; in addition to Fisherman's Ministry, a weekly evangelistic visitation min-istry; catered Fellowship suppers each Wednesday night; and age-graded, midweek family night programs, including Kid's Praise for ages five through fifth grade, R.I.O.T. Youth Ministry, and L.I.F.E adult life skills classes.[11] Although the congregation does not have the specialized therapy, special needs, or occupational support groups of Hebron, a thera-peutic and self-help ethos is evident in the daily workings of Trinity Christian Fellowship as well. For example, fitness and diet guru Susan Powter's book *Stop the Insanity!* (1993) was assigned to the women's Sunday school class. The congregation's welcome letter, tied with a burgundy bow to match the auditorium's color scheme and distributed to all newcomers, excerpts the writings of an unnamed young African pastor. It begins:

> I'm part of the fellowship of the unashamed. I have Holy Spirit Power. The dye has been cast. I have stepped over the line. The decision has been made. I'm a disciple of His. I won't look back, let up, slow down, back away, or be still. My past is redeemed, my present makes sense, my future is secure. I'm finished and done with low living, sight walking, small planning, smooth knees, colorless dreams, tamed visions, mun-dane talking, cheap living, and dwarfed goals.

Although Trinity Christian Fellowship has explicit goals for an-nual growth, it seeks to diminish the negative connotations of ex-pansion in its mission statement. The fellowship's brochure states its mission this way

> The vision God has given us is bold, exciting and full of opportunity. It is not our desire to be a "Megachurch" with thousands of members. It is our desire to be a family oriented, nurturing, loving body of believers who understand the true goal of being Christian. . . . The goal of Trinity Christian Fellowship is to minister the love of Jesus to today's families.

Despite the formal mission statement, most members believe Trinity could grow to megachurch status. Not only does Gerhard have close association with Wynn, especially in the mid-1980s when Hebron Baptist was just attaining megachurch status, but Trinity Christian Fellowship is also affiliated with Trinity International Fellowship of Churches, led by Reverend Mark Rutland, who directed a 4,000-member congregation in Winter Park, Florida. Thus Trinity's stated intention of foregoing megachurch designs is not because either the congregation or its pastor believes that such a goal is unattainable, even in an organizational field already dominated by a megachurch. Rather Gerhard and Trinity members have aims of "mothering" numerous other local congregations.[12] In essence, the congregation intends to expand its sphere of influence by decentralization and franchising instead of by centralization and consolidation.[13] A significant aspect of many services is the ritual of "sending out." For example, a young couple from the congregation was commissioned to pastor Promiseland Bible Church in Woodstock, Georgia—a exurb northwest of Atlanta. Sponsored by Trinity Christian Fellowship and Trinity International Fellowship of Churches, another congregant sought to establish a Bible study and worship group at Georgia Tech where he was a first-year student. Members of TCF committed to making weekly treks to downtown Atlanta to assist with guitar playing and evangelism.

Gerhard uses the mothering concept both to reinforce the congregation's self-identity as a family serving other families and to establish strong patterns of evangelistic outreach followed by vigorous discipleship programs. He states often, "We can't give them birth and then expect them to grow up on their own." His sermons on missions are peppered with vivid physical metaphors and analogies comparing spawning nascent congregations to human parenting. Congregants are expected to do the spiritual equivalent of "wiping babies' butts," "burping out the gas," and "holding them through the night when they can't sleep."[14] But Gerhard abides no coddling of spiritual newborns. In a series of sermons entitled "Victorious Christian Living," he cited two reasons why Christians fail to mature and five keys to spiritual maturity. His reasons included that mature Christians permit spiritual infants to stay immature. He preached sternly, "God is clear. Here's the thing. You have to seek God and walk in right relationship with Him. If you're not doing that, *grow up!* [speaker's emphasis]" After a short pause, he added "I mean that in a loving way."

Gerhard, like a strict father, often vehemently rails against the shortcomings of hypothetical congregations, sometimes pounding vigorously on the oak cross-shaped pulpit. But the raging quickly turns to parental concern. The congregation's altar call most clearly exhibits this. Proclaiming "we're all family here, and, besides, Jesus says confess your sins one to another and you will be forgiven," Gerhard often rejects the all-eyes-closed, all-heads-bowed traditional call, opting instead for the all-eyes-open, all-heads-up variety. As individuals file toward the front of the congregation, and most do every service, congregants reach out to caress or hug their neighbors. Gerhard awaits at the steps of the burgundy platform to embrace each person as he or she arrives. On their way to the front of the auditorium, several grab the white baskets of facial tissue positioned under the first seat of every other row of chairs. They are needed as Trinity members weep together and confess aloud their faults and pains. The altar service typically lasts no longer than ten minutes and is usually followed by several upbeat praise choruses projected on the front wall. During this time, congregants roam the sanctuary hugging, patting, and stroking one another.

Trinity Christian Fellowship's ritual practice conforms to its identity as a family whose mission it is to mother other congregations in its immediate environs. Although the church clearly perceives megachurch status as an option, it has chosen a strategy of growth that, while it may one day extend its sphere of influence throughout the Atlanta metro region and beyond, does so through a decentralized network of satellite congregations and groups. This arrangement has clear organizational benefits for a congregation with limited financial support from national or regional governing bodies. By capitalizing on its most ready resource—energetic young believers—the congregation sends people out to establish outposts in other areas, rather than to bring more and more people together in a single facility. This approach has the added benefit of diffusing leadership tensions within the congregation, as emergent religious entrepreneurs are given their own locales in which to ply their religious wares. Within its organizational field, Trinity Christian Fellowship has embraced a strategy for taking advantage of changes in their focal population while avoiding head-to-head competition with an already established megachurch. The success of this tactic will be related in no small degree to Gerhard's ability to mobilize people for spiritual homesteading. Leaving nothing to chance, congregants are alerted by a sign on the way down the driveway, "You are now entering the mission field."

First Baptist Church–Dacula

First Baptist Church–Dacula is the congregation most hamstrung by Hebron's phenomenal growth in the past decade. Even without Hebron nearby, First Baptist would have stiff competition within its field from New Hope, New Life, New Covenant, Union Grove, Pleasant Grove, Hog Mountain, Alcovy, and Ebenezer Baptist Churches, all located within a relatively thinly populated 15-mile radius. Although a saturation point for Baptist churches in the rural and semirural South has not yet been found, such a concentration of separate congregations bespeaks the area's checkered history of church splits and raids. Including Hebron, the congregations represent an even division between independent and Southern Baptist affiliations. Attendance numbers range from approximately 15 people at Alcovy to Hebron's near 3,400 regular attendants. The majority of the congregations, however, have between 50 and 150 Sunday worshipers.

Such is the case with First Baptist–Dacula, the only church of any affiliation located in what passes for Dacula's downtown. One of the independent Baptist congregations, the church is loosely affiliated with the General Association of Regular Baptists, which Reverend Ivan Palmer, the pastor for the past eight years, identified as more theologically conservative than the Southern Baptist Convention. Palmer characterizes the congregation as fundamentalist—"although we're not fighting fundies. It's just not my style." The First Baptist does, however, have a long history of strident conservatism, breaking with the Southern Baptist Convention in the 1970s in protest over the denomination's leftward drift (see Ammerman 1990:44-71).

Much more than Hinton Memorial, First Baptist Church, founded during the Great Depression, is the true artifact of the community's blue-collar past. Adjacent to Dacula's general store and ancient gas station, the church's brick facility was built in the mid-1950s by local farmers and factory workers. The small foyer of the church sports a display case with David C. Cook publications and several dog-eared copies of *Closer Walk*, a Christian sports newsletter. The wall above the display often contains a carefully arranged collage of photos. One Sunday it highlighted the church's family retreats at Amicalola Falls in the northern Georgia mountains. The church's spare sanctuary seats approximately 225, although at most services, no more than 50 people are present. At the front of the room are milky, stained-glass windows with a crown and a dove. The white pulpit is immediately below the window. As the minister stands at the pulpit, the crown and dove appear to hover over his head. Above is a sign reading "'Til the Whole World Knows," which was left up all year after an annual mission conference.

As worshipers pull up for services in their pick-up trucks and late model GM cars, the church's bells peal. As they climb the stairs to the church, worshipers are greeted by the sounds of a modern synthesizer, electric guitar, and drums belting out the tune of a peppy Christian chorus. The church's part-time music minister, Palmer's son-in-law, was a music major and recent graduate of Southeastern Bible College in Birmingham, Alabama. The contemporary music represents one innovation that First Baptist adopted in its efforts to draw Dacula's exurban newcomers. Although many congregants enjoy the praise choruses and worship songs—"I'm so Glad I'm a Part of the Family of God" and "In My Life Lord, Be Glorified"—that begin each service, Phyllis Kennington, a 52-year-old long-time member, confessed that they "jangled" her nerves. She much prefers singing such standards as "'Tis So Sweet to Trust in Jesus," "There is Power in the Blood," and "Victory in Jesus" from the hymnbook. She and other traditionalists in the congregation are accommodated with a traditional hymn "set," as the music minister refers to the musical medleys. Even during the 11:00 o'clock Sunday morning service, congregants call out page numbers of hymns that they favor. This juxtaposition of musical styles epitomizes this heterogeneous body and its ambivalent responses to changes in and around Dacula.

Despite his efforts to update the congregation's practices, programs, and style, Palmer was more at home with a traditional storytelling format. He was wont to ramble and veer off during services, relating long and circuitous narratives. For example, on one Sunday morning, Palmer recounted in detail his meeting with a member's brother-in-law who had recently lost his leg in an industrial accident, including a mention of the Red Velvet cake he was served. During the same service, he called on a woman in her mid-30s to tell about her trip to Bolivia to see her missionary parents. Worried that he was putting her on the spot with his impromptu invitation, he told her "don't panic it's just family here." With no evidence of panic, the woman followed Palmer's example and spoke for approximately ten minutes. Palmer also invites considerable spontaneous lay participation during the service, often asking a congregant to come to the pulpit to lead a song, offer prayers, or testify. Services here often run nearly two hours.

Scripture passages are read from the King James Version. Sermons often highlight the Bible's lessons for helping us handle our anxieties, worries, and fears. Palmer preached a series of sermons in 1993 on how to establish a calm heart in a strife-torn world. He spoke about living in a nasty, fearsome world where no one and nothing can be counted on all the time. He used long, detailed examples of being out of work, health problems, business reversals, and betrayal. One Sunday morning after about 15 minutes of enumerating the dangers of the modern world, he said, "But we don't have to focus on that." Instead he urged a concentration on the peace of heaven, although "the promise of heaven will not always ease the problems of today." Palmer's itemization of the hazards of this world was countered by his detailed description of the beauties of heaven. He spoke about the mansions in heaven, which most people erroneously think are like the homes on Harbins Road, an upper middle-class neighborhood of newcomers near Dacula. Directing the congregants to turn to Revelation in their Bibles, Palmer assured them that "We understand that heaven will be more fabulous than anything we can imagine." In heaven, he reported, "there is plenty of room in the family for the young and the old," unlike the homes on Harbins. He also said that there would be no "pecking order" in heaven, like there is on earth.

In addition to the otherworldly comfort provided in the Bible, Palmer regularly highlights the direction for everyday life contained in the Word of God. He admonishes congregants that "All we need for life and godliness is found in the Bible" and that the Bible had "practical, down-to-earth truth with handles." He often speaks about people whom the world would "throw away," but that God never throws anyone away so neither can we. This commitment is acted out as services close with an altar call, often with strains of "Just as I Am" swelling in the background. Congregants are assured that although changes in their community are often frightening and that they may feel like the throw-aways of the community's coming culture, there is always room for them, "just as they are" at the altars of First Baptist.

However, First Baptist has no coherent strategy for growth or even self-maintenançe in Dacula's realigned religious organizational field. Like the blue-collar workers who fill its pews, this church has been largely sidestepped by the area's growth and transformation. The congregation's attempts to modernize have satisfied neither the newcomers who want both energetic worship experiences and additional programs, nor the oldtimers who are disoriented by the changes. Although Palmer has implemented several new programs and services in the congregation, including an AWANA youth group, seniors meetings, and a nursery, he has had little help from congregants. Many of the programs are staffed by Palmer's family. His two daughters and their families, as well as a nephew and his mother, attend the church. Lois Palmer, his wife, single-handedly organizes the week-long Vacation Bible School.

This lack of programming made it nearly impossible for First Baptist to retain young adults, teenagers, and their families. Palmer commented bitterly, "Hebron has sucked teenagers out of here like a vacuum cleaner." Particularly critical of what he deemed to be the megachurch's overprogramming that separates children from their parents at church and takes them out of the home too often, he accused Hebron of collusion in modern society's efforts to tear apart the family. Joan Swallow, a stay-at-home mother and wife of a missionary sponsored by a Lawrenceville-based independent Baptist mission agency, shared this atittiude:

> But they have a nursery at the church and you *have* [speaker's emphasis] to leave them, and I wouldn't leave my children there. Of course, I've heard that they've had two kidnappings over there. They're so big, you see. They don't know who's in the nursery and who's not. And I know that [kidnapping] happens. One of the Mom's sisters told me. And then I heard that it happened again last year.

Hebron leaders deny that their nursery has been plagued by kidnappings. Swallow's comment, however, reveals how much First Baptist's members feel threatened. Their children are being kidnapped, in a manner of speaking—drawn away by Hebron's programming and mystique.

First Baptist is traveling the road of organizational decline. Without a marketable sense of the congregation's history and connection to the community, they have been unable to carve out a niche catering to exurbanites craving a sense of embedded community; without a viable vision of manageable growth and the institutional resources of a denomination or similar organization, their attempts to update their worship and to implement their minimal growth strategies have been ill conceived and underfunded. Although the congregation may continue to make half-hearted attempts to conform to the growing programming and stylistic demands of part of its focal population and may survive for the foreseeable future in its paid-off building, First Baptist–Dacula is unlikely, under current circumstances, to be a real player in the community's religious institutional environment.

Conclusion

In recent years, sociologists of religion have begun to trace numerous implications of the "declining significance of denominationalism" (Wuthnow 1988). At various levels, this weakening of denominations is restructuring the religious institutional environment. Historical denominations must now compete with nascent religious consortiums, such as Trinity International Fellowship of Churches, for congregational loyalty (Eiesland 1994). This being the case, it becomes all the more important for sociologists of religion to explore the new pressures exerted on congregations within their local organizational field.

In this chapter, I have used the religious organizational field of Dacula, Georgia, to investigate some of these additional dynamics at the local, congregational level. As new institutionalist theorists would predict, congregational responses are conditioned not only by such internal factors as the availability of material resources, the ready pool of human skills and ideas, and type and skill of pastoral leadership, but also by pressures exerted by other religious organizations in the local field. In particular, the case of Hebron's success and wide-ranging influence in its organizational field testifies to the fact that early and successful innovators place unique constraints and afford distinctive opportunities for congregations. However, neither institutional isomorphism (DiMaggio and Powell 1991), nor a staged theory of early mimesis with developing diversity following the centralization of authority, fully accounted for the responses of congregations to the success of an early innovator.

In this case, the presence of a megachurch obliged other congregations to develop and maintain specialized growth or survival strategies. Like a WalMart, the discount giant, setting up shop in another small town, Hebron Baptist's phenomenal growth evoked considerable antipathy from other congregations. Hinton Memorial, like many downtown pharmacies and five-and-dime stores faced with the threat of a WalMart on the edge of town, has developed a market niche by buttressing local loyalties and nursing fears of the community's takeover by large-scale, impersonal organizations. Trinity Christian Fellowship has developed a growth strategy designed to maintain a relatively low financial overhead, to respond quickly to changes in their focal population and organizational field, and to lessen leadership rivalries among energetic religious entrepreneurs, while continuing to expand their sphere of influence. First Baptist–Dacula has engaged in an ambivalent response of jumbled, stylistic adaptation and modest programming innovation, which has failed to stem the tide of congregational defectors, has dissatisfied long-time, blue-collar homefolk, and has fallen short of attracting exurban newcomers to the Dacula area. This array of response leads not to isomorphism, but to an ongoing stable variety of local religious-organizational forms as congregations adapt to the exigencies of the new exurban environment.

NOTES

1. This project was partially funded by the Congregations in Changing Communities Project, directed by Nancy Ammerman. My work was also supported by a 1993 research grant from the Society for the Scientific Study of Religion, for which grateful appreciation is expressed. Thanks are also due to colleagues who commented on earlier drafts: Nancy Ammerman, Penny Becker, John Boli, Mark Chaves, Shoshanah Feher, Fred Kniss, Scott Thumma, and R. Stephen Warner.

2. Pseudonyms have been used for individuals involved in the congregations related here, with the exception of Reverend Larry Wynn, who is a well-known leader in the community and in the Georgia Baptist Convention, in which he served as president; and Reverend Mark Rutland, who is a well-known evangelist and leader in the charismatic movement. Hebron Baptist Church, Hinton Memorial United Methodist Church, First Baptist Church–Dacula, and Trinity Christian Fellowship are the true names of congregations located in and near Dacula, Georgia, although Hinton Memorial UMC changed its name after I concluded my study.

3. A field is composed of those organizations whose services or products are similar (DiMaggio and Powell 1991:64). The congregations of Dacula constitute an organizational field (cf. Becker 1997). Although no formal ministerial or congregational association exists among them, there are numerous informal relations and ties, including conducting common Thanksgiving and Fourth of July services, devising collective processes for serving indigent families, and appointing members to the educational advisory council of Dacula's elementary school.

4. Vaughan (1993) notes that the changes in urban and suburban demographics, including the growth of exurbs, have affected religious patterns. He contends that megachurches are uniquely suited to suburban and urban life (73). However, no study has yet plotted the locations of megachurches to determine where they are located, e.g., near interstate thoroughfares or near or on the periphery of metropolitan regions.

5. One quandary in defining and designating megachurches is dealing with Catholic parishes. These congregations differ considerably from the current picture of megachurches, but many urban parishes fit the criteria of size and theological conservatism. Yet they are not typically included in counts of megachurches (Thumma 1993).

6. According to Thumma's numbers, slightly more than 75 percent of these megachurches are located in the Southeast and West (1993).

7. In addition to the newsletter, which is free, the congregation offers cassette tapes of the weekly sermons for a nominal fee and low-cost video tapes of special services—including cantatas and religious plays—that keep nominal members attached to the church.

8. *The Vision,* the weekly newsletter, contains a short commentary by Wynn, signed "I Love You, Larry;" a schedule of weekly events at the church; requests for workers and resources; prayer needs; miscellaneous announcements; notice of new members by name, separated by those who were baptized and those who transferred membership; and personal notes, including thanks to workers and notices of weddings, births, and deaths. Wynn's commentaries focus largely on events happening in the congregation or in the Dacula community, such as the success of the Dacula High School football team. Occasionally, events in the Atlanta metropolitan area warrant mentioning, such as the 1994 Billy Graham Crusade. From 1992 to 1993, the newsletter distributed before national elections in November contained no mention of politics.

9. A sample of 30 newsletters from 1993 to 1994 reveals that the average number of baptisms per week was 8.9, and the average number of membership transfers per week was 9.1. The average number of baptisms in each of the four Sunday morning services was three. In 1994, the church reported 530 converts.

10. Wade Clark Roof, in his study of religious patterns among baby boomers, contends that a high degree of interfaith marriages and blended families has resulted in the decline of denominationalism. He predicts that this trend will only intensify. He writes: "Denominational boundaries within Protestantism will likely erode further, as increasing numbers of Americans grow up knowing very little about their religious heritages" (1993:249). Others also note the prevalence of religious voluntarism (cf. Warner 1993; Hammond 1992; Roof and McKinney 1987). In a study of five Baptist congregations, Olson (1989, 1993) notes another disincentive to religious participation among seekers. He demonstrates churches with the highest numbers of church friends per attendants have either stable or declining membership. He argues that this finding is due to a saturation of people's friendship networks, so that new attendants tend to find the congregation cliquish and do not persist in attending.

11. When asked, several congregants could not identify what these acronyms signified. One commented, "I don't know, but it seems about right to name a youth group RIOT, don't you think?"

12. This strategy includes developing smaller, dependent congregations that use the church's resources, including office personnel of the "mother" congregation until they are mature enough to stand on their own.

13. Although it is beyond the scope of this article, it could be argued that contrary to the proposals of some contemporary theorists (e.g., Miller 1993) who detect in these megachurches a postmodern organizational form, these very large congregations exhibit a significant modern influence in their valorization of bigness and centralization. More plausibly, congregations that adopt deliberate "mothering" strategies, for instance, may exhibit a postmodern organizational shift toward smallness and decentralization. For a careful discussion of the pros and cons of identifying organizations as modern or postmodern, see Hassard and Parker (1993).

14. It is worth noting, as a sideline, that actors in these spiritual dramas are just as likely to be male as female. Men and women are expected to nurture "newborn" Christians. This equalitarian imagery does not, however, translate into equal power sharing within the congregation. Although women serve extensively on the program staff, none sits on the Pastor's Committee, the local governing body.

References

Ammerman, Nancy. 1990. *Baptist Battles: Social Change and Religious Conflict in the Southern Baptist Convention.* New Brunswick: Rutgers University Press.
___. 1993. "SBC Moderates and the Making of a Postmodern Denomination." *The Christian Century* (September 22–29, 1993):896–99.
___. 1994. "Telling Congregational Stories." *Review of Religious Research* 35:289–301.
Becker, Penny Edgell. 1997. "Congregational Models and Conflict: A Study of How Institutions Shape Organizational Process." Pp. 231–55 in *Sacred Companies: Organized Aspects of Religion and Religious Aspects of Organization*, edited by Jay Demerath, Peter Dobkin Hall, Terry Schmitt, and Rhys H. Williams. New York: Oxford University Press.
DiMaggio, Paul J. and Walter W. Powell. 1991. "The Iron Cage Revisited: Institutional Isomorphism and Collective Rationality in Organization Fields." Pp. 63–82 in *The New Institutionalism in Organizational Analysis*, edited by Walter W. Powell and Paul J. DiMaggio. Chicago: University of Chicago Press.

Dobriner, William N. 1963. *Class in Suburbia*. Englewood Cliffs, NJ: Prentice-Hall.

Eiesland, Nancy L. 1994. "Irreconcilable Differences: Conflict and Schism in a Small-town/Suburban United Methodist Congregation." Unpublished paper, Pentecostal Currents in the American Church Project of the Institute for the Study of American Evangelicalism.

———. 1995. "A Particular Place: Exurbanization and Religious Response in a Southern Town." Ph.D. dissertation, Graduate Division of Religion, Emory University, Atlanta, GA.

Fligstein, Neil. 1991. "The Structural Transformation of American Industry: An Institutional Account of the Causes of Diversification in the Largest Firms, 1919–1979." Pp. 311–36 in *The New Institutionalism in Organizational Analysis*, edited by Walter W. Powell and Paul J. DiMaggio. Chicago: University of Chicago Press.

Fuguitt, Glenn V. 1984. "The Nonmetropolitan Population Turnaround." *Annual Review of Sociology* 21:259–80.

Hammond, Phillip E. 1992. *Religion and Personal Autonomy: The Third Disestablishment in America*. Columbia: University of South Carolina Press.

Hannan, Michael T. and John Freeman. 1989. *Organizational Ecology*. Cambridge: Harvard University Press.

Hassard, John and Martin Parker. 1993. *Postmodernism and Organizations*. Newbury Park: Sage Publications.

Hoge, Dean R. and David A Roozen. 1979. *Understanding Church Growth and Decline, 1950–1978*. New York: The Pilgrim Press.

Jepperson, Ronald L. 1991. "Institutions, Institutional Effects, and Institutionalism." Pp. 143–63 in *The New Institutionalism in Organizational Analysis*, edited by Walter W. Powell and Paul J. DiMaggio. Chicago: University of Chicago Press.

Matlock, Glenn. 1993. "Hebron to Hold Saturday Services." *Gwinnett Post Tribune* (April 7):B1.

Meyer, John W. and W. Richard Scott. 1983. *Organizational Environments: Ritual and Rationality*. Beverly Hills, CA: Sage.

Miller, Donald E. 1993. "Postmodern Characteristics of Three Rapidly Growing Religious Movements: Calvary Chapel, the Vineyard Christian Fellowship, and Hope Chapel." Presented at the annual meetings of the Society for the Scientific Study of Religion, Raleigh, NC.

Miller, Donald E. and Paul Kennedy. 1991. "The Vineyard Christian Fellowship: A Case Study of a Rapidly Growing Non-Mainline Church." Presented at the annual meetings of the Society for the Scientific Study of Religion, Pittsburgh, PA.

Olson, Daniel V. A. 1989. "Church Friendships: Boon or Barrier to Church Growth?" *Journal for the Scientific Study of Religion* 28(4):432–47.

———. 1993. "Fellowship Ties and the Transmission of Religious Identity." Pp. 32–53 in *Beyond Establishment: Protestant Identity in a Post-Protestant Age*, edited by Jackson Carroll and Wade Clark Roof. Louisville, KY: Westminster/John Knox Press.

Olson, Richard. 1988. *The Largest Congregations in the United States: An Empirical Study of Church Growth and Decline*. Ann Arbor, MI: University Microfilms.

Ostling, Richard N. 1991. "Superchurches and How They Grew" *Time* (August 5):62–63.

Powter, Susan. 1993. *Stop the Insanity!* New York: Simon and Schuster.

Richardson, James. 1991. "Calvary Chapel: Mergers, Coalitions, and Denominationalization." Presented at the Conference on Evangelicals, Voluntary Association, and the American Public Life, Wheaton, IL.

Roof, Wade Clark. 1993. *A Generation of Seekers: The Spiritual Journeys of the Baby-Boom Generation*. San Francisco: HarperSanFrancisco.

Roof, Wade Clark and William McKinney. 1987. *American Mainline Religion*. New Brunswick: Rutgers University Press.

Roozen, David A. and Jackson Carroll. 1979. "Recent Trends in Church Membership and Participation: An Introduction." Pp. 21–41 in *Understanding Church Growth and Decline, 1950–1978*, edited by Dean R. Hoge and David A. Roozen. New York: Pilgrim Press.

Schaller, Lyle E. 1990. "Megachurch!" *Christianity Today* (March 5):20–24.

———. 1992. *The Seven-Day-a-Week Church*. Nashville: Abingdon Press.

Scott, W. Richard and John W. Meyer. 1991. "The Organization of Societal Sectors: Propositions and Early Evidence." Pp. 108–40 in *The New Institutionalism in Organizational Analysis*, edited by Walter W. Powell and Paul J. DiMaggio. Chicago: University of Chicago Press.

Sewell, Jr., William H. 1992. "A Theory of Structure: Duality, Agency, and Transformation." *American Journal of Sociology* 98(1):1–30.

Sibley, Celia. 1993. "Six-Night Starlight Crusade: A 'Love Offering' from Hebron." *Atlanta Journal and Constitution*, Gwinnett Extra (May 22):J7

Silk, Mark. 1993. "The Church that Swallowed Dacula." *Atlanta Journal and Constitution* (February 13):E6.

Spectorsky, A.C. 1957. *The Exurbanites*. New York: Berkley.

Swidler, Ann. 1986. "Culture in Action: Symbols and Strategies." *American Sociological Review* 51:273–86.

Thumma, Scott L. 1993. "Sketching a Mega-Trend: The Phenomenal Proliferation of Very Large Churches in the United States." Presented at the annual meetings of the Association for the Sociology of Religion, Miami, FL.

Vaughan, John N. 1993. *Megachurches & America's Cities: How Churches Grow.* Grand Rapids: Baker Books.

Warner, R. Stephen. 1993. "Work in Progress toward a New Paradigm for the Sociological Study of Religion in the United States." *American Journal of Sociology* 98(5):1044–93.

———. 1994. "The Place of the Congregation in the Contemporary American Religious Configuration." Pp. 54–99 in *American Congregations: New Perspectives in the Study of Congregations,* Volume 2, edited by James P. Wind and James W. Lewis. Chicago: University of Chicago Press.

Wuthnow, Robert. 1988. *The Restructuring of American Religion: Society and Faith Since World War II.* Princeton: Princeton University Press.

———. 1994. *Sharing the Journey: Support Groups and America's New Quest for Community.* New York: Free Press.

Chapter 9

THE RELIGIOUS CONSTRUCTION OF A GLOBAL IDENTITY

An Ethnographic Look at the Atlanta Bahá'í Community[1]

MICHAEL MᶜMULLEN

The Bahá'í faith began in 1844 in Persia with the advent of the Bábí movement founded by Siyyid `Alí Muhammad (known as the Báb), who foretold the coming of a prophet who would fulfill all the promises of the world's religious traditions and inaugurate the long hoped-for King-dom of God. In 1863, Mírzá Husayn `Alí, who became known as Bahá'u'lláh to Bahá'ís, declared himself to be that promised one. After suffering imprisonment and exile throughout the Middle East, Bahá'u'lláh died in 1892. The Bahá'í movement was then governed by Bahá'u'lláh's son, `Abdu'l-Bahá until 1921, followed by Bahá'u'lláh's great-grandson, Shoghi Effendi Rabbani, the "Guardian" of the Bahá'í faith until 1957. After Rabbani's death, the first Universal House of Justice was elected in 1963, which continues to govern the world's 5.5 million Bahá'ís from its global headquarters in Haifa, Israel.[2]

The World Congress of a Global Religion

During Thanksgiving week 1992, more than 27,000 Bahá'ís from 180 countries gathered in New York City to celebrate the Second Bahá'í World Congress. It marked the centennial anniversary of the death of the Bahá'í faith's prophet-founder and assembled the largest gathering in the Bahá'ís' 153-year history. The events of the World Congress captured the symbols and rhetoric of the global community and world civilization envisioned in Bahá'í scripture.[3]

Upon entering the convention center, Bahá'ís filed past dozens of brightly colored, quilt-sized banners proclaiming verses from Bahá'í scripture and bearing symbols of cultures from around the globe. Once seated, many believers donned headset receivers that translated the proceedings in English into Spanish, French, Japanese, or Persian. On the front stage, four large projection screens surrounded the lectern.

According to many attendants, the first day's procession of Bahá'í representatives of the races and nations of the world set the tone for the week and remained one of the Congress' most meaningful rituals. As music played, each representative—arrayed in native or traditional dress—walked down the aisle to the center stage of the convention center. It took more than a half-hour for the ceremony, which concluded with a sustained standing ovation that celebrated the diversity of humanity and brought tears to the eyes of many in the crowd. In addition, prayers were read in a variety of languages at each session; using native instruments and songs, music was performed in Persian, Chinese, Hispanic, Pacific Islander, African, Indian, and African American gospel styles. The event culminated in live satellite broadcasts from the Bahá'í World Center in Haifa, Israel, and from Bahá'í centers in Western Samoa, Argentina, Romania, India, Russia, Kenya, Panama, Malaysia, and Australia.

During the four days of meetings, Bahá'ís experienced unity in diversity, a central Bahá'í spiritual principle, as the sounds, sights, and symbols of the World Congress reminded them of their common allegiance to Bahá'u'lláh. Worshiping in the presence of more than 27,000 fellow Bahá'í from all walks of life reinforced their hope for a united planet. For one 43-year-old Bahá'í from Atlanta who attended the Congress, it strengthened his Bahá'í identity as one who celebrates unity in diversity:

> I think it gave me a little real appreciation of the global perspective because I had never been to an international event before. I saw people from all over . . . I think it's given me . . . a heightened awareness or appreciation for the changeable power in the faith, the power to actually change the world. That maybe comes from seeing folks from all over.

The display of diverse language, culture, and nationality illustrated for participants the vision of global unity and peace outlined in Bahá'í scriptures. This global solidarity will come about, Bahá'ís feel, through adherence to a common ideology and recognition of a common global authority institutionalized at the local, national, and international levels of social life.

This chapter highlights the individual and collective rituals that link local Bahá'í community life with a globalized ideology and network of institutions. The World Congress gives a vivid example of how participation in a global ritual reinforces universal Bahá'í identity. But I argue that the practices of local community life function in this way as well, linking the local and global. Local practices particularize a universal identity. My study of the Atlanta Bahá'í community allows me to examine this linking of universal and particular religious identity.

Globalization and Identity

Roland Robertson has defined globalization as "both the compression of the world and the intensification of consciousness of the world as a whole" (1992:8). Robertson sees globalization as the mechanism by which the world has become a single place—where political, economic, and cultural spheres of life are becoming more and more interdependent. However, the world is not a harmonious, integrated system in Robertson's view. Historically, this process has been rife with conflict and reactionary movements, and it cannot be attributed to monocausal forces like capitalist development (Robertson and Lechner 1985).

Issues of social identity are at the forefront in the cultural analysis of globalization processes. The evolution of the world into an increasingly interdependent system constrains societies and other collectivities to identify and legitimate themselves in relationship to the "global-human condition." This identification involves the alteration, retrenchment, or invention of new social identities and a transformation of symbolic and ritual boundaries. Anthony Giddens has said that "transformations in self-identity and globalisation . . . are the two poles of the dialectic of the local and the global in conditions of high modernity" (1991:32). Particularistic identities are reinforced or transformed by universalizing processes that threaten the "plausibility" of a traditional world view, culture, or sense of individual or collective self. However, at the same time, globalization processes "universalize" and blend identities as travel, communication, and political and economic interactions bring people into regularized patterns of contact. This "particularization of universalism" and "universalization of particularism" both constitute the globalization phenomenon (see Robertson 1992).

This chapter will focus on the processes whereby a "universalized" Bahá'í ideology gets "particularized" in a local setting. The Bahá'í faith is a unique religious movement responding to globalization processes by creating a worldwide religious identity for its adherents through both ideological and organizational means, systematically linking the practices of a local Bahá'í community with a world center and the ideological coherence and institutional coordination it fosters. An ethnographic study of such a movement reveals the ways in which local and global institutions are actively created, connected, and ordered. It also gives us a detailed account of how attempts at global identity formation become reinforced and lived in local community ritual. Robertson and Lechner (1985:112) point out: "There is of course no shortage of academically produced alternative images of future world order. There is, on the other hand, a paucity of academic discussion of rival images of world order among the movements of our time." An ethnographic picture of a local Bahá'í community in Atlanta addresses this deficiency and represents one of the relatively unstudied religious responses to globalization processes.

Converting to a Global Faith

The overwhelming majority of Bahá'ís with whom I spoke emphasized two factors vital in their conversion. The first was the character of the Bahá'ís as a diverse group of religious people; and the second was their discontent with other organized religions. The two quotes below are typical of the themes that emerged in many interviews.

My main problem at that age was racism. And I tried to reconcile myself to it over the years, based on belief in Jesus and teachings of the other prophets, and [I knew] this was not of God, but it seemed it was getting · stronger. Sometimes it looked like none of the prophets had ever showed up, in terms of the racism that was around. . . . But the main teaching that attracted me was that Bahá'u'lláh taught that the whole earth is but one country, and mankind its citizens. God hadn't taught or created racism. It's men who instituted that.

Catholicism as I knew it, and even . . . Catholic education as I had had, didn't permit me to use my own mind and arrive at my own conclusions about a lot of things; and the other was the exclusivity of Christianity and Christ. . . . Anything else was not and could not have been God driven. And I couldn't accept that.

The Bahá'í emphasis on unity in diversity and the rational and progressive beliefs of the faith drew many of the converts in the Atlanta community.

Unity in Diversity

Social principles that captured the attention of Bahá'í converts included commitment to the elimination of all prejudice, the equality of men and women, universal education, national disarmament, and a federated world government. To find a group with such racial, ethnic, and economic diversity was novel and intriguing for one convert:

There was such a wide range of people there. . . . There were old people, young people and different races and different economic classes and different parts of the country, the globe, and all that—and it looked so peculiar. . . . I remember that was really a shocking experience.

Especially in the 1950s and 1960s, the diversity of nearly all Bahá'í meetings was unusual among religious organizations that were then, and often are still, segregated by class and race (see Roof and McKinney 1987).

A Rational and Progressive Religion

Interviews confirmed not only the "pull" of the diversity within the Bahá'í community, but the "push" resulting from respondents' disillusionment with their previous religious communities. The Bahá'í faith satisfied many converts' search for a more logical, progressive religion. Others said that their church or synagogue could not give them satisfactory answers to their questions and that they could no longer participate in what they considered to be a hypocritical or secular institution. One woman said

I left the church (Presbyterian) when I was 13, and, the last Sunday that I went to church, I'd asked the minister after he did his real aggressive sermon, what would happen if a group of people on an island that never

heard of Christ, but they worshiped a rock, and as a consequence of this
they treated each other well, and they loved each other and took care of
each other. And he said they'd go to hell. And that's when I left. So, it
was a long time before I even thought about religion on a consistent
basis again.

A man expressed the same sentiments concerning divisions among the
religions:

> It is the exclusivity of religions that I think has been the impetus for
> most of us to look at the Bahá'í faith. Some people appear not to be
> bothered by the exclusivity of Christianity, or Islam, or whatever, but I
> think that most of us who have accepted the faith, we really have found
> that bizarre—that only those of us in this [religious tradition] are "saved."

Others found their prior religions lacking in spiritual depth or vitality. A psychologist said that he was disillusioned with his Jewish upbringing before he met his wife-to-be, a Bahá'í:

> I was pretty much formally distanced from Judaism in a corporate sense. . . . I
> slowly developed a disillusionment around Jewish practice . . . as we know
> it in the synagogues and Jewish cultural life. . . . It was without spiritual-
> ity. . . . I was just feeling nothing there was drawing me that was truly mean-
> ingful in a core sense, and I just floated away.

One woman described how the Bahá'ís' spiritual principle of the unity
of science and religion brought her into the faith, thus resolving her
personal struggle with religion. She related a formative experience in
eighth grade, when she had discovered Darwin's theory of evolution
and identified strongly with his scientific quest. When she was finally
introduced to the Bahá'í faith as an adult, she saw that for Bahá'ís an
evolutionary principle was operating in spiritual matters as well as in
biology. Science and religion fit together in harmony within a Bahá'í
world view.

For these converts, the Bahá'í faith resolves what Berger (1967) called
the problem of plausibility in a pluralistic, globalized world. Not only
are various Christian denominations in competition with a secular world
view, but, also as a result of globalization processes, Christian groups
must now vie for ideological coherence and cohesiveness amid the
world's other religions. One response promotes dogmatism, or an insis-

tence on one true faith. Instead of declaring one religion valid for all time and the others anathema, the Bahá'í faith claims all are valid within a given historical framework or dispensation. This ideology—called "progressive revelation" in Bahá'í scripture—provides adherents with a world view that interprets religious history as a global, evolutionary, and teleological progression of individual and collective maturation revealed from the one God.

In general, Bahá'ís are disillusioned with organized religion, searching for a logical or rational religious faith that makes sense in a globalized, pluralistic world. They are also attracted by either the religious ideology or by the example of unity in diversity found in nearly all Bahá'í meetings. Both the ideology and ritual are critical aspects of Bahá'í identity, reflecting the global world view of this faith. The universal character of the Bahá'í faith provided its initial attraction for "seekers" dissatisfied with their current religious tradition and for the small number of converts with no previous religious affiliation.[4] The unity in diversity required by Bahá'í scripture is manifest in the diversity of racial, income, and previous religious backgrounds from which the Atlanta Bahá'í community has been drawn.

Questionnaire data provide a general demographic profile of Atlanta's Bahá'í community. The group is racially and ethnically diverse. While one-half of the community identify themselves as white, nearly one-fourth were black or African American, and 13 percent indicated "Persian" and "mixed/other," respectively. On average, they are well-educated, middle-class professionals.[5] Most are married to other Bahá'ís.

The vast majority of the community were not reared by Bahá'í parents; 70 percent are converts. Of those who converted, more than half of Atlanta's Bahá'ís are from 12 different Protestant denominations: 16 percent of them were previously Baptist; and 11 percent, Methodist. And, more than 11 percent were originally Roman Catholics before declaring their faith in Bahá'u'lláh. Less than 4 percent converted from a Muslim background, and an equal proportion (2 percent) claim Jewish backgrounds or no religious upbringing. The remainder of respondents— approximately one percent—included Buddhists and Hindus. As occurs in most conversions, many Bahá'í converts first learned of the faith through personal relationships. Of those not growing up as Bahá'ís, the primary source of exposure to the Bahá'í faith was through friends who were themselves Bahá'ís; almost 40 percent of the respondents indicated this source. Twenty-four percent were introduced to the faith by spouses or other family members; and another 14 percent discovered the faith through more impersonal relations with Bahá'ís (such as a colleague at work, a doctor, a teacher, or even the one woman who learned about the faith through her priest). These results substantiate the importance of interpersonal networks in the conversion process.[6]

Community Observances of a Global Faith

As Geertz (1973) and Durkheim (1965) have noted, religious ritual symbolizes the unity and solidarity of a faith community. Bahá'í scripture discourages overly formalized and dogmatic rituals; their rituals are flexible. Bahá'í rituals reinforce the authority of their organizational system (called the "Administrative Order") and link them to the global center of their faith. Bahá'í ritual particularizes the universal; a local community and its members live out a global ideology by following the laws of Bahá'í scripture. As a local community engages the universal, Bahá'í practices conform to the contours of the particular cultural topography. The basis for all Bahá'í practices comes from the *Kitab-I-Aqdas* or *Most Holy Book*. I will discuss collective observances first, and then personal devotional practices.

The organizational participation of the average Bahá'í is dictated by the rhythm of the Bahá'í calendar. The Bahá'í year is divided into 19 months of 19 days each (totaling 361), with the insertion of extra days (four in an ordinary year, five in a leap year) between the 18th and 19th months to adjust the calendar to the solar year. Each month is named after an "attribute of God"—virtues that Bahá'ís are supposed to acquire (mercy, knowledge, honor). On the first day of each Bahá'í month, Bahá'ís gather for a 19-Day Feast, which is the central worship experience in the Bahá'í faith.

As I arrived at the Atlanta Bahá'í Center for feast, I saw the sign to the right of the doorway proclaiming: "Atlanta Bahá'í Center, Built by Leroy Burns, Sr. as a place for all races to come together and worship." The first floor is a large meeting room used for potluck dinners and children's religious classes and is dominated by a six-foot photograph of the Shrine of the Báb in Haifa. Along the stairway to the worship service are photos of interracial Bahá'í groups at picnics and classes. Other pictures of Bahá'í shrines in the Holy Land surrounding Haifa decorate the walls, as well as a painting of the Master—`Abdu'l-Bahá, the son of Bahá'u'lláh. Posters on the walls are decorated with popular

Bahá'í phrases, such as "The earth is but one country, and mankind its citizens" or "One Planet, One People, Please."

A prayer read from a Bahá'í prayer book began the service, followed by five to seven members reading from the Writings that had been chosen by the host.[7] Since this particular feast was the Feast of Bahá (Glory), all the readings revolved around the glory of God, of God's creation, and of God's kingdom imagined in the Bahá'í dispensation. Interspersed with the readings was a taped recording of a Persian song sung by Narges, a famous Iranian Bahá'í exile; an interpretive dance expressing the Bahá'í perspective on marriage and the equality of men and women; and a nominally Christian hymn—"Be Still My Soul"—with Bahá'u'lláh replacing references to Christ. Closing prayers were recited in Spanish, Persian, and English.

After devotions, the chair of the Local Spiritual Assembly (LSA), the local governing body of nine Bahá'ís elected annually from the community, led the worshipers in the administrative part of feast. The LSA secretary read the monthly correspondence from the National Spiritual Assembly (NSA), letters from other communities in the Atlanta area concerning inter-LSA collaboration on teaching and service projects, and a letter of encouragement from the Universal House of Justice (UHJ) to the younger Bahá'ís of Atlanta concerning an upcoming teaching project for the city's youth.

In this particular month, the regular communication from the NSA included news of a recent execution of a Bahá'í in Iran and encouraged Bahá'ís to write their elected representatives in Washington, D.C., to support the most recent Senate resolution condemning the Iranian government's treatment of its Bahá'í minority.[8] A Persian member of the community stood and related a recent conversation with her parents who still could not secure a visa to the United States. She said that the anxiety in the beleaguered Teheran Bahá'í community had increased since the execution, but that their faith remained in Bahá'u'lláh.

A treasurer's report updated the Bahá'ís on the financial health of the community and recounted the previous month's contributions and expenditures. The treasurer pointed to the fund box and asked those attending for voluntary contributions. Various community members made announcements, including news of weekly Arabic classes at the Bahá'í Center for those who wanted to read Bahá'í scripture in its original language. A guest from South Africa who had been "pioneering" (living and working in another country to establish Bahá'í communities and teach people about the faith) gave a report on Bahá'í efforts to promote racial unity in the postapartheid society. Another Bahá'í related his experience on pilgrimage to Haifa and his meetings with Bahá'ís from all over the world and with members of the UHJ. Finally, the administrative portion of the feast ended with a group consultation on the deepenings (daily scripture reading) for 75 new declarants who converted as a result of a citywide teaching campaign.

After a closing prayer, the social part of the feast began with a light meal and fellowship. Discussions ranged from how the Atlanta Braves baseball team was doing, to global economic trends, to abstract ideas from Bahá'í theology. Police sirens and shouts from the pavement below punctuated the conversation. The Atlanta Bahá'í Center is located near the famed Sweet Auburn district of historic African American Atlanta, and the surrounding neighborhood has suffered from urban decay common in large cities. However, the Atlanta Bahá'í Center maintains itself as a sacred space in the midst of the extremes of urban poverty on the one hand, and African American cultural treasures, such as the Martin Luther King, Jr. Center and historic Wheat Street Baptist Church, on the other.

The flow of the feast allows all members of the local Bahá'í community to speak on relevant issues, exchange ideas, and communicate news. Recommendations that require official approval are referred to the LSA. Each feast represents a kind of town meeting, where Bahá'ís practice a form of spiritual democracy. The observance of the feasts, therefore, receives a high priority in Bahá'í communities. Every 19 days, the whole community participates in spiritual fellowship and democratic administration.

Feasts also stress the local/global link of Bahá'í faith. Most feasts occasion a letter from the NSA informing communities of decisions made by the NSA or of global activities of interest to the Bahá'í world. Several times a year, the United States' NSA distributes a videocassette called the "Bahá'í Newsreel," describing Bahá'í activity happening around the world as well as new developments at the World Center. These rituals of communication linking the global with the local via national institutions deliberately fortify and strengthen local Bahá'ís' identity as members of a worldwide movement.

While the feast described above took place at the Atlanta Bahá'í Center, typically feasts are held in members' homes when funds are not available to build or purchase a center. Although most communities attempt to rotate the responsibility for holding feasts among all community members, issues like non-Bahá'í spouses, who, like all non-Bahá'ís, may not attend, and the presence of children often require small communities to designate two or three homes as permanent feast sites. The host or hostess of the feast normally prepares refreshments and chooses readings from Bahá'í scripture. This decentralized character of ritual reinforces the democratic nature of Bahá'í collective observances. Every Bahá'í has the chance to personalize the devotional services in a faith with no clergy. Most feasts have no music during devotions; but during my 18 months of fieldwork, it had become a more prevalent part of worship in various locales.

Not only is the feast format (devotions, administration, socializing) flexible enough to incorporate the proclivities of the individual host or hostess, but it also accommodates the cultural diversity of the communities themselves. I encountered this diversity throughout my participant observation fieldwork. Each community took on a distinct character, influenced by its individual strengths and the cultures represented. The flavor of the feast changed with the community, as well. Because of housing segregation in Atlanta and because Bahá'í communities are organized geographically in parishlike structures, some communities have a dominant ethnic group. The feast, therefore, takes on characteristics of the dominant ethnic group. In Atlanta and the southern and southeastern metropolitan area where a large African American population resides, elements of the black church experience surfaced during feast. Feasts often incorporated gospel music (even singing nominally Christian songs like "How Great Thou Art," or "Be Still My Soul") and the practice of raising hands during prayer. Frequently, "Amen," or "Yá Bahá'u'l-Abhá" (the Bahá'í equivalent of "Hallelujah") could be heard during devotions, and individuals would "testify" during consultation to the miracles Bahá'u'lláh had worked in their lives that month. Worship tended to be much more expressive than in the LSA jurisdictions dominated by white members.

Communities with a large Persian population predictably had more Arabic and Persian chanting, and a large array of Persian dishes enlivened the social portion of the feast. When older Persians not fluent in English attended, a second-generation son or daughter translated the NSA message (or read the duplicate copy provided in Persian) or interpreted the conversation during consultation. Persian believers who suffered persecution before and after the Iranian revolution of the late 1970s sometimes told stories about Iran and related news from relatives remaining in the country. For the non-Persians at the feast, these practices raised their awareness of the Bahá'í faith as a beleaguered movement not immune to difficult times in this country, as many expressed to me during interviews. The Persian influence in the Atlanta area increased the solidarity of the Bahá'í community. The stories of the "martyrs for the faith" gave Bahá'ís a glimpse of the internationality of their beliefs.

Historically, rich members have attended feast in the homes of the poor and vice versa; and blacks, Persians, and whites visited one another's homes every 19 days. Although racial and ethnic tensions troubled the Atlanta community prior to the 1940s (primarily from Bahá'ís' white neighbors who did not approve of "race mixing"), they are no longer an issue. People of all colors and social strata invariably greeted each other with hugs, mixed socially at the end of feast, and went out for meals together after meetings.[9] The only hint of segregation came from elderly Persians, many of whom could not speak English and who, thus, tended to stick together.

The other major collective observances in the Bahá'í calendar are the Holy Days and special events that commemorate occasions in Bahá'í history. Holy Days take on one of two distinct moods: either festive and celebratory or reverent and somber. For example, the festival of Ayyám-i-Há, before the month of fasting, is a joyful occasion. It is celebrated much like a birthday party with cake and balloons and games for children. On the other hand, the Ascension of Bahá'u'lláh, commemorating his death on May 29, 1892, has a more subdued feel, evoking reverence and veneration and featuring a prayer vigil that starts at 3:00 in the morning.[10] These and other communal rituals engage Bahá'ís in practices that affirm and strengthen their faith while constructing individual and community identities that are both global and local.

Personal Observances

Personal devotions also aid members in constructing religious identity. Most Bahá'ís engage in prayer, fasting, readings, and pilgrimages, as well as donating money to Bahá'í causes. Not only do personal observances reinforce boundaries between the believer and the nonbeliever, they also reinforce the global character of the Bahá'í religious orientation.

Prayer

Bahá'ís have hundreds of prayers written by the Báb, Bahá'u'lláh, and 'Abdu'l-Bahá, which members use in private devotion and recite at Bahá'í gatherings. Although the completeness of an individual Bahá'í's library may vary, nearly all Bahá'ís possess a prayer book. In fact, during my entire association with Bahá'ís, I cannot recall ever hearing a Bahá'í pray spontaneously in his or her own words. Although extemporaneous prayer is not strictly forbidden, Bahá'ís almost always turned to the prayers revealed by their three central figures.

Usually arranged by topics, prayers appear in prayer books under headings such as aid and assistance, family members, detachment, spiritual qualities, firmness in the Covenant, protection, steadfastness, or success in teaching. This arrangement has the effect of rationalizing and standardizing, in a Weberian sense, devotional practice within the Bahá'í faith.

Frequently, a Bahá'í at a meeting recites a healing prayer by Bahá'u'lláh for an ailing relative, or `Abdu'l- Bahá's prayer for America asking God that this country "become glorious in spiritual degrees even as it has aspired to material degrees." Bahá'u'lláh forbade the recitation of congregational prayer, as is done by Muslims five times a day, with the exception of the Prayer for the Dead, which is usually said at a funeral.

Otherwise, prayers are done individually or recited by one individual while others listen. There are also different forms of daily obligatory prayer, including some requiring genuflection. Some respondents told me that they found this practice somewhat difficult to get used to; nevertheless, daily prayer is part of the lives of most Atlanta Bahá'ís. My survey results indicated that 82 percent of Atlanta-area respondents pray at least once daily.

Reading the Writings

Bahá'ís are enjoined to read daily from Bahá'í scripture—a process known as deepening. Deepenings take place alone or in small groups.[11] Deepenings are often referred to as Bahá'í Bible study, and those held on Sunday morning are often called Bahá'í Sunday school. At most group deepenings I attended, Bahá'ís sat in a circle and took turns reading from scripture—such as the writings of Bahá'u'lláh or `Abdu'l-Bahá. People gave their interpretation or understanding of a particular passage, and sometimes lively discussions ensued. Deepenings are the core of Bahá'í socialization—where Bahá'í ideology firmly establishes a global world view.

Pilgrimage

At the present time, the World Center in Haifa is the sole pilgrimage destination for Bahá'ís around the world. Bahá'ís sign up for a three- or nine-day visit; the wait is sometimes several months to several years. While on pilgrimage, Bahá'ís visit the Shrines of Bahá'u'lláh and the Báb, the tomb of `Abdu'l-Bahá, and the grave of his sister, as well as the International Teaching Center, the archives building, and the Universal House of Justice. Pilgrims may meet with a House of Justice member after dinner for discussion or possibly a member of the International Teaching Center. Thirty percent of Atlanta Bahá'ís indicated that they have fulfilled this obligation of their faith.

Fund Contributions

Like members of other religious organizations, Bahá'ís are encouraged to contribute money to their faith. Various Bahá'í funds support local, national, and international levels of Bahá'í organization.[12] Bahá'ís consider their projects—whether a health clinic in India or the House of Worship in Illinois—to be "gifts to the world." It is thus a privilege reserved only for Bahá'ís; outsiders are not allowed to contribute.

Fasting

The Bahá'í devotional life also follows the scriptural obligations for the month of fasting, the month of `Alá', comparable to March 2–21, and the last month in the Bahá'í year. Bahá'ís between the ages of 15 and 70 must observe the month of `Alá'. Fasting is similar in form to Muslim practice during Ramadan. Bahá'ís fast from sunup to sundown, refraining from eating, drinking, and smoking. There are some exemptions, however, for those who are traveling or pregnant.

The fast is a time of additional prayer and reflection for Atlanta Bahá'ís—although many say adhering to this spiritual discipline is difficult in a culture unaccustomed to the practice. Bahá'ís frequently gather to "break the fast" during the month of `Alá', assembling at sunset for large meals in one anothers' homes. In addition, predawn breakfasts reinforce a distinctive collective identity. Survey results indicate that more than half the respondents fully observed the 1994 fast, while another 20 percent partially observed it.

Personal devotional practices reinforce the Bahá'ís' sense of global identity by bringing the faithful into contact with the authority that undergirds a universal ideology. Reading scripture or reciting prayers written by the founders personalizes the Bahá'í's relationship to this authority. Giving material resources to local, national, and global funds helps Bahá'ís feel they are personally contributing to and sacrificing for a global institution-building project. Additionally, fulfilling pilgrimage requirements brings believers in contact with their World Center in all its symbolic grandeur. Thus, devotional practices are an essential element in creating a religious identity that is globally oriented.

Global Identity in Local Practice

The creation of a Bahá'í identity is fostered by two dialectical processes. The previous section focused on the particularization of the universal, as community members engage in collective and personal ritual that reinforces a world-embracing perspective. Geertz noted that ritual "shape[s] the spiritual consciousness of a people" (1973: 113). Not only does ritual establish local solidarity among a group of gathered believers, but Bahá'í ritualized activity also brings them into regular contact with higher levels of authority, thus "globalizing" their local identities. For example, in participating in the 19-Day Feast, Bahá'ís always receive communications from the national and global centers, helping the faithful to think globally. Messages of encouragement, advice, and hope periodically come directly from the Universal House of Justice—an institution held by Bahá'í writings to be infallible. The "Bahá'í Newsreels" reinforce the global compass of the individual's faith, as believers see Bahá'ís from Bangkok and Lagos engaging in teaching efforts and administrative duties similar to those carried out in Atlanta. Ritual brings "unity in diversity" to life on a global scale.

The inductive character of Bahá'í identity develops as local activity becomes a metaphor for the universal mission of societal transformation and world order anticipated in Bahá'í scripture. Feasts also encourage Bahá'ís to "[en]act locally" certain key features of their ideology. The administrative portion of the feast gives individuals a chance to participate in community-wide consultation, itself a democratic element in Bahá'í worship. Every 19 days, Bahá'ís discuss issues of relevance to their collective lives, with direct access to LSA participants. This interchange ensures that local authorities hear community concerns. The community supports local, as well as national and global, funds and projects.

The Bahá'í focus on racial unity and the "oneness of humanity" constitutes the ideological social principle at the heart of an emerging Bahá'í identity. Not only does the ideal of a united humanity undivided by racial or ethnic intolerance provide an initial attraction for converted Bahá'ís, but it constitutes much of the focus of Bahá'í activity. This focus is especially salient for Bahá'ís in Atlanta, who speak with dignity about their 85 years of affecting racial unity in a city known both for its institutionalized Jim Crow segregation and for the birthplace and headquarters of Dr. Martin Luther King, Jr. Atlanta Bahá'ís promote racial unity not only within their community, but also as a general societal goal. Thus, advocating racial unity and promoting the Bahá'í faith go hand in hand.

The Bahá'ís with whom I spoke explicitly linked their efforts at racial unity within the community to their global ideology and identity. A commonality that emerged from informal discussions, participant observation, and interviews with Atlanta Bahá'ís emphasized their intentional connection of local practices and activity to their global vision of world order. Seeking a united planet through obedience to the laws and principles of Bahá'u'lláh began in one's backyard: thus Bahá'ís embodied the popular phrase "think globally, act locally."

Racial unity was a recurrent theme in several of the Bahá'í meetings at which I was a participant-observer. Bahá'ís often recounted stories from their faith as models for their own behavior. One common theme was the trip made by 'Abdu'l-Bahá throughout Europe and North America in 1911–1913. While in America, he traveled from New York to San Francisco, teaching the Bahá'í faith and preaching about the desperate need for Bahá'ís to practice racial unity among themselves. One popular anecdote relates how 'Abdu'l-Bahá upset protocol in racially segregated Washington, D.C., by inviting a young black lawyer, Louis Gregory, to sit in the seat of honor at a dinner of Washington's elite society. Gregory—a new Bahá'í—went on to become one of the most prominent teachers of the Bahá'í faith in the United States. Bahá'ís in Atlanta, especially African American Bahá'ís, look to him as an important role model for dealing with a racist culture, a culture where separatism is often considered more attractive than unity. Stories of Gregory's actions in difficult situations—including his interracial marriage and his deportment in the face of prejudice—inform African American Bahá'ís in a way that Martin Luther King, Jr. or Malcolm X cannot. The regular narration of such stories links the Bahá'ís' global ideology, their faith's founders, and the unique racial history of the American South.

A willingness to address and resist racism is one of the characteristics of the Bahá'í community that has most appealed to many of its converts and certainly is one of the most widely communicated themes of the Bahá'í message. For many non-Bahá'ís, the assumed inevitability of racial unity is the hallmark of Bahá'í utopianism—a sort of naive vision of the world shorn of its hard political realities. However, for Bahá'ís, the unity of humanity is already a spiritual reality prevailing since the advent of the Bahá'í dispensation, eventually to become a social reality through the work of the Bahá'ís.[13]

One example of Atlanta Bahá'ís promotion of racial unity is their involvement with the Martin Luther King, Jr. Center for Nonviolent Social Change. Bahá'í involvement in the MLK Center has grown ever since the Bahá'ís marched as a group in the center's first parade in January 1986. Over the years, Bahá'ís have returned as one of many participants, entering a large float, comarshalling the televised parade, and contributing two members to the federal holiday commission that oversees the national King holiday. In recent years, Bahá'ís have sponsored an interfaith prayer service at the King Center during King Week in January, and a former UHJ member and a NSA member have spoken at various King Center–sponsored events. Survey results revealed that Bahá'í participation in these events is very high (nearly three-fourths report attending a Bahá'í-sponsored event during King Week), and is equally supported by all ethnic groups within the faith. During the 1994 King Week parade, more than half of all participants (by my count) were Bahá'ís, who showed up on an unusually cold, rainy winter day to witness to their belief in racial unity.

In Atlanta, the efforts for racial unity most tangibly express how Bahá'ís "think globally, but act locally." But racial unity is just one theme in a global world view that Bahá'ís themselves refer to as "the Bahá'í perspective"—the adoption of which is critical in the crystallization of a Bahá'í identity. When issues in the news were discussed at Bahá'í meetings, I would frequently hear Bahá'ís say, "Well, the Bahá'í perspective on that is. . . ." Many Bahá'ís referred to their perspective as if every member of the faith sees an issue in the same way. This presumed unanimity does not exist, as the often spirited discussions during deepenings make apparent. However, during my numerous conversations and interviews with Bahá'ís, an explicit Bahá'í perspective emerged in the crucible of Bahá'í institutions. That perspective is, in a word, global.

Although some Bahá'ís come into the faith with a universal outlook, it is enriched and deepened through reading Bahá'í scripture and serving in Bahá'í institutions. One Bahá'í said that he definitely sees the Bahá'í perspective as being different from the Christianity of his childhood:

> [Bahá'ís] are as concerned about Bahá'ís in China as we are in Europe, or anywhere—New Guinea—as we are those that are similar to us, in Europe or Australia. . . . I don't think Christians see Christians on the other side of the globe as part of their family. But I think Bahá'ís do.

He went on to talk about his global family

> You become global in the sense that your family is scattered around the globe. That was one of the things that I remember when I first came into the faith, realizing that no matter what city I was in anywhere, that if there is a Bahá'í community there, I've got family. And I think that contributes to a closeness in the Bahá'í community.

The Bahá'í perspective not only includes concepts, such as "the human family" and "the oneness of humanity," but it also highlights the universality of Bahá'ís' homes and communities. Bahá'ís frequently repeat Bahá'u'lláh's passage: "The earth is but one country, and mankind its citizens." One man explained how his experience outside the United States had opened up his world: "As a Bahá'í [in Europe and Africa], the world had grown, I had embraced the world. The world was my home. Wherever I was, it was home; wherever I laid my head was home."

Most Bahá'ís with whom I spoke agreed that the large Persian influx into the metro Atlanta Bahá'í community has added to and enriched their global perspective. One man said the following about the influence of Persian believers: "Yea, I think it's changed the way we [Bahá'ís] view ourselves . . . how we see ourselves as a community, that we are an international community." His wife added, "It also woke [Atlanta Bahá'ís] up to some degree, and made whole bunches of provincial folk realize it is an international religion."

They went on to mention that the Persian community has also taught Atlanta Bahá'ís about their faith, as well as introduced new tensions.

Having access to Bahá'u'lláh's writings in their original language long before the English translations, Persians were more educated on the nuances of the laws of fasting and the prescribed way of performing certain prayers, such as the obligatory prayers. Several respondents said that Persians also were more conscious of celebrating the Bahá'í holy days and festivals, which led to further incorporation of the Bahá'í calendar into non-Persian Bahá'ís' identity.

It is not only those who grow up in America and convert to the faith who appreciate the Bahá'í faith's globality. One Persian man, who with most of his family converted in Iran from Shi'ite Islam, also talked about the universality of the Bahá'í perspective. When asked to compare the faith in Iran and Atlanta, he said

> Not really [any difference]. That is the beauty of the Bahá'í faith. Everybody does it the same. As I said, I was in Africa before I came here. The Bahá'í faith . . . made the whole concept of religion so unique, you just go to Africa, you see Bahá'ís. The only thing you don't know about them is their name. When you find their name, then you have the same religion, the same beliefs, they are striving for the same oneness of mankind, and unity of mankind, and reduction of all prejudices. Basically striving for the same thing, not like Christianity or Islam with all the sects.

Another Persian man expressed these sentiments concerning the globality of his faith:

> If you want to know what means Bahá'í faith, you better leave your country, and go to another country. Then you will see really the power of Bahá'í faith . . . you will see regardless of your race, regardless of your nationality, regardless of your background, immediately you are home. Immediately you have friends. Friends who are better than your relatives, in some cases.

The Dialectic of the Local and the Global

This chapter has outlined the process by which a Bahá'í identity is socialized and lived. Bahá'ís develop their world view through the interaction of local and global institutions and by the practice of a specifically global ideology. Collective rituals following the Bahá'í calendar bring local Bahá'ís into frequent contact with institutional authority that teaches adherents to be "world citizens" by manifesting a Bahá'í perspective and thus particularizing a universal faith. The organization of Local Spiritual Assemblies requires Bahá'ís to learn consultation and power sharing amid a diverse membership, thus "universalizing" the particular social arrangements of the community by practicing just and democratic administration.

Even personal devotional practices of the Bahá'í faith facilitate this universal-particular or global-local dialectic. Prayer, fasting, reading Bahá'í writings, and especially pilgrimage and financial contributions inspire Bahá'ís to work for the "oneness of humanity"—a core value in the Bahá'í faith—in their local community. When Bahá'ís meet collectively to deepen their faith, they are required to practice unity in diversity, since no one individual can dictate the meaning of scripture for another.

As a global religion, the Bahá'í faith is distinguished from the more studied, fundamentalist movements, in that it inculcates in its adherents a universalizing, rather than particularizing, ethos and world view.[14] This world view is cultivated through various ideological and ritual mechanisms that link local community life to a global identity and social structure. Their beliefs include progressive revelation, a focus on racial unity, and the spiritual principle of unity in diversity. The center of community ritual—the 19-Day Feast—is a local act that reinforces the global expanse of the Bahá'í faith and repeatedly exposes community members to the authority of their universalizing movement and world view—"thinking globally."

NOTES

1. The author would like to acknowledge the Faculty Research and Support fund grant # 111640 at the University of Houston–Clear Lake for assistance in preparing this chapter.

2. For further background on the history of the Bahá'í faith, see Hatcher and Martin 1985, Esslemont 1970. The 1992 *Britannica Book of the Year* declared that the Bahá'í faith had established significant communities in 205 countries, second only to Christianity in its geographic distribution. *The World Christian Encyclopedia*, published in 1982, estimated that the worldwide Bahá'í community grew by 3.63 percent since 1970—the fastest growing of the independent world religions.

3. My attendance at the World Congress began 18 months of intensive ethnographic fieldwork which included participant observation, in-depth interviews,

archival research, and distribution of a questionnaire to nearly 500 members of the metropolitan Atlanta Bahá'í community.

4. While most converts were seekers who were dissatisfied with their previous religion, a small minority were pulled into the faith by the prophetic claims found in Bahá'í scripture (such as Bahá'u'lláh being the return of Christ, or the promised one of Islam, the Mahdi) rather than pushed by disaffection with their church, synagogue, or mosque.

5. More than 65 percent of the survey respondents indicated having a college diploma or higher level of education. Nearly 70 percent worked in white-collar or professional occupations.

6. Conversion to the Bahá'í faith parallels many features discussed in the sociology of religion conversion literature (see Lofland and Stark 1965; Snow and Phillips 1980). Empirical evidence indicates that social networks are the most crucial factor in pulling individuals into nontraditional religious movements (Stark and Bainbridge 1980). These relationships with trusted friends and family help potential converts to overcome the "foreignness" of the Bahá'í religion. The host of Islamic references, the unfamiliar Persian names, and the practice of ritual fasting and obligatory prayers all create boundaries that many converts found difficult to cross. At one point during my fieldwork, a recent convert became embarassed when she stumbled over a Persian word while reading aloud. An elderly Persian woman reassured her that no matter how she pronounced, "God *heard* [speaker's emphasis] you correctly."

7. Duties of the host or hostess rotate among the active members of the community—allowing each member to shape the worship experience.

8. Since 1982, six resolutions have been passed by the U.S. Senate at the urging of the NSA.

9. Although survey data cannot address the issue of interracial friendship, I observed that interracial unity was not limited to official Bahá'í gatherings. I attended many informal Bahá'í gatherings where people of all ethnic backgrounds readily socialized. This was especially evident among Bahá'í youth, whose parents told me their kids had always had interracial playmates and these relationships continued into young adulthood.

10. Although Bahá'ís are to suspend work on the more important Holy Days, many Bahá'ís are unable or unwilling to take the day off. Survey results indicate that more than 60 percent of Bahá'í respondents attend Holy Day celebrations "most of the time" or "often."

11. Almost 45 percent of survey respondents said that they regularly attended one of several advertised deepenings in the metropolitan Atlanta area.

12. International funds are monies used by the UHJ for social and economic development projects around the world such as schools, health clinics,

242 MICHAEL M^CMULLEN

and similar services. One such fund supports construction projects at the World Center on Mount Carmel in Haifa. Nearly 92 percent of those I surveyed contributed to their local funds, while 70 percent had given to national funds in the last year.

13. Several Bahá'í deepenings that I attended revolved around the 1991 NSA publication, "The Vision of Race Unity: America's Most Challenging Issue," a 12-page pamphlet that outlines the "spiritual solution" to racism in this country and invites other to investigate the Bahá'í faith as a model for bringing about social change. Bahá'ís distributed the pamphlet widely to introduce nonbelievers to the faith and to teach them its ideology.

14. Robertson, along with most scholars, focuses on those movements that revitalize traditional identities (while modifying them for the modern context). He does, however, admit that: "The fundamentalist movements concerned with the revitalization of their own particular societies . . . are indeed attempting to bring back the tribal gods of society or community, while those movements which are more explicitly oriented to the global scene are attempting to vitalize and establish a universal God for a global community" (Robbins and Robertson 1987:48). This latter attempt accurately characterizes Bahá'ís efforts to universalize social and religious identity and establish the mechanisms that link a Bahá'í world view to a local community.

References

The Bahá'ís: A Profile of the Bahá'í Faith and its Worldwide Community. 1994. New York: Office of Public Information, Bahá'í International Community.

Berger, Peter L. 1967. *The Sacred Canopy: Elements of a Sociological Theory of Religion*. New York: Doubleday.

Durkheim, Emile. [1915] 1965. *The Elementary Forms of the Religious Life*. New York: Free Press.

Encyclopaedia Britannica. 1992 *Britannica Book of the Year*. New York: Encyclopaedia Britannica.

Esslemont, J. E. 1970. *Bahá'u'lláh and the New Era*. Wilmette, IL: Bahá'í Publishing Trust.

Geertz, Clifford. 1973. *The Interpretation of Cultures*. New York: Basic Books.

Giddens, Anthony. 1991. *Modernity and Self-Identity: Self and Society in the Late Modern Age*. Stanford: Stanford University Press.

Hatcher, William S. and J. Douglas. 1985. *The Bahá'í Faith: The Emerging Global Religion*. New York: Harper and Row.

Lechner, Frank J. 1991. "Fundamentalism Revisited." Pp. 77–97 in *In Gods We Trust: New Patterns of Religious Pluralism in America*, edited by Thomas Robbins and Dick Anthony. New Brunswick: Transaction Books.

Lofland, John and Rodney Stark. 1965. "Becoming a World-Saver: A Theory of Conversion to a Deviant Perspective." *American Sociological Review* 30:862–75.

National Spiritual Assembly of the Bahá'ís of the United States. 1991. *The Vision of Race Unity: America's Most Challenging Issue*. Wilmette, IL: Bahá'í Publishing Trust.

Rabbani, Shoghi. 1963. *The Advent of Divine Justice*. Wilmette, IL: Bahá'í Publishing Trust.

Robbins, Thomas and Roland Robertson. 1987. *Church-State Relations: Tensions and Transitions*. New Brunswick: Transaction Books.

Robertson, Roland. 1992. *Globalization: Social Theory and Global Culture*. London: Sage.

Robertson, Roland and William R. Garrett, eds. 1991. *Religion and Global Order*. New York: Paragon House Publishers.

Robertson, Roland and Frank J. Lechner. 1985. "Modernization, Globalization, and the Problem of Culture in World-systems Theory." *Theory, Culture and Society* 2(3):103–17.

Roof, Wade Clark and William McKinney. 1987. *American Mainline Religion: Its Changing Shape and Future*. New Brunswick: Rutgers University Press.

Snow, David A. and Cynthia L. Phillips. 1980. "The Lofland-Stark Conversion Model: A Critical Reassessment." *Social Problems* 27(4):430–47.

Stark, Rodney and William Sims Bainbridge. 1980. "Networks of Faith: Interpersonal Bounds and Recruitment to Cults and Sects." *American Journal of Sociology* 85(6):1376–95.

Taherzadeh, Adib. 1992. *The Covenant of Bahá'u'lláh*. Oxford: George Ronald.

Universal House of Justice. 1985. *The Promise of World Peace*. Haifa: Universal House of Justice.

Weber, Max. 1922. *The Sociology of Religion*. Boston: Beacon Press.

Conclusion

THE CULTURAL TURN

Stories, Logic, and the Quest for Identity in American Religion

ROBERT WUTHNOW

In the *Eclogues*, Virgil (1984: I, l. 5) writes triumphantly of the "great cycle of the ages" that comes about through the renewal of each generation. The chapters in this book are perhaps a modest example of what Virgil had in mind. They are written by a new generation—by younger scholars who bring critical vision and fresh energy to the study of American religion. There is an implicit critique in these essays of the ways in which previous generations have conceptualized their material. Most of the authors suggest that American religion has become more complicated than earlier theories could have predicted. Through the case studies they examine, they challenge us to adopt new ways of thinking.

But how well do they succeed? I am hardly a disinterested party to this question. Some of the formulations that these authors find inadequate are ones to which I have contributed; other suggestions that receive more favorable remarks can also be traced to my work (Wuthnow, 1988). Certainly, I am of a different generation. Yet, it is for this reason that the editors have asked me to offer some concluding observations. I do so in the spirit of extending current debates about American religion, seeking both to illuminate some of the underlying assumptions in the present essays and to situate them within larger developments in the scholarly study of religion.

Ethnography in the Study of Religion

The single thread that does most to unify these essays is their shared methodology: all are grounded primarily in ethnographic research. Shoshanah Feher knows her fellowship of Messianic Jews thoroughly. Penny Becker's study of congregational conflicts in Oak Park emerges from observations in these churches and synagogues. Timothy J. Nelson spent several years studying the AME church in Charleston. All the chapters provide verbatim quotes from real people and an inside look at a particular expression of American religion. An initial question for consideration is thus what we learn from these studies about the strengths (and weaknesses) of ethnographic research.

One lesson worth emphasizing is that ethnography is itself a highly diverse set of techniques and practices (see also Bell 1994; Burawoy 1991; Davidman 1991). In some of the chapters, it comes close to being what anthropologists have always considered most important: direct observation of social events while they are happening through firsthand research in the field. For example, Nancy L. Eiesland's two-year study of an Atlanta-area megachurch involved personal observations that permit her to describe in rich detail the character of its programs and services. But in other cases, ethnography clearly means something else. Some of the evidence was collected by examining church records to learn about events that had already transpired. Some of it came from interviewing people who had been party to these events. Through these interviews, the researchers solicited comments and reflections that might not have been present during the event itself.

The meaning of ethnography that fits most of these studies is that it consists of qualitative research, especially research that permits people to use their own language and to express their own ideas. But even this definition falters; for instance, Becker presents some quantitative summaries of the events in her 23 congregations, and many of the other chapters make some use of secondary information provided by surveys.

To call these ethnographic studies stretches the meaning of the term in another way. In sociology the term "ethnography" is often used pejoratively to mean a study that is primarily descriptive. These studies are rich in descriptive detail. But they also are concerned with theoretical questions. They are not strictly inductive, but reflect questions that the researchers brought with them as a result of having read and thought about theoretical generalizations.

In my view, this is an instructive way in which to understand the role of ethnography. It is internally diverse, permitting researchers to make firsthand observations, to interview respondents, to examine texts, and even (I would add) to conduct an occasional survey or make enumerations on the basis of their field notes. Ethnography serves best when it provides an *in-depth* examination of its subject matter. Thus, a good ethnography of a congregation builds on the researcher's extensive familiarity with its people, its public services, its backstage deliberations, and perhaps its history. An ethnography of a small group within a congregation may be richer and more thorough than one of an entire congregation. But it is also conceivable to do an ethnography of an entire community, again recognizing that certain limitations will be invoked by the wider scope of its coverage. I would also insist that some of the best studies of entire denominations, regions, ethnic subcultures, and institutions within the broader society are characterized by an ethnographic quality: extensive familiarity with a subject that comes from combining data from a variety of sources.

Ethnography is, as the editors emphasize, particularly well suited to an interest in the cultural aspects of religion. Through the words of people that are quoted in the foregoing chapters, we learn something of how they view their worlds. Although we gain only a selective impression of what religion means to them, we are able to see that it is meaningful. The description provided in some of the chapters of how the worship service was conducted or of where the church was located serves a similar function. This is the *texture* that permits the reader to judge whether or not the author's interpretations are believable. When theoretical generalizations are offered, ethnography provides the details that help us decide whether these generalizations are credible.

From this perspective, there may be little disagreement about the value of good ethnography. The difficulty comes only when ethnographers pit their own particular kind of ethnography *against* other methods, as if a choice were required (Eliasoph and Lichterman 1996). Take the following example. Suppose an ethnographer says, well, you cannot really understand the family unless you spend time sitting in people's living rooms talking to them and observing their interaction, and for this reason the data collected by the U.S. Bureau of the Census on families is worthless! Of course this would be a ridiculous claim. Yet some of the carping about attitude surveys that ethnographers register takes the same form. One does not have to choose. One should recognize the contribution that different methods make.

In this sense, then, the present studies have the greatest value when viewed as complementary to those using other methods, rather than being regarded as an alternative. If some of the chapters suggest a need to nuance discussions of American religion that treat it in terms of denominational identities or in terms of left-right distinctions, then there is merit in considering what the authors add to these broader discussions. The point is not "one or the other," but "both-and."

Religious Complexity

A second strand that runs through these essays is their insistence on the complexity of American religion, an argument that also appears increasingly in studies of the history of American religion (e.g., Albanese 1991; Butler 1992). This complexity is evident in that chapter topics range from Jewish and Catholic groups to African American Protestants and include observations of large and small congregations located in suburbs and inner-city areas, as well as among gays, Bahá'ís, and religious pressure groups. To some extent, this complexity is prefigured in the use of ethnography itself. Especially when multiple methods are used or when in-depth observations are made in a single congregation or community, one is more likely to perceive complexity than if one only observes a phenomenon from afar.

But the present emphasis on complexity is a reflection of a larger tendency in the study of American religion (and probably in the human sciences generally). The one feature that most clearly distinguishes contemporary scholarship from that of, say, the 1950s or 1960s is its rejection of what the editors of this volume refer to in their introduction as "linear narratives of disembodied trends." Recent studies not only dispute the claims of theories that emphasize, for instance, secularization and modernization; they also reject the value of such theories, preferring instead to talk about gender differences, multiple vocabularies, local cultures, contradictory impulses, negotiation, and the construction of meaning.

Taken to an extreme, an emphasis on complexity leads away from theory building and from the search for meaningful empirical generalizations. It robs the human sciences of any capacity to generate cumulative knowledge by arguing that only the idiosyncratic details of a particular case, in all its complexity, can be observed. This extreme is what some scholars decry as a shift toward postmodernism (Lyotard 1984; Wyschogrod 1990).

The chapters in this volume do not illustrate an extreme emphasis of this kind. Most of them provide low-level generalizations that help the reader to understand the central aspects of the case under consideration and to imagine how other cases might be similar or different. The role that complexity plays here is partly to suggest simply that American religion, by any indication, has been complex throughout its history and is now more diverse than it was understood to be in the past. New immigrant communities, gay and lesbian organizations, cults, and syncretic forms of religious expression illustrate this diversity. In addition, these chapters emphasize that social processes are complex—meaning that multiple languages and motives are present, that groups are subject to crosspressures, and that many factors may be involved in determining how groups arrive at decisions.

It is too early to tell whether the current research will lead to some new theories in the future. At present, the debunking of received theoretical wisdom still appears to be useful, especially when it leads to a greater appreciation of the ways in which established theories have been influenced by accepting as normative certain scientific, Christian, or masculine experiences. It also appears likely that the result of studies like the ones in this volume will be a shift toward greater levels of theoretical abstraction as guiding metaphors, rather than the creation of substantive propositions. Thus, a rational-choice perspective dominates some discussions of religion, but it seldom provides hypotheses that can be proven or disproven as evidence of the unique validity of this perspective. Much the same might be said about theories of conflict, resource mobilization, or subcultures.

The Construction of Identity

Another claim that finds prominence in these essays is the idea that religion is centrally concerned with the construction of identity. The editors highlight this emphasis in the introduction, where they suggest, as other writers have (Fontinell 1993; Gergen 1991; Taylor 1989) that religious identity has become problematic because of the changing cultural and religious landscape in which we live. When individuals move from one religious community to another, they often experience a sense of dislocation (as one of my interviewees did in remarking, "I'm a Presbyterian who's still a Baptist underneath"). Whole communities also find themselves having to carve out hyphenated identities (for example, as Korean Presbyterians or as Hispanic Catholics).

In emphasizing the problems of religious identity, these essays do not succumb to a focus that privileges only the inner workings of individual lives. Much to their credit, each of the authors situates the quest for religious identity in a social context. Nelson shows how African Americans in Charleston acquire an identity as Christians amid a neighborhood with exceptionally high levels of crime and drug abuse. Edward R. Gray and Scott L. Thumma situate their understanding of gay Christians in relation to churches, movements, and the wider culture.

Religious identity, as described in these essays, is often what might be called a "deep" aspect of an individual's self-concept. It becomes, as it were, internalized to the point that an individual can take it for granted. Yet the more important point is that identity is constantly being negotiated and renegotiated. Michael McMullen's Bahá'í followers do not simply think of themselves as members of a group but think often and in diverse ways about what it means to be a Bahá'í. At Eastside Chapel, Nelson's church members symbolically draw distinctions between themselves and others, doing so ritually (as they listen to sermons) and investing these distinctions with a strong sense of emotion. Feher's Messianic Jews and Janet Stocks's feminist evangelicals also struggle to define themselves, in these cases in relation to at least two cultural traditions that are often at odds with each other.

The quest for religious identity is part of the broader phenomenon of spiritual seeking that has been associated with baby boomers (Hoge, et al. 1994; Roof 1993) but that appears to be increasingly characteristic of older and younger Americans as well. As people shop for the religions that satisfy them, they often display a consumer mentality (just as when they shop for fast food), and this mentality has led a number of observers to worry that spirituality has become too much focused on personal identity and too little rooted in the "collective memory" of an authoritative religious tradition. The lack of an anchoring community also prompts concerns among social observers about whether or not people who make up their own identities (perhaps adopting several identities) can function as stable and responsible citizens. Thus, a person who offers several religious identities to describe herself (such as an interviewee of mine who said her religious preference was "Methodist Taoist Native American Quaker Russian Orthodox Buddhist Jew") encourages critics to assume that religious identities have simply become too shallow to be taken seriously.

Yet the foregoing chapters cast the quest for religious identity in a different light. They show that people can negotiate complex definitions of themselves *and* participate seriously and loyally in a religious community. For instance, the Messianic Jews that Feher examines display an ability, as she suggests, to engage in complicated boundary work that is at once flexible and supportive of commitment to the congregation. Although their loyalty is more tenuous, Stocks's evangelical feminists (especially those from Reformed Protestant backgrounds) are also sufficiently rooted in their tradition to "stay and fight," even though they have defined themselves differently from other people who have similar backgrounds.

Some of what appears to be happening in cases such as these is that multiple communities are being invoked. Evangelical feminists may be ostracized by the leaders of their denomination or congregation, but the declining significance of these communities makes it possible for them to receive support through informal networks, telephone calls, and newsletters. Similarly, in the case of my "Methodist Taoist . . . ," she could still maintain a complex identity because her particular Methodist church openly questioned narrow interpretations of Methodist tradition and provided its members a wide variety of opportunities including sweat lodges, support groups, and protest marches. Identity can, therefore, be reconciled with participation in religious communities, even though the negotiation of identity takes considerably more effort than it may have in more tightly bound settings in the past.

A Focus on Culture

Perhaps the broadest contribution that these essays make lies in their emphasis on the cultural aspects of religion. Becker's analysis of congregational conflicts provides perhaps the clearest example. Her chapter privileges what she terms "moral logics." She finds that congregants are often torn between a moral logic of caring and a moral logic focusing on the application of authoritative truth. When confronted with difficult issues, these logics come to the foreground. Congregational debates provide an occasion for deciding which logic will prevail. Certainly there are other factors involved as well. For example, pastoral leadership, the size of a congregation, how rich or poor it is, and its relationship to a denomination might be worthy of consideration. But Becker is most interested in the cultural aspects of these conflicts. Similarly, Stocks is concerned about loyalty to particular denominations, and she understands the reasons for loyalty or defection, not in terms of an economistic logic, but as a process that is negotiated through cultural understandings. Eiesland, too, is especially interested in the cultural styles of congregations, here focusing on those that have become, or that are competing with, megachurches.

These examples are part of a broader development that has been re-shaping the study of religion in recent years. Researchers have given greater attention to the role of stories in the lives of individuals and in the collective lives of congregations (Wind and Lewis 1994; Ammerman 1997). The substantive and formal aspects of sermons have been exam-ined (Witten 1993). How moral reasoning is influenced by religious convictions has been emphasized (Tipton 1982). The symbolic demar-cations that religious groups draw between themselves and others, and the ways in which these demarcations create religious identities, have also sparked interest.

It is important to acknowledge that cultural factors have been promi-nent in studies of religion since the inception of the human sciences. Marx and Engels's *German Ideology* (1947) provides an insightful un-derstanding of the ways in which religious consciousness is constructed, while Durkheim's *Elementary Forms of the Religious Life* (1915) can be read for its interpretation of religious rituals and symbolic bound-aries, and Weber's writings on religion in *The Protestant Ethic and the Spirit of Capitalism* (1958) and elsewhere are replete with ideas about the moral implications of various ways of construing ultimate meaning. In the work by American scholars that was deeply influenced by these classical contributions, such as that of Talcott Parsons (1951, 1971), Peter L. Berger (1969), Clifford Geertz (1973, 1983), and Robert N. Bellah (1970), the role of meaning, values, and symbols was also given central attention.

To an important extent, the work of the past decade or so has been influenced by these theoretical contributions, most of which remain re-quired reading for American graduate students specializing in the soci-ology of religion. Some additional perspectives have been incorporated into recent thinking (for example, from Pierre Bourdieu, Victor Turner, or Jurgen Habermas). But the greatest contributions have been simply to provide a much richer empirical sense of what we mean by culture as well as an understanding of how it operates. Ideas as different as "tool kits" (Swidler 1985) and "culture wars" (Hunter 1991) have helped to legitimate the study of culture, and scholars have spared no effort in examining its manifestations in religious movements and in established settings alike.

The decision to focus on culture cannot be understood only in terms of its prominence in theoretical tradition, however. Certainly it is possible to study religion in terms of the rational choices of its actors or the resources that its leaders mobilize or its organizational dynamics. But, in a word, culture is what makes religion interesting. Religion is, after all, centrally concerned with beliefs and convictions, with texts and their interpretation, with the dissemination of the revealed word, with the ways in which meaning and purpose is constructed, and with the traditions that accumulate around particular religious communities. To avoid focus on these aspects of religion would be like trying to understand apple pie without paying attention to apples.

None of this is meant to suggest that religious culture can be understood fully without paying attention to the power plays that characterize leaders and their followers, for example, or the finances on which religious organizations depend. But the contribution of sociological work to, say, the study of church finances differs from that of an economist precisely in paying attention to the beliefs about work and money, the content of stewardship sermons, and the tacit rituals that make up the economic culture of congregations. In addition, some of the current emphasis on culture also stems from the fact that these other characteristics can often be left in the background. That is, American religion has largely been free of government restrictions, and it has enjoyed the legitimacy and the financial resources that have allowed it to flourish as a marketplace of beliefs and practices.

The present essays help to clarify some of what may be meant by religious culture. Matthew P. Lawson's essay is particularly helpful because it begins with familiar understandings of religious culture, moves to a consideration of stories, and then shows how these stories may be capable of guiding social action. His discussion extends my own work and that of Greeley (1981), Linde (1993), and others who have been interested in the narrative dimenson of religious culture. In this work, the value of narrative has been taken to lie in its ability to present concrete exemplars around which social action may be modeled, to contain the multivocality that may be required in formulations of complex motives, to unify the intellectual and emotional aspects of religion, or to point to the ineffable quality of religious experience. In Lawson's formulation, stories also become important because of the relationships among social actors (or objects) that may be encoded within them. Thus, stories about charismatic believers' relationships to God, Christ, or the Holy Spirit provide models for these believers' relationships to their spouses or employers. As Lawson also emphasizes, these stories become effective, not simply by being heard, but by being ritually enacted in ways that help to dramatize the symbolic distinctions on which they are based.

An important byproduct of Lawson's analysis is also his suggestion that social researchers make greater use of personal narratives in their studies of religion. This is a novel suggestion because it flies in the face of criticisms that have been raised about the uses of interviews more generally, especially criticisms emphasizing the role of interviewers in guiding respondents' answers and ones suggesting that interviews cannot be properly interpreted without observations of subjects in other real-life contexts. Lawson's own interviews are greatly enriched by the fact that he was able to observe his respondents in the prayer group he studied. Yet his analysis also shows that people construct their relationships with others based on events that may be invisible to the ethnographer and that they do so over a long period of time. Personal narratives should not be taken as a factually accurate rendition of these events, but as first-person efforts to make sense of one's life. Most people, it appears, develop narratives that help them understand the major continuities and discontinuities in their spiritual journey. As individual biographies have gained legitimacy in the wider culture (through the use of curriculum vitaes, court cases that emphasize personal responsibility, schooling, and the like; see Thomas, et al. 1987), their importance in religious settings also merits serious consideration (perhaps especially in settings where testimonials, journaling, and concepts of faith development or spiritual formation are emphasized).

Although Lawson's chapter is concerned with normative action, this concern comes more fully to the forefront in the chapters that attempt to formulate understandings of moral discourse itself. Following the example of Bellah, et al. (1985), Wolfe (1989), and others, these chapters take up the idea that sociology needs to contribute to our understanding of the ways in which moral judgments are made and legitimated. Elfriede Wedam focuses on the ways in which pro-life activists make such judgments. Becker's use of the idea of moral logics is another example. A moral logic is an argument about what should be done in a given situation. Unlike a story, it emphasizes following a course of action based on the assertion of a primary principle. Although Becker does not emphasize it as such, a moral logic can also be a rationale given after the fact for an action taken.

The study of moral logics is a particularly promising area for further research. Philosophical work often presumes to know how people think about moral issues and poses hypothetical examples to illustrate strengths or deficiencies in moral logic. Yet the ways in which people actually talk about moral issues are often more complex than such work acknowledges. One contribution that empirical studies make is to show how people draw on basic principles (such as principles of right or wrong, justice, truth, or goodness) to legitimate specific courses of action. Another contribution is to examine more closely the styles of reasoning that are encoded in these legitimating arguments. Some studies have suggested that people can perhaps be classified into broad categories, depending on which kind of moral reasoning they exercise. An additional contribution is the examination of "secondary warrants" that are invoked to explain why a course of action is reasonable despite evidence to the contrary (for example, why it makes sense to trust people even though they have violated one's trust in the past). Yet another contribution shows how social contexts temper the application of absolute principles. As Wedam suggests, these contextual considerations may provide the common ground on which efforts to resolve major culture wars may be based (see also Rudy 1996).

Beyond such general issues as stories and moral logics, several of the chapters also supply insights about particular aspects of religious culture. Nelson's chapter on the AME church in Charleston, for instance, illustrates one way in which ethnographic studies contribute to our understanding of substantive issues. Nelson emphasizes the suspicion and mistrust that prevails in many low-income, inner-city neighborhoods. This observation is one that he buttresses with evidence from other case studies; it might also be supported through the many surveys that have recently examined the social correlates of mistrust, showing its prominence among people in lower-income groups, among African Americans, in cities, and in other areas with high crime rates (Kohut 1997). What Nelson usefully contributes is insight into the ways in which religious language gives expression to mistrust. Although one might suppose that religious participation would encourage greater levels of trust (as students of social capital would suggest; e.g., Coleman 1990), Nelson shows that religious language can legitimate mistrust, by suggesting, for example, reasons why fellow believers may be hypocrites or "not really saved." He also shows that mistrust may have mixed consequences when viewed from the standpoint of the congregation. On the one hand, it may encourage people to stick to themselves, rather than truly cooperating with others; on the other hand, as in some religious cults, mistrust can become an instrument by which high levels of commitment are encouraged among the faithful.

Another substantive contribution is illustrated in the chapter by Gray and Thumma. It provides vivid evidence of the importance of the performative aspects of religious culture. Although several other chapters also emphasize these aspects (especially Lawson, Nelson, and Feher), the gay bar that Gray and Thumma studied provides an occasion for considering the ways in which people may actively create their own performances in order to dramatize certain commitments. Unlike some conceptions of traditional religious services that assume rituals to be "there," simply for the taking, Gray and Thumma point to the self-conscious or reflexive character of some rituals. That is, participants may deliberately take on several identities, pose in ways that aim to challenge or violate conventional social categories, or adopt a playful stance toward their performances.

An extension of work such as this would perhaps raise questions about the roles of intentionality, staging, and reflexivity in other religious settings as well. For example, Harding's (forthcoming) research among fundamentalists in Jerry Falwell's congregation in Virginia suggests that there may be a kind of postmodernism even in a setting such as this that permits believers to entertain doubts about what they are doing and saying or that better enables them to interact with nonbelievers. Or for a different example, Schmidt's (1997) research on ventriloquism reveals ways in which the boundaries between magic and religion, veracity and deception, and belief and hypocrisy have been contested over the entire course of American religious history (see also Halttunen 1982).

Another lacunae that these essays help to fill is the relationship between religious culture and the specific social contexts in which it occurs. Much of what is commonly known about religious culture in the United States comes from national surveys and from broad characterizations (e.g., having to do with narcissism, therapy, and culture wars), both of which may be unduly influenced by the mass media and are certainly likely to miss the nuances of particular locations. Studies that draw on neoinstitutional theory (DiMaggio and Powell 1991), such as Eiesland's chapter, recognize the role of culture in shaping the character of formal organizations, while studies of congregational subcultures, such as the chapter by Nelson, pay attention to the interplay between what happens in congregations and what takes place in their communities.

Eiesland's chapter is especially helpful because it emphasizes the influence that local churches have on one another. Particularly when there are large disparities in membership size among these churches, it is likely that efforts either to imitate or distance themselves from one another will occur. Extending this analysis, other studies might usefully consider the ways in which megachurches themselves form reference groups for one another.

Characterizing American Spirituality

Apart from the specific claims that the authors put forward, I want to consider what we may learn from these essays about the character of spirituality itself. Perhaps the point that comes through most clearly in these essays is the tension that presently exists in American culture between a spirituality that finds itself at home in churches, synagogues, mosques, fellowship halls, and other places of worship, on the one hand; and, on the other hand, a spirituality that exists in the interstices between congregations, for example, through the private encounters of individuals with the sacred, or through innovative social forms, such as small groups or activist networks. Many Americans continue to practice their faith by affiliating with formal religion, but many more express their spirituality most deeply in other ways.

This point is worth emphasizing because it raises questions that remain unanswered in the foregoing chapters. Ethnographic studies are particularly well suited to making observations about groups. They are less suited to examining the private lives of individuals. In my study of small groups (such as Bible studies and prayer fellowships), for example, my fellow researchers and I were able to learn a lot about the dynamics of these groups by spending between six months and two years participating in them (Wuthnow 1994a). Yet my thinking about their role in spiritual formation was sharply challenged one day when an interviewee who had spoken at length about her group responded to a question about her spiritual journey, "Oh, well, that's a different subject; let me tell you about that." In fact, her comment provoked me to launch a separate study focusing on private devotional practices and their role in the spiritual formation of individuals. For this research, neither a survey nor ethnographic observation made sense; lengthy personal interviews (sometimes supplemented by interviews with spouses, parents, grandparents, or children) proved most useful.

Some social spaces are also more open to outside observers than others. Congregations have generally been an amenable place in which to make observations. In comparison, most corporations do not permit social scientists free access to their corridors and business meetings.

Thus, when I was engaged in research on the relationships between religious faith and work and money, I made extensive use of in-depth interviews to ask people about their work (Wuthnow 1994b). In such interviews, stories often become the vehicles by which respondents describe events. An experienced interviewer learns to ask questions that encourage respondents to tell stories they have actually heard or told in other settings, as well as questions that elicit more direct responses. In this study it also proved helpful to compare stories told by people in widely differing occupations, to compare responses given when people thought they were supposed to be talking about religion with those given when people thought the topic was simply their work, and to compare these qualitative responses with the more structured answers given in a national survey.

The danger in drawing too many conclusions about American religion from ethnographic observations in congregations is partly that spirituality occurs in many places besides congregations. As Gray and Thumma demonstrate, it may be present at a gay bar; or as Lawson suggests, it may need to be understood in the rivalries and differences that characterize sibling relationships. Of course, one could argue that such settings pale in significance compared with congregations as the *institutions* in which spirituality is shaped. Yet there is mounting evidence that many other institutionalized settings play a prominent role in shaping American spirituality as well. Certainly the material culture of the family—Bibles, candles, religious pictures—is proving to be a rich subject of study (Joselit 1994; McDannell 1986). For the many Americans who view community service as a kind of religion, the soup kitchen and the volunteer center are places in which spirituality is expressed. Other locations that may have a profound impact on Americans' spirituality include the recording studio, the concert hall, the athletic stadium, and the publishing house.

Researchers have also raised questions that suggest a need for deeper probing into the life of congregations themselves. In her study of women's Bible study groups, for example, Jody Davie (1995) realized that what was not being said was probably as important as what was being said. After participating in several of these groups for a period of months, she interviewed members privately to ask whether they agreed with what was being said in the groups and why they did not speak about certain subjects. She found that silence played a significant role in maintaining a semblance of consensus in the groups. Another aspect of congregations that seldom receives attention involves the private relationships between clergy and laity (Warner 1988). In my study of congregational finances (Wuthnow 1997), I found that few laity ever talked with clergy about their views on this topic. Numerous discussions that took place in counseling settings and in committee meetings are also off-limits to the typical ethnographer.

The larger point illustrated by these examples is that American religion is as complex as the essays in this volume suggest—and considerably more so. To the typical pastor, church leader, or seminary professor, much of this diversity may be easy to ignore. The people who attract the leaders' attention are the ones who fill the pews, pay the bills, and participate actively at congregational meetings. To the typical journalist, the portrait of American religion may seem more diverse, but only in stylized ways. News reportage of necessity focuses on events and thus ranges from a visit by the pope, to a controversial ruling by a denominational assembly, to a PromiseKeepers' stadium rally, to a mass suicide among cult members. When Americans stop to think about it, many know that their own experiences in religion are rather different from those captured either by clergy or journalists. They know that their deepest experience with spirituality came, for example, from deciding to give birth at home or from home schooling their children. They know that their father's spirituality was shaped largely by participating in the Masons. They know that their own spirituality is shaped by a recent television program or book about angels (Anderson 1992), by the book they picked up recently about wiccans and Druids, by their search for their roots (Norris 1993), or by the death of one of their children (Wolterstorff 1987).

Diversity of this kind can be sufficiently bewildering that any effort to make sense of it seems hopeless. Yet such diversity is not without pattern or causes. In the largest terms, the market economy in which we live, the individualism that characterizes American culture, and the prominence of the mass media and the entertainment industry are among the factors that have encouraged this high level of diversity. As the essays in this volume suggest, both the entrepreneurialism of religious leaders and the ways in which religious groups adapt to their social context (perhaps inadvertently, as Nelson shows, or through deliberate "niche marketing," as Eiesland documents) also contribute to this diversity. Certainly the extent to which the United States is once again becoming a nation of immigrants will continue to enhance its religious diversity.

Spiritual Practices

The conceptual development that is proving helpful for sorting out some of the more personalized kinds of religious diversity is the idea of spiritual practices. Drawn in some cases from the work of moral philosophers such as MacIntyre (1984) and Stout (1988) and in other cases from cultural theorists such as Bourdieu and Bakhtin (Turner 1994), practices are understood to be patterned clusters of activities organized around the pursuit of some intrinsically desirable good or purpose. Practices are inevitably social, because they conform to certain social expectations, but they are not necessarily performed communally or in firsthand contact with other people (for instance, praying or playing chess against a computer are social practices, even though they are performed alone). Practices are thus ways of understanding what may take place in congregations but also draw attention to the more individualized or loosely connected activities of which spirituality may be composed (Dykstra and Bass 1997).

The idea of spiritual practices is consonant both with the diversity of American religion and with the present emphasis on understanding its cultural aspects. McMullen's chapter on Bahá'ís clearly exemplifies such diversity. Bahá'í followers often engage in private devotional practices that explicitly recognize religious diversity but also seek to provide unity through these personal rituals. Bahá'í faith also aims to deepen devotional life beyond what may be evident among more casual seekers, thus providing a corrective to the dabbling that is sometimes associated with other universalistic religions or New Age expressions of spirituality (Heelas 1990, 1993, 1996).

More generally, practices are usually pieced together in creative ways, perhaps even by combining elements of different religious traditions. They are given coherence by core narratives, which generally focus on an individual's spiritual journey. Yet they are also governed by the moral logics of religious communities (Taves 1986; Kerr 1993; Orsi 1996). For instance, hospitality is a practice that has long been emphasized in religious settings, and it can be performed in as diverse ways as volunteering at a homeless shelter or inviting guests to a seder (Pineda 1997). Other examples of practices include finding ways to honor the body through one's conceptions of spirituality, engaging in contemplative prayer, or expressing spirituality through art or literature (Ketchin 1994). To emphasize practices is to recognize that individuals bear responsibility for the expression and development of their own spirituality. Practices shape a person's identity, but they are more about behavior than about identity itself. Practices such as worship, rearing children, showing compassion, and being responsible stewards of the earth are essentially about the pursuit of intrinsic goods (Wuthnow 1991).

But, of course, the present volume is not intended only for readers who may be interested in learning about American spirituality; it is for readers who expect to contribute to the study of religion through their own writing and research (perhaps a new generation of readers). To these readers, it is well to emphasize that no single method or theoretical perspective can provide answers to all the important questions for which we would like answers. Most of us are compelled to learn a variety of methods and theories and to employ them in our work, and yet we also adopt those methods and theories with which we feel most comfortable. Most of us, therefore, benefit from collaborating with others. Indeed, the candid admissions of most scholars suggest that they appreciate the work of others because they know wherein their own gifts and limitations lie. Some are gifted ethnographers, others may function better as historians or as theorists or as quantitative researchers. Each of us contributes by doing what we can. Virgil (1984, VIII, l. 63) reminds us of this, too, when he cautions: "We are not all capable of everything."

References

Albanese, Catherine L. 1991. *Nature Religion in America: From the Algonquin Indians to the New Age*. Chicago: University of Chicago Press.

Ammerman, Nancy Tatom. 1997. *Congregation and Community*. New Brunswick, NJ: Rutgers University Press.

Anderson, Joan Wester. 1992. *Where Angels Walk: True Stories of Heavenly Visitors*. New York: Barton & Brett.

Bell, Michael Mayerfeld. 1994. *Childerly: Nature and Morality in a Country Village*. Chicago: University of Chicago Press.

Bellah, Robert N. 1970. *Beyond Belief: Essays on Religion in a Post-Traditional World*. New York: Harper & Row.

Bellah, Robert N., Richard Madsen, William M. Sullivan, Ann Swidler, and Steven M. Tipton. 1985. *Habits of the Heart: Individualism and Commitment in American Life*. Berkeley and Los Angeles: University of California Press.

Berger, Peter L. 1969. *The Sacred Canopy: Elements of a Sociological Theory of Religion*. Garden City, NY: Doubleday.

Burawoy, Michael, ed. 1991. *Ethnography Unbound: Power and Resistance in the Modern Metropolis*. Berkeley and Los Angeles: University of California Press.

Butler, Jon. 1992. *Awash in a Sea of Faith: Christianizing the American People*. Cambridge: Harvard University Press.

Coleman, James S. 1990. *Foundations of Social Theory*. Cambridge: Harvard University Press.

Davidman, Lynn. 1991. *Tradition in a Rootless World: Women Turn to Orthodox Judaism*. Berkeley and Los Angeles: University of California Press.

Davie, Jody Shapiro. 1995. *Women in the Presence: Constructing Community and Seeking Spirituality in Mainline Protestantism*. Philadelphia: University of Pennsylvania Press.

DiMaggio, Paul J. and Walter W. Powell. 1991. "Introduction." Pp. 1–38 in *The New Institutionalism in Organizational Analysis*, edited by Walter W. Powell and Paul J. DiMaggio. Chicago: University of Chicago Press.

Durkheim, Emile. [1915] 1965. *The Elementary Forms of the Religious Life*. New York: Free Press.

Dykstra, Craig and Dorothy C. Bass. 1997. "Times of Yearning, Practices of Faith." Pp. 1–12 in *Practicing Our Faith: A Way of Life for a Searching People*, edited by Dorothy C. Bass. San Francisco: Jossey-Bass.

Eliasoph, Nina and Paul Lichterman. 1996. "The Practice of Meaning in Civil Society." Presented at the annual meetings of the American Sociological Association, New York.

Fontinell, Eugene. 1993. "The Return of 'Selves.'" *Cross Currents* 43: 358–74.

Geertz, Clifford. 1973. *The Interpretation of Cultures*. New York: Basic Books.
———. 1983. *Local Knowledge: Further Essays in Interpretive Anthropology*. New York: Basic Books.

Gergen, Kenneth J. 1991. *The Saturated Self: Dilemmas of Identity in Contemporary Life*. New York: Basic Books.

Greeley, Andrew M. 1981. *Religion: A Secular Theory*. New York: Free Press.

Halttunen, Karen. 1982. *Confidence Men and Painted Women: A Study of Middle-Class Culture in America, 1830-1870*. New Haven: Yale University Press.

Harding, Susan. Forthcoming. *The Afterlife of Stories*. Princeton: Princeton University Press.

Heelas, Paul. 1990. "The Sacralization of the Self and New Age Capitalism." Pp.139–55 in *Social Change in Contemporary Britain*, edited by Nicholas Abercrombie and Alan Warde. Cambridge: Polity Press.

————. 1993. "The New Age in Cultural Context: The Premodern, the Modern, and the Postmodern." *Religion* 23: 103–16.

————. 1996. *The New Age Movement: The Celebration of the Self and the Sacralization of Modernity.* London: Blackwell.

Hoge, Dean R., Benton Johnson, and Donald A. Luidens. 1994. *Vanishing Boundaries: The Religion of Mainline Protestant Baby Boomers.* Louisville: Westminster/John Knox.

Hunter, James Davison. 1991. *Culture Wars: The Struggle to Define America.* New York: Basic Books.

Joselit, Jenna Weissman. 1994. *The Wonders of America: Reinventing Jewish Culture, 1880–1950.* New York: Hill and Wang.

Kerr, Hugh T. 1993. "Spiritual Discipline." *Theology Today* 49: 449–53.

Ketchin, Susan. 1994. *The Christ-Haunted Landscape: Faith and Doubt in Southern Fiction.* Jackson: University Press of Mississippi.

Kohut, Andrew. 1997. *Trust and Citizen Engagement in Metropolitan Philadelphia: A Case Study.* Washington, DC: Pew Research Center for the People and the Press.

Linde, Charlotte. 1993. *Life Stories: The Creation of Coherence.* New York: Oxford University Press.

Lyotard, Jean-Francois. 1984. *The Postmodern Condition: A Report on Knowledge.* Minneapolis: University of Minnesota Press.

MacIntyre, Alasdair. 1984. *After Virtue: A Study in Moral Theory.* Notre Dame, IN: University of Notre Dame Press.

Marx, Karl and Frederick Engels. 1947. *The German Ideology.* New York: International Publishers.

McDannell, Colleen. 1986. *The Christian Home in Victorian America, 1840–1900.* Bloomington: Indiana University Press.

Norris, Kathleen. 1993. *Dakota: A Spiritual Geography.* New York: Ticknor and Fields.

Orsi, Robert A. 1996. *Thank You, St. Jude: Women's Devotion to the Patron Saint of Hopeless Causes.* New Haven: Yale University Press.

Parsons, Talcott. 1951. *The Social System.* New York: Free Press.

————. 1971. *The System of Modern Societies.* Englewood Cliffs, NJ: Prentice-Hall.

Pineda, Ana Maria. 1997. "Hospitality." Pp. 29–42 in *Practicing Our Faith,* edited by Dorothy C. Bass. San Francisco: Jossey-Bass.

Roof, Wade Clark. 1993. *A Generation of Seekers: The Spiritual Journeys of the Baby Boom Generation.* San Francisco: Harper San Francisco.

Rudy, Kathy. 1996. *Beyond Pro-Life and Pro-Choice: Moral Diversity in the Abortion Debate.* Boston: Beacon.

Schmidt, Leigh Eric. 1997. "The Magic of the Enlightenment: Ventriloquism, Religion, and Personal Identity." Presented at the Religion and Culture Workshop, Princeton, NJ.

Stout, Jeffrey. 1988. *Ethics after Babel: The Languages of Morals and Their Discontents*. Boston: Beacon Press.

Swidler, Ann. 1985. "Culture in Action: Symbols and Strategies." *American Sociological Review* 51: 273–86.

Taves, Ann. 1986. *The Household of Faith: Roman Catholic Devotions in Mid-Nineteenth-Century America*. Notre Dame, IN: University of Notre Dame Press.

Taylor, Charles. 1989. *Sources of the Self: The Making of the Modern Identity*. Cambridge: Harvard University Press.

Thomas, George M., John W. Meyer, Francisco O. Ramirez, and John Boli. 1987. *Institutional Structure: Constituting State, Society, and the Individual*. Beverly Hills, CA: Sage.

Tipton, Steven M. 1982. *Getting Saved from the Sixties: Moral Meaning in Conversion and Cultural Change*. Berkeley and Los Angeles: University of California Press.

Turner, Stephen. 1994. *The Social Theory of Practices: Tradition, Tacit Knowledge, and Presuppositions*. Chicago: University of Chicago Press.

Virgil. 1984. *The Eclogues*, rev. ed. New York: Penguin.

Warner, R. Stephen. 1988. *New Wine in Old Wineskins: Evangelicals and Liberals in a Small-Town Church*. Berkeley and Los Angeles: University of California Press.

Weber, Max. 1958. *The Protestant Ethic and the Spirit of Capitalism*. New York: Charles Scribner's Sons.

Wind, James P. and James W. Lewis, eds. 1994. *American Congregations*, 2 vols. Chicago: University of Chicago Press.

Witten, Marsha G. 1993. *All Is Forgiven: The Secular Message in American Protestantism*. Princeton: Princeton University Press.

Wolfe, Alan. 1989. *Whose Keeper? Social Science and Moral Obligation*. Berkeley and Los Angeles: University of California Press.

Wolterstorff, Nicholas. 1987. *Lament for a Son*. Grand Rapids, MI: Eerdmans.

Wuthnow, Robert. 1988. *The Restructuring of American Religion: Society and Faith Since World War II*. Princeton: Princeton University Press.

———. 1991. *Acts of Compassion: Caring for Others and Helping Ourselves*. Princeton: Princeton University Press.

———. 1994a. *Sharing the Journey: Support Groups and America's New Quest for Community*. New York: Free Press.

———. 1994b. *God and Mammon in America*. New York: Free Press.

————. 1997. *The Crisis in the Churches: Spiritual Malaise, Fiscal Woe.* New York: Oxford University Press.

Wyschogrod, Edith. 1990. *Saints and Postmodernism: Revisioning Moral Philosophy.* Chicago: University of Chicago Press.

INDEX

`Abdu'l-Bahá, 221, 228, 232, 233, 234, 236
abortion, 148, 154, 157
    and legal restrictions, 159–63, 164
    and religious beliefs, 153–54
    as violence, 150
    innocent victims of, 154, 155, 164
    insensitivity of, 153
    men's approach to, 151–52
    moral nature of, 151–55, 157, 161, 165
    women's approach to, 151–52
abortion activists, 141
accommodation thesis, 123–24
Adat huRuach, 25, 27, 28, 29, 31, 37, 38, 39, 41–42, 43, 45
Adler, Jonathan E., 165
afikomen, 26-27
African Methodist Episcopal church, 169–70, 173, 179, 186-87
Al-Anon, 57, 61, 66, 74
Albanese, Catherine L., 248
alcoholism, 57–60, 61, 63–64, 182, 184
Alford, Robert, 141, 143
aliyah, 31
American religion:
    complexity of, 248–49, 259
    cultural aspects of, 247, 256
Ammerman, Nancy Taton, 16, 17, 92, 117, 124, 143, 209, 214, 252
Anderson, Elijah, 174

Anderson, Joan Wester, 259
Anderson, Leon, 21
Anderson, Robert Mapes, 183
Anderson, Sherry Ruth, 117
anti-abortion movement. *See* Pro-life movement
anti-Semitism, 12, 123, 128

Baer, Hans A.. 182
Bahá'í, 18, 19, 21, 22, 221–42, 248, 250, 260
    collective identity of, 232, 234, 235
    deepenings, 233, 237, 241, 242
    Holy Days, 232, 239, 241
Bahá'í perspective, the, 237–38, 239–40. *See also* global world view
Bahá'í scripture, 229, 233
    global ideology in, 228, 236, 237
    progressive revelation of, 227
Bahá'í World Center, 222, 230, 234, 242
    pilgrimages to, 234, 235, 240
Bahá'í World Congress, 221–22, 223, 240
Bahá'u'lláh, 221–22, 224, 227–29, 232–33, 236, 238–39, 241
Bainbridge, William Sims, 186, 241
Balmer, Randall, 39
Bane, Mary Jo, 171
Barth, Fredrick, 44
Bass, Dorothy C., 260
Bateson, Gregory, 64, 71